OLMSTED SOUTH

Recent Titles in
Contributions in American Studies
Series Editor: Robert H. Walker

OLMSTED SOUTH

OLD SOUTH CRITIC / NEW SOUTH PLANNER

edited by Dana F. White
and Victor A. Kramer

Contributions in American Studies, Number 43

GREENWOOD PRESS
WESTPORT, CONNECTICUT . LONDON, ENGLAND

Library of Congress Cataloging in Publication Data

Main entry under title:
Olmsted South, old South critic, new South planner.

(Contributions in American studies; no. 43 ISSN 0084-9227)
Bibliography: p.
Includes index.
1. Olmsted, Frederick Law, 1822-1903.
2. Southern States—Social conditions.
3. Regional planning—Southern States. 4. Cities
and towns—Southern States—Civic improvements.
5. Social scientists—United States—Biography.
6. Landscape architects—United States—
Biography. I. White, Dana F. II. Kramer,
Victor A.
HN79.A13O55   309.2'5'0924   78-20019
ISBN 0-313-20724-0

Copyright © 1979 by Dana F. White and Victor A. Kramer

Visual Materials Compiled and Arranged by Howard L. Preston
and Dana F. White with Colleen Keegan

Library of Congress Catalog Card Number: 78-20019
ISBN: 0-313-20724-0
ISSN: 0084-9227

First published in 1979

Greenwood Press, Inc.
51 Riverside Avenue, Westport, Connecticut 06880

Printed in the United States of America

10 9 8 7 6 5 4 3 2 1

The mountain ranges, the valleys, and the great waters of America, all trend north and south, not east and west. An arbitrary political line may divide the north part from the south part, but there is no such line in nature: there can be none, socially. While water runs downhill, the currents of trade, of love, of consanguinity, and fellowship, will flow north and south.

Frederick Law Olmsted
"Introductory. The Present Crisis"
The Cotton Kingdom, 1861

Very soon all our northern cities will have been provided with parks. . . . I am moved by a desire to get a footing at the South, from Southern men, and willing to pay for it.

Frederick Law Olmsted to John C. Olmsted
March 13, 1894

CONTENTS

ILLUSTRATIONS

FOREWORD
History and the Rediscovery of Frederick Law Olmsted*

Frederick Law Olmsted's writings about the antebellum South have long been recognized by historians as a primary source of documentation. This fact is evident in most major works which deal with the institution of slavery. The continued relevance to the South of Olmsted's writing and planning is the general subject of this volume of essays which draws imaginatively—often in an exegesis of text—on his publications. In thus honoring Olmsted, the contributors to this anthology are part of a larger body of historians, from various disciplines, who, since the 1950s, have introduced Olmsted as a major witness to many aspects of nineteenth-century American society—not limited to the South. Such an upsurge of scholarly attention is reflected in the frequency with which Olmsted's personal and professional papers, housed at the Library of Congress, are consulted and in the corresponding number of significant works of scholarship in which he is treated either as a major or supporting figure.[1]

Central to any explanation of the scholars' rediscovery of Olmsted is the recognition that the forces shaping American society, like those of other industrialized nations, are rooted in the nineteenth century. During that period, massive growth in population, industrialization, urbanization, and economic structure, dependent upon changes in science and technology, began to transform the social and physical environments of home, work, and play. The full impact of this revolution on the nation—particularly its cities—was not felt until the 1950s, when a reinterpretation of the past began in terms of social and environmental issues.[2]

As historians moved to better comprehend the origin of these changes, it soon became apparent that Olmsted and those associated with him were among the first to grasp the full magnitude of the transformation. In addition, it was discovered that they applied principles of physical planning which remain viable. It is significant that most of the recent literature concerning Olmsted has dealt with his contributions to the development of parks, communities, cities, and regions where social changes are most visually apparent. Indeed, a volume on Olmsted and the South could not have been written until now—after the post-World War II changes in Southern economy and society and their regional physical effects. In short, the rediscovery of Frederick Law Olmsted as a protomodern figure is linked to the pervasive concern of most Americans about their homes, communities, cities, and recreational areas as environments that reflect and influence their daily quality of life.[3]

It is particularly appropriate that Olmsted's work should be rediscovered by historians seeking a fuller understanding of the times in which they live—perhaps hopeful that their scholarship may influence public policy—for Olmsted, like other noted figures in nineteenth-century American life, can be considered a historian. One of the underlying reasons for the emergence of historians such as John Lothrop Motley, William Hickling Prescott, George Bancroft, Francis Parkman, and Henry Adams in this period was the widespread appreciation and practice of the historian's craft by so many in public life. Olmsted sought fact and interpretation in the works of the historians of his age, some of whom he came to know.[4] Research and writing of history were important to his evolution as a social critic and physical planner, guiding his career development as well as providing a conceptual basis for his theories and practice of physical planning and design.

In a similar sense, this illustrated anthology of fifteen scholarly essays is unified by the aim of each contributor to examine some facet of Olmsted's work in the South in order to retrieve a more usable past. Historical relevance pervades the entire text, from the editors' "Introduction," which calls for "a new beginning . . . a new generation of Olmsted scholarship," to the last essay, which points to the critical issue of regionalism as "the great and challenging theme" of Olmsted's environmental planning effort (1888–1895) at George W. Vanderbilt's estate "Biltmore," near Asheville, North Carolina.[5]

Through a broad spectrum of subjects—ranging from historiography, literary criticism, and analysis of art and landscape design to the planning of specific projects such as parks and suburbs—the editors have sought to make Olmsted relevant to our time. In so doing , they have disclosed luminously the extent to which Olmsted's life reveals in breadth and depth a unique synthesis of American and English culture. Generally, efforts at historical synthesis focusing on a single person have been directed toward political personalities like Andrew Jackson or "Boss" Tweed.[6] It is logical, perhaps inevitable, given the trend of modern historiography toward more socially oriented subjects, that this synthesis now develop around someone like Olmsted, who never held elective office and whose life and work were rooted in social, ecological, and aesthetic concerns. A reformer, he worked to make the political system more responsive to public needs.

To support such an interpretation, the evidence must demonstrate that Olmsted's multifaceted career—as scientific farmer, author, publisher, social reformer, administrator, landscape architect, and city and regional planner—was linked sufficiently with persons and events to warrant his being recognized as a symbol of this age. The essays in Part One, "Old South," augment an already rich literature showing Olmsted's relationship to such developments as the radical antislavery New England Emigrant Aid Society and the artistic and literary achievement of John W. Orr and Harriet Beecher Stowe. The second part of the volume, "New South," provides the most detailed description and analysis yet available of his influence on the South's most important post-Civil War city—Atlanta, Georgia. In sum, then, this volume extends his relationship to the one region that traditionally has been critical of his accounts of its antebellum history and an area thought to have been largely removed from the kind of physical planning he advocated.

As we have already noted, the fact that for more than a century Olmsted has occupied, with ebbs and flows, a unique place as a witness to antebellum Southern life is not a new revelation. What is more recent, however, is the extent to which historians today can see his "separate" efforts—as social critic and planner—as more integrated aspects of cultural development. Such a unified understanding was furthered by Laura Wood Roper in five articles published between 1950 and 1965, culminating in *FLO: A Biography of Frederick Law Olmsted* (1973).[7]

Roper's research paralleled that of other scholars working on separate themes of nineteenth-century society, each study tied to a concern with the emergence of a modern urban America. Neil Harris in *The Artist in American Society* describes Olmsted as one of a group who were creating social landscapes for American cities. George Fredrickson treats him in *The Inner Civil War* as a member of a social elite of Northern urban intellectuals whose collective point of view altered dramatically as a result of that war. Seymour Mandelbaum in *Boss Tweed's New York*, a largely theoretical account of the development of American cities, used Olmsted's writings on urbanism and park planning to illustrate his own thesis concerning the governmental process and the role of the political boss. As for Olmsted's relationship to the built environment, we have the conclusion of James F. O'Gorman, a Henry H. Richardson scholar, that the noted architect's achievement was his "ability to focus in the most direct and lasting architectural terms the currents of nineteenth-century theory which found broader expression in . . . the panoramic landscape of Olmsted's vision." A serious effort to place Olmsted's urban contributions within "a profoundly conservative concept of reform" has been made by Geoffrey Blodgett in "Frederick Law Olmsted: Landscape Architecture as Conservative Reform." And, most recently, Robert Lewis, in "Frontier and Civilization in the Thought of Frederick Law Olmsted," has extended this group analysis to include Olmsted's relationship to a European—largely English—cosmopolitan tradition of culture and civilization.[8]

Therefore, all of these works, which explicitly use Olmsted as historical evidence, reflect the growing recognition that his significance is broader than any one—or all—of his achievements. His biography becomes a comprehensive history of many facets of the American experience, interfacing significantly with the lives of a whole group of Americans and Europeans who were attempting to create a new urban society out of an agrarian order. Hence, it matters little whether the particular tradition, event, or set of institutional ideas is scientific agriculture, publishing, the Civil War and Reconstruction, New York City politics, or the physical design of such cities as Boston, Louisville, and Atlanta; theory and facts substantiate a central role for Olmsted and his work. In scientific agriculture, he was early recognized and supported by Andrew Jackson Downing, a key figure in the popularization of horticulture and landscape design; in publishing, among his closest associates were such literary notables as George W. Curtis, Edwin L. Godkin, Parke Godwin, and Charles A. Dana. During the Civil War, as executive director of the United States Sanitary Commission (1861–1863), his colleagues included the influential Unitarian minister Henry W. Bellows and the famous attorney-diarist George Templeton Strong; in New York City, his relationship with Andrew Haswell Green, the silent but politically powerful partner of Governor Samuel J. Tilden, was fundamental to the planning process; and in his career as a designer he worked with or influenced almost every important architect and land designer in the nation.[9]

The level of Olmsted's contribution to the shaping of a modern tradition of urbanism also can be documented by the research of scholars specializing in the history of science, social institutions, and environmental planning and design. For example, in *The Cholera Years* Charles E. Rosenberg, a noted historian of science, describes the attitudes that led to a more scientific understanding of urban public health needs. Rosenberg emphasizes the considerable efforts of pioneer public health physician Elisha Harris, one of Olmsted's chief assistants on the Sanitary Commission and co-author of the 1871 *Report to the Staten Island Improvement Commission*, probably the most comprehensive environmental-planning study completed in this country in the nineteenth century.[10]

A scholar of nineteenth-century social work, Joseph M. Hawes, has provided the fullest account to date of Charles Loring Brace's leadership in reducing juvenile delinquency in the nation's cities. Brace, a founder of the Children's Aid Society, and Olmsted were friends from childhood; they held similar attitudes regarding planned intervention in the lives of homeless children. John B. Jackson's *American Space: The Centennial Years* reveals—for the first time, virtually—the achievements of a group of Americans actively involved in physical planning and design, most of whom were close to Olmsted. Among them were George Waring, Jr., whose first major public project was the drainage system of Central Park and who was responsible, too, for the much-valued Tenth Census of the United States and for organizing New York City's first modern Department of Sanitation.[11]

Hence, perhaps the most interesting aspect of these essays on the South is the extent to which they reveal in Olmsted's writings "new" ways of perceiving nineteenth-century society—all of which speak to concerns of our own day. For a historian of folklife, Olmsted's writing is significant because he often captured in dialogue and dialect the daily habits and customs of various sections and social classes.[12] One of the essays draws attention to Olmsted's treatment of a variety of work environments in which blacks found themselves and the impact of their work on their personality:

The works of Frederick Law Olmsted are also an invaluable source for the occupational differentiation and variations in life style among slaves. He observes, in fine detail, slaves working in an unexpectedly broad range of jobs, many with an equally surprising degree of autonomy: black men working in the coal mines of Virginia alongside Welsh miners; black fishermen and divers working off the North Carolina coast; black lumbermen and blacks in the turpentine industry, who labored off in the swamps and forests. Olmsted postulated that the incentive of virtual freedom or money encouraged in these workers the expression of positive character traits . . . [And] that the lumbermen . . . "were more sprightly and straight-forward in . . . manner and conversation than any field-hand plantation negroes that I saw at the South."[13]

A literary historian, Robert Detweiler, provides the first coherent stylistic analysis of *The Cotton Kingdom*, emphasizing the aesthetic unity of the work in terms of "image, diction, [and] syntax."[14] His essay adds a new and important dimension to our understanding of Olmsted's literary career, paralleling the extension of our knowledge of Olmsted's work as a designer of landscapes. Olmsted's books, which have long been read and used for their social interpretation, can now be better perceived as aesthetic achievements, just as his parks, mostly admired before the 1960s for their design qualities, are studied more today as social landscapes.

The diversity of the essays attests to the modernity and relevance of the volume. The whole work argues implicity that Olmsted's career was too intricately engaged with the social and environmental fabric of his time to be limited to any special branch of history. Contemporary relevance must be sought from different vantage points of the past. In discussing Olmsted's multiple relevance to the present, these essays, as already noted, substantiate the work of other historians who also represent different specializations. They underscore Olmsted's own awareness and use of diverse historical sources more than a century ago.

Olmsted's writing and planning were informed by an interpretation of history as a society-shaping process as much as a factual record of the past. He drew upon the works of such English historians as Thomas Carlyle, Thomas Macaulay, and Henry Buckle. Among American scholars, he found the efforts of George Bancroft, John Lothrop Motley, and Richard Hildreth most useful. In addition, he was much influenced by the sermons of his teacher and friend, the formidable Hartford Congregational theologian Horace Bushnell, for whom historic analysis was a key to understanding theology.[15]

Nor was Olmsted alone in treating the past so seriously. History was a popular form of literature in a new democracy seeking a sense of purpose. Regarding Macaulay's *History of England*, editors at *Harper's* wrote in 1849 that "we have already sold 40,000 copies, and we presume that over 60,000 copies have been disposed of. Probably within three months of this time the sale will amount to 200,000 copies."[16] And while not all authors had such success, most of the historians Olmsted read had influential—if not substantial—audiences.

Not so well recognized is the extent to which some of the men and women with whom Olmsted associated (like him, not primarily historians) actually wrote serious history or integrated it with their other writings. In 1868, the editor-politician-statesman John Bigelow—to whom Olmsted turned for assistance during his early political difficulties with Andrew Haswell Green over the administration of Central Park—edited *The Autobiography of Benjamin Franklin*, containing the famous manuscript autobiography which Bigelow had found. Parke Godwin, one of the chief contributors to *Putnam's Monthly Magazine* during the period 1855–1857, when Olmsted was co-owner, in addition to completing a two-volume biography of his father-in-law, William Cullen Bryant, projected a history of France, of which only one volume was published. And for Charles Loring Brace in *Home-Life in Germany*—as in his many other works—history was an indispensable tool. "No one," he wrote, "can understand even the modern domestic life of Germany, without knowing something of its Past. . . . I have accordingly devoted several chapters to Political and Theological History, as indispensable to a right understanding of my subject."[17]

But political and theological history were not the basic concerns of either Brace or Olmsted. The analysis that gave structure to their respective efforts was what today would be termed social or environmental history. Correspondence between the two men reveals Olmsted's insistence on greater emphasis upon a fuller social record of the past. For it was only by appraising the fundamental forces in the development of civilization that one could come to terms with its problems and aspirations and, most important, employ this knowledge in a useful way. "Give us all the real life . . .," Olmsted wrote Brace in Germany. "Tell us what you do and what people do to you—and in what way your impulses are moved as much as you can. It's worth more than your thoughts to us who know you." In short, according to Brace, history was "not merely a journal of battles and the reigns of kings." It was a description of "the Life of Man."[18]

To understand a culture or a society, one must strive to set aside stereotypes and biases. Olmsted made the point more explicitly in *Seaboard Slave States*—which Stephan Thernstrom has quoted as the introduction to his influential book *Poverty and Progress*:

Men of literary taste . . . are always apt to overlook the working-classes, and to confine the records they make of their own times, in great degree, to the habits and fortunes of their own associates, or to those of people of superior rank to themselves of whose sayings and doings their vanity, as well as their curiosity, leads them to most carefully inform themselves. The dumb masses have often been so lost in this shadow of egotism, that, in later days, it has been impossible to discern the very real influence their character and condition has had on the fortune and fate of nations.[19]

In both England and America, there was emerging a studied effort to remedy this neglect in trying to understand the total fabric of the past. The initial English source for Olmsted in this emphasis on social history was Thomas Babington Macaulay, whose first volume of *The History of England from the Accession of James the Second* (1849) was so popular that study groups were formed to discuss it in depth. "I continue to meet the Macaulay club every day," Olmsted wrote his brother, "and enjoy it very much." Brace applauded the good effect that Macaulay's writings had in Germany in fostering national unity. And Brace's friend, the fiery Unitarian minister Theodore Parker, whom Olmsted knew, praised Macaulay's famous "third" chapter, which emphasized the development of "a high degree of [popular] physical, moral, and intellectual improvement."[20]

Olmsted's first career choice in scientific agriculture was shaped by an understanding of the past. In the America of the 1840s, he looked to a Jeffersonian tradition for such purpose, revealed in part in Jefferson's own social record, *Notes on the State of Virginia*. "Rural pursuits," Olmsted wrote his brother, ". . . tend to elevate and enlarge the ideas, for all the proudest aims of Science are involved in them. . . . I believe that our farmers are, and have cause to be, the most contented men in the world." In fact, until he was nearly thirty years of age he regarded agriculture as an ideal occupation for any intelligent young man seeking a socially useful and personally satisfying profession. His book *Walks and Talks of an American Farmer in England* (1852) was written "especially for farmers and farmers' families." And the signature "Yeoman" followed his initial description of the seaboard slave states, published a year later as a series in the *Times*. Like Jefferson, whom he admired, Olmsted, until the age of thirty, remained committed to scientific farming as the most socially useful of occupations.[21]

Olmsted's journeys through the South in the years 1852–1854 were the turning point in his attitude toward the agrarian way of life and in his interpretation of the past. This experience was reinforced by the Civil War, which began one year after the publication of the third volume of his account of the antebellum South. Ironically, the purpose of the trips had been to help prevent the war by presenting an "objective" picture of Southern life and manners. Henry Raymond, the *New-York Daily Times* editor who commissioned the project, believed that the war could be averted by offsetting the extreme image of the South and slavery drawn by Northern abolitionists such as William Lloyd Garrison.

Raymond, who had just recently founded the *Times*—partly as a reaction against the social and economic views of Horace Greeley and his *New York Tribune*—was looking for exactly such a man as Olmsted. Olmsted's book on England, published in 1852, had been well received by the press as a fair and interesting depiction of English social life. In it, Olmsted had noted with disdain that America's foreign image was being distorted by proselytizing abolitionists. Of the English view of slavery he had written that "they are usually greatly misinformed, and view it only as an unmitigated and wholly excusable wrong, injustice, and barbarous tyranny for which all Americans are equally responsible, and all equally condemnable, and with regard to which all are to be held responsible and everlastingly to be scolded at (except a few martyrs, called abolitionists, that obtain a precarious livelihood through their contributions)." In addition, he and Raymond, both supporters of the Free-Soil Whigs, held similar political views opposing the extension of slavery into the territories. It was logical, then, for Raymond to select Olmsted to do an objective Northern study of the South.[22]

Olmsted began his trips with the view that slavery was "an unfortunate circumstance." He felt that the people of the South themselves were blameless and that immediate abolition was impracticable. He hoped, therefore, to foster a conciliatory spirit in the North by presenting an objective study of the "condition and habits of the people of the South." Olmsted's earliest reports, published in the *Times*, do maintain such an objectivity. The final volumes, however, do not. Although the major emphasis is on the disastrous effects of slavery on the entire South, an equally important unifying theme is the defense of a democratic, commercial, and urban society dependent on free labor in contrast to an aristocratic, fundamentally agrarian order based on slave labor.[23]

There are several reasons for this change, but one of the most apparent in Olmsted's writings was his use of history and his appreciation of the work of Motley, Bancroft, and particularly Hildreth. Olmsted did not rely simply on his recorded observations, nor even on his diligent research into census and other primary sources, to more fully understand and explain his perceptions; history was a principal tool of his analysis of the South. "I have been studying Virginian history and slavery on the conditions of the State," he wrote his father in 1854, "and have still one more chapter to write upon it to bring the sketch down to our modern times."[24]

His sources were not only the impressions of an investigating journalist but also a body of analytical literature that provided an intellectual synthesis important in his development as a historian. In *Seaboard Slave States*, he referred to Bancroft's "Essay on the Decline of the Roman People," published in 1855 in *Literary and Historical Miscellanies*. Bancroft's point was that the Barbarians did not ruin Italy; rather, the Romans themselves did. Slavery had brought about the decline of the Roman people and had wasted the land even before the entry of any invader.[25]

That same volume contained Bancroft's famous essay on the necessity of progress, a panegyric to commerce and urbanization. "Look round this beautiful earth," wrote Bancroft, "and see how much man has done for its subjection and adornment; making the wilderness blossom with cities, and the seemingly inhospitable sea cheerfully social with the richly freighted fleets of world-wide commerce." In 1858, Bancroft—along with Washington Irving—served as a member of an appointed group of distinguished citizens who advised New York City on the selection of the plan for Central Park. And both he and Olmsted during the pre-Civil War sectional debate over slavery supported the efforts of the German-born Friedrich Kapp to bolster German-American loyalty toward the North.[26]

In *Back Country*, Olmsted drew upon Motley's *History of the Dutch Republic* and Washington Irving's *Life of George Washington* to prove that a democratic, peaceloving nation can defeat an aristocratic warlike state, pointing to the victory of Holland over Spain and to that of the colonies over Great Britain. And Olmsted could scarcely have ignored Motley's published address applauding the growth of New York City, with special emphasis on its "stately parks—than which nothing more luxurious is to be found in older and imperial cities."[27]

Olmsted also quoted from Hildreth's *History of the United States* to prove the failure of Southern society to promote social mobility. "Poverty and the want of education on the part of the mass of the freedmen," said Hildreth—Olmsted wrote in *Seaboard*—"kept them, too often, in a subservient position, and created in the Middle as well as the Southern colonies an inferior order of poor whites, a distinction of classes and an inequality almost unknown in republican New England." More significantly, perhaps, Hildreth was a regular contributor to *Putnam's* during Olmsted's tenure there; and Hildreth's book on the South, *Despotism in America*, published in 1854, contains many insights that Olmsted probably incorporated into his own work. Olmsted also must have known of Hildreth's important little book, *A Theory of Politics* (1853), which offered, among other things, a stage-analysis of history and an emphasis upon cities which may have influenced Olmsted's study of the South as well as his future work as a city planner.[28]

Olmsted's diaries, therefore, were more than critical evaluations of slavery and its impact on the land and its people. They were also a fundamental defense of the value and importance of cities. The very structure of the presentation of the diaries was strengthened—if not sparked—by the writings of contemporary historians.

But if an interpretation of history had informed—perhaps prompted—and helped to guide Olmsted's move from scientific farmer to publicist and social critic, it had not yet compelled him to undertake an original analysis and synthesis of his own. Such an effort, however, began even before he left the Sanitary Commission in 1863 to work on the Mariposa Estate in California. Devotion to history dictated careful recordkeeping by the Commission and motivated his contribution to *Hospital Transports* as a partial account of the activities of the organization.[29] Olmsted also supported Charles J. Stillé's more complete and official *History of the U.S. Sanitary Commission* (1866), with chapters written by such members of the organization as Henry W. Bellows and George Templeton Strong. In later years, he was the one most responsible for preserving the voluminous files of the Commission now housed in the New York Public Library and still awaiting a fresh and more critical survey than Stillé's work provides.

Several factors moved Olmsted to undertake (although never to complete) a major and original synthesis of the American past. There was the war itself, which he and almost every other American intellectual understood had assumed the proportions of a secular crusade—not only the victory of good over evil, of freedom over slavery, and of order over chaos, but a demonstration of a democracy's capacity to unite on common principles, although beset by many internal disharmonies. But rhetoric and desire were one thing and the reality of the national condition another. Olmsted's war experience provided sufficient reason to question whether these goals were attainable without new social policy. More significant, perhaps, were the serious doubts being expressed abroad, notably in England, by some of the very persons whom Olmsted most admired—such as Thomas Carlyle and John Ruskin—that the war was a failure of democracy rather than one of its successes.[30]

To still similar doubts within himself, Olmsted determined sometime in 1863 to undertake a major work of original historic documentation and analysis, which would offer a new synthesis of the American experience.[31] By this time close to physical and mental collapse—broken down by the burden of his position as well as the demands he placed upon himself and unwilling to return to the political battles of New York City—he needed to use history as a guide not so much to what to do but to the context in which his work should take shape.

There was a public dimension to his dilemma, which pertained to the emancipation of slaves in this country and the future of black Americans. Few understood as well as Olmsted that the challenge was not simply that of emancipation, but that of preparing a dependent population for full participation in all aspects of American life. Therefore, in 1862, he urged that the federal government create a special supportive social environment in Port Royal, one of the South Carolina Sea Islands captured by the North in 1861. The essential elements of the proposal are clearly discussed in Laura Roper's article on the subject. The Sea Island slaves, some eight or ten thousand of whom had been left behind when their masters and overseers fled, had become the responsibility of the Union Army.[32]

For Olmsted, this presented a perfect opportunity to demonstrate to the South, to the nation, and to the world the commitment of the government to prepare black Americans for fuller participation in the total society. Writing to his father in 1863, Olmsted indicated how much he wished to have an opportunity to assume responsibility for managing a large Negro settlement: "I want to demonstrate the feasibility of the plan which I advocated in one of the Georgia chapters of Seaboard Slave States, of navigating one ship out of Slavery." Olmsted's plan, Laura Roper tells us, crumbled, and two years later he declined to be a candidate for the position of head of the Freedmen's Bureau, in part because he recognized that the instrumentality being created was too weak to accomplish the task involved. In short, it was clear to him quite early that the nation would not assume responsibility for the social programs required.[33]

Hence, it became doubly important for him to understand where the nation was heading and in what ways he could contribute to its improvement. What made such a study more realizable—but not easy—was the publication in 1857 of Henry Thomas Buckle's influential *History of Civilization*. This work was important for three reasons. First, it was a most optimistic book not only about how English civilization had changed, but also about how it was developing. Second, it was the most satisfying synthesis of attitudes toward the "new"—social—history formulated by an earlier generation of European and American scholars—one which emphasized the importance of cities as creative centers of civilization. "Have you seen," wrote Theodore Parker to an English friend, "a quite remarkable book by H. T. Buckle? It is a *History of Civilization in England*. It is one of the most remarkable and instructive books I have seen from the English press in this century. . . . I think it a great book and know none so important since the Novum Organum of Bacon. . . . This is a Novum Organum in the department of history." For the historian-biographer James Parton it was "the most valuable work of the century." A decade after its publication—by which time Buckle had died without completing the projected work—the historian Motley considered the two volumes of the *History* so important to the future progress of the nineteenth century that he wished "to linger in the stately portico to the unbuilt dome which the daring genius of Buckle consumed his life in devising." Third, at the heart of that genius was a startling new methodology for its time: the use of social statistics to document both the failures and progress of civilization.[34]

For Buckle, history was part of political economy, which in the nineteenth century had developed a more scientific basis. Reliable statistics about most of society were now available, offering a means by which to apply the methods of physical science to the study of history. For the first time, scholars could measure such essential data as rates of birth and marriage, mortality, fluctuation of wages, and the cost of living. A corollary to this thesis was Buckle's complete dedication to environmentalism. Even in discussing the causes of murder, he wrote that facts of this kind "force us to the conclusion, that the offenses of men are the result not so much of the vices of the individual offender as of the state of society into which he is thrown." The social law which Buckle was enunciating was that "the moral actions of men are the product of their antecedents, not of their volition."[35] And for Buckle, as for Olmsted and other Americans, it was in the great cities that such a scientific analysis of society could and should be undertaken.

Olmsted seized upon the methodology. The Sanitary Commission already had an active Bureau of Statistics directed and staffed by some of the nation's most important pioneer statisticians. Hence, in 1863 he began to acquire data for a major work, a study of "civilization in the last fifty years" in the United States, using the Union Army as a laboratory in which to measure social progress. He worked most intensively on the project during the years 1863–1865, while in California, where he encountered what was still a violent and barbaric frontier society.[36]

How to reconcile California's physical and social environment with progress? How to prove that the Civil War, from a retrospective point of view, was not democracy defunct, but an inevitable step toward the realization of a unique social destiny? To do both, Olmsted reasoned, using Buckle's approach, it was necessary to prove scientifically—that is, through the use of statistics—that social progress was discernible in the personal development of most Americans regardless of birth or social origin. Such a study, he hoped, would demonstrate that despite failures America was succeeding in the most difficult task ever to confront a Western nation: the assimilation of many groups whose unity would be evident in an improved social condition.[37]

While Buckle provided the methodology for such a study, it was the noted Hartford Congregational minister, Horace Bushnell, who had formulated a theory to explain the challenge of the American experience. "Get me a copy of Dr. Bushnell's discourse of Barbarism the first Danger," Olmsted urged his father in 1864. "If you can't get any other wise ask the Doctor—and then advertise. I would give $10 or $20 for a copy if necessary."[38]

Bushnell's essay offered hope for the future. First published in 1847, it was a statement of a theme which was to appear in most of the minister's essays in the 1840s and 1850s: the need to develop civilized communities adequate to the social needs of a population—including homes, public schools, libraries, and churches. But such a development, Bushnell pointed out, in a very mobile and still immature nation, could not be a consistently upward movement. Rather, a study of Western history revealed an almost periodic swing between progress and barbarism. The history of the United States in particular was the result of a movement of population away from civilized communities toward a more primitive frontier. Nothing was more certain, he wrote, based on a study of the past, than that *"emigration or a new settlement of the social state, involves a tendency to social decline."*[39]

Civilization, Bushnell persisted in reminding his young friend, was a consequence of time and of the establishment of those social institutions, embodied in physical structures, that transmitted knowledge, morals, and beauty. It was, he concluded, a law of "humanity, in all of its forms of life and progress, that the physical shall precede the moral. The order of nature is—what is physical first, what is moral afterwards." Hence, a moral society depended not primarily on the existence of churches, but on "schools of a high order . . . stone bridges durable and safe, macadamized roads . . . weaving all the hamlets together, in a network of easy correspondence, indicating and also promoting the advanced wealth and civilization of the people."[40]

Olmsted never completed this history. But he did publish as part of his and Calvert Vaux's *Report for Prospect Park* (1868) a social analysis of urban development which incorporated and reflected his considerable work as a historian and which helped to structure his most creative period as a physical designer.[41] Underlying his plans for each park, parkway, campus, and suburb was an understanding of the past expressed in the natural history of the site as well as in the growth and development of American society. These physical designs—meant to serve the social and environmental needs of millions—today not only offer a basis for studying the art and science of a socially useful design discipline but are evidence as well that belief in historical relevance can affect public policy.

By expanding our understanding of the ways in which Olmsted's writings and works in the South are relevant to scholarship today, the editors of *OLMSTED SOUTH*—both of whom live and work in Georgia—have widened the frame of reference for thoughtful public policy with respect to various issues that concerned Olmsted and which continue to confront us. It is timely—perhaps inevitable—that a major work on Olmsted should be written in the South during a period when the nation's elected leader is a former governor of the state of Georgia, trained as a farmer and engineer, who projected in his campaign an independent nonpolitical stance symbolizing the transformation of that region in terms of racial policy, effective planning, and conservation of natural resources. In the continuing effort to meet the awesome challenges confronting the nation with regard to each of these problem-issues, it is important that we have the widest and fullest understanding possible of their origins as well as of earlier efforts to resolve them. The contributors to this volume have assisted those who seek these answers today, just as Olmsted found relevant and useful the written history of the nineteenth century.

Albert Fein

NOTES

1. For a recent listing of Olmsted scholarship, see "Selective Bibliography," in Elizabeth Stevenson, *Park Maker: A Life of Frederick Law Olmsted* (New York, 1977), pp. 457–61.

2. This theme, implicit in most significant works since the 1950s about the nineteenth century, has been more explicitly developed in studies about England and France, such as the following works by Raymond Williams: *Culture and Society, 1780–1950* (London, 1958), *The Long Revolution* (London, 1961), and *The Country and the City* (New York, 1973), and in David H. Pinkney, "A Historian's Movable Feast — France," *French-American Review* 2 (Winter 1977 and Spring 1978): 28–44.

3. A seminal study was Hans Huth, *Nature and the American* (Berkeley, Calif., 1957). As a reflection of this interest, two anthologies of Olmsted's planning reports have been issued: Albert Fein, ed., *Landscape into Cityscape: Frederick Law Olmsted's Plans for a Greater New York City* (Ithaca, N.Y., 1967), and S. B. Sutton,

ed., *Civilizing American Cities: A Selection of Frederick Law Olmsted's Writings on City Landscapes* (Cambridge, Mass., 1971). In addition, there have been two major visual exhibits treating mainly of Olmsted's physical planning and design, and many articles in both national and local newspapers dealing with this aspect of his career.

4. Among the historians whom Olmsted came to know socially were Charles Francis Adams, Henry Adams, and Francis Parkman. For his relationship with the Adams brothers, see Laura W. Roper, *FLO: A Biography of Frederick Law Olmsted* (Baltimore, 1973), p. 156, and Stevenson, *Park Maker*, p. 352. Both Parkman and Olmsted were members of Boston's prestigious Saturday Club, composed of many of the nation's leading intellectual figures.

5. See Victor A. Kramer and Dana F. White, "Yankee Visitor," pp. xxxi–xxxvi, and Frederick Gutheim, "Olmsted at Biltmore," pp. 239–246.

6. As examples of this type of scholarship, see John W. Ward, *Andrew Jackson: Symbol for an Age* (New York, 1955), and Seymour Mandelbaum, *Boss Tweed's New York* (New York, 1965).

7. Each of the following opened up different aspects of Olmsted's career: "Frederick Law Olmsted and the Western Texas Free-Soil Movement," *American Historical Review* 56 (October 1950): 58–64; Frederick L. Olmsted "The Yosemite Valley and the Mariposa Big Trees: A Preliminary Report, 1865," *Landscape Architecture* 43 (October 1952): 12–25 (ed. L. Roper); "Frederick Law Olmsted in the 'Literary Republic'," *Mississippi Valley Historical Review* 39, No. 3 (December 1952): 459–82; " 'Mr. Law' and *Putnam's Monthly Magazine*: A Note on a Phase in the Career of Frederick Law Olmsted," *American Literature* 26, No. 1 (March 1954): 88–93; "Frederick Law Olmsted and the Port Royal Experiment," *Journal of Southern History* 31, No. 13 (August 1965): 272–84.

8. Neil Harris, *The Artist in American Society: The Formative Years 1790–1860* (New York, 1966), pp. 215–16; George M. Fredrickson, *The Inner Civil War: Northern Intellectuals and the Crisis of the Union* (New York, 1965), pp. 100–108; Mandelbaum, *Boss Tweed's New York*, pp. 74–75, 116–17; James F. O'Gorman, "The Making of a 'Richardson Building,' 1874–1886," in *Selected Drawings, H. H. Richardson and His Office: A Centennial of His Move to Boston 1874* (Harvard College Library, 1974), p. 30; Geoffrey Blodgett, "Frederick Law Olmsted: Landscape Architecture as Conservative Reform," *Journal of American History* 62 (March 1976): 869–87; Robert Lewis, "Frontier and Civilization in the Thought of Frederick Law Olmsted," *American Quarterly* 24 (Fall 1977): 385–403.

9. Roper, *FLO*, passim; Stevenson, *Park Maker*, passim; Albert Fein, *Frederick Law Olmsted and the American Environmental Tradition* (New York, 1972), passim.

10. Charles E. Rosenberg, *The Cholera Years: The United States in 1832, 1849, and 1866* (Chicago, 1962), pp. 187–88; Fein, ed., *Landscape into Cityscape*, pp. 173–300.

11. Joseph M. Hawes, *Children in Urban Society: Juvenile Delinquency in Nineteenth-Century America* (New York, 1971), passim; John B. Jackson, *American Space: The Centennial Years, 1865–1876* (New York, 1972), passim; Richard Skolnick, "George E. Waring, Jr.: A Model for Reformers," *New-York Historical Society Quarterly* 47 (July 1963): 257–87.

12. See Kay L. Cothran, "Olmsted's Contributions to Folklife Research," pp. 59–66.

13. Karla J. Spurlock-Evans, " 'Old' Sources for a 'New' History: Frederick Law Olmsted's Journeys in the Slave South," pp. 51–58.

14. Robert Detweiler, "Transcending Journalism: Olmsted's Style in *The Cotton Kingdom*," pp. 67–80.

15. As an example of Olmsted's consciousness of the process of history as it reflected his age and the need for constant documentation of the recent past, of the Europoean revolution of 1848 he wrote: "Some one can render a service to civilization by publishing precisely what feudal rights, so called, were abolished in large parts of Germany and Hungary in 1848, and what results to the commerce of the districts affected the greater freedom and impulse to industry arising therefrom has had." See Olmsted, *A Journey in the Back Country in the Winter of 1853–54* (New York, 1907), 2: 124–25; originally issued in 1860.

16. John Bach McMaster, *Thomas Babington Macaulay (1800–1859)* (New York, 1899), p. 139.

17. For an example of Olmsted's relationship to Bigelow, see John Bigelow, *Retrospections of an Active Life*, 5 vols. (New York, 1909–13), 1: 340–44. The 1868 publication was expanded into a three-volume work, *The Life of Benjamin Franklin Written by Himself* (Philadelphia, 1874); see Margaret Clapp, *Forgotten First Citizen: John Bigelow* (Boston, 1947), pp. 261, 272; Olmsted made use of Bigelow's antislavery book, *Jamaica in 1850; or, the Effects of Sixteen Years of Freedom on a Slave Colony* (New York, 1851), to counter the argument that the emancipation of slaves had been injurious to West Indian society. Olmsted, *Back Country*, 1:110. Regarding Olmsted's appreciation of Godwin's contribution to *Putnam's*, see Frederick Law Olmsted to Parke Godwin, January 19, 1856, Bryant-Godwin Papers, New York Public Library; Parke Godwin, *The History of France* 1 (New York, 1860); Charles Loring Brace, *Home-Life in Germany* (New York, 1856), pp. iv–v.

18. Olmsted to Brace, July 27, 1851, Olmsted Papers, Library of Congress—hereafter cited as Olmsted Papers, Brace, *The Races of the Old World: A Manual of Ethnology* (New York, 1863), p. iv.

19. Olmsted, *A Journey in the Seaboard Slave States, with Remarks on Their Economy* (New York, 1856), pp. 214–15; quoted in Stephan Thernstrom, *Poverty and Progress; Social Mobility in a Nineteenth Century City* (Cambridge, Mass., 1964), p. 1.

20. Olmsted to John Hull Olmsted, February 24, 1849, Olmsted Papers; Brace, *Home-Life in Germany*, p. 138; Theodore Parker, "Macaulay's History of England," in George W. Cooke, ed., *The American Scholar* (Boston, 1907), p. 326.

21. Olmsted to John Hull Olmsted, June 23, 1845, Olmsted Papers; Olmsted, *Walks and Talks*, Part I, p. 1; Roper, *FLO*, p. 90; as an example of Olmsted's use of Jefferson as a source, see *Seaboard Slave States*, pp. 257–70.

22. For a similar interpretation of the objectives of this journey, see Roper, *FLO*, pp. 84–85; Stevenson, *Park Maker*, pp. 71–72; Olmsted, *Walks and Talks*, Part I, p. 221.

23. Olmsted, *Back Country*, 1:v; this theme of the increasing emotional quality of Olmsted's writing on the South was further developed in Fein, ed., *Landscape into Cityscape*, pp. 15–26.

24. Olmsted to John Olmsted, December 31, 1854, Olmsted Papers.

25. Olmsted, *Seaboard Slave States*, pp. 514–15.

26. George Bancroft, "The Necessity, the Reality, and the Promise of the Progress of the Human Race," in *Literary and Historical Miscellanies* (New York, 1855), p. 493; Roper, *FLO*, p. 102; George Bancroft, "Introduction," in Friedrich Kapp, *Life of William von Steuben, Major General in the Revolutionary Army* (New York, 1859). Kapp's continued willingness to support the Northern cause is evidenced in Friedrich Kapp to Olmsted, September 20, 1861, Olmsted Papers.

27. Olmsted, *Back Country*, 2:248–49; John Lothrop Motley, *Historic Progress and American Democracy: An Address Delivered Before the New-York Historical Society at Their Sixty-Fourth Anniversary* (New York, 1869), p. 2.

28. Olmsted, *Seaboard Slave States*, p. 231; Donald Eugene Emerson, *Richard Hildreth* (Baltimore, 1946), pp. 154, 172.

29. [Frederick Law Olmsted and others], *Hospital Transports, A Memoir of the Embarkation of the Sick and Wounded from the Peninsula of Virginia in the Summer of 1862* (Boston, 1863).

30. Olmsted was also addressing a constant stream of criticism from nineteenth-century Europeans concerning the inadequacies of American civilization; see Roper, *FLO*, p. 247.

31. These doubts were heightened by the outbreak of draft riots in New York City in July 1863. Olmsted to Mary Olmsted, July 15, 1863, Olmsted Papers.

32. Roper, "Frederick Law Olmsted and the Port Royal Experiment"; the fullest account of this failed effort at comprehensive reconstruction is Willie Lee Rose, *Rehearsal for Reconstruction: The Port Royal Experiment* (New York, 1964).

33. Olmsted to John Olmsted, April 18, 1863; A. J. Bloor to Olmsted, April 28, 1865; Calvert Vaux to Olmsted, March 24, 1864; regarding decision to reject offer, see Olmsted to John Olmsted, August 28, 1865, Olmsted Papers.

34. For Buckle's views on cities, see Giles St. Aubyn, *A Victorian Eminence: The Life and Works of Henry Thomas Buckle* (London, 1958), p. 126; quote in ibid., p. 33; see also Theodore Parker, "Buckle's History of Civilization," in *The American Scholar*, pp. 364–418, 522; James Parton, *Smoking and Drinking* (Boston, 1868), p. 50; Motley, *Historical Progress*, p. 30; Roper, *FLO*, p. 247.

35. Quoted in Parker, "Buckle's History of Civilization," pp. 371–72.

36. It is ironic that in a recent, widely publicized and controversial econometric study of slavery, Robert William Fogel and Stanley L. Engerman, *Time On the Cross: The Economics of American Negro Slavery* (Boston, 1974), Olmsted should be criticized in that his "attempt to make use of census data to evaluate the performance of the slave economy was deeply flawed" (p. 176). The irony is that there is ample documentation in the preparation for his proposed history of American civilization to prove that Olmsted was a pioneer proponent of the application of the most advanced statistical methods to the study of history; see, for example, Olmsted to Ezekiel Brown Elliott, April 6, 1864; Olmsted to Dr. John Foster Jenkins, November 7, 1864; Olmsted to Frederick Newman Knapp, December 13, 1867, Olmsted Papers. The subject of scientific validity, as defined by statistical data, was so fundamental to Olmsted's process of study and analysis that at one time he gave serious thought to seeking appointment as commissioner of a newly formed Bureau of Agriculture and Statistics—Olmsted to John Olmsted, April 19, 1862. For an example of the kind of statistical work the Sanitary Commission

produced, see B[enjamin] A. Gould, *U.S. Sanitary Commission; Statistical Bureau Ages of U.S. Volunteer Soldiery* (New York, 1866).

37. That this was the hypothesis which structured Olmsted's collection of data is clear from (1) the historians who influenced him and (2) fragments of his uncompleted work, which remain among his papers at the Library of Congress—"History of Civilization in the United States During the Last Fifty Years."

38. Olmsted to John Olmsted, March 11, 1864, Olmsted Papers.

39. Horace Bushnell, *Barbarism the First Danger* (New York, 1847), p. 4.

40. Horace Bushnell, "A Discourse on the Moral Tendencies and Results of Human History" (New York, 1843), pp. 3–4; Horace Bushnell, "Agriculture in the East [1846]," in *Work and Play: Or, Literary Varieties* (New York, 1864), p. 255.

41. Frederick Law Olmsted and Calvert Vaux to the Brooklyn Park Commissioners, January 1, 1868, in the *Eighth Annual Report of the Brooklyn Park Commissioners* (Brooklyn, 1868), reprinted in Fein, ed., *Landscape into Cityscape*, pp. 135–64.

ACKNOWLEDGMENTS

Over the years that it has taken to shape this volume, we have become indebted to a great many individuals and institutions for their support and assistance: the University Research Committee of Emory University, which awarded the grant that supported our initial work; the Department of English of Georgia State University (GSU) for supplementary support; Mary Bankster and the secretarial staff of GSU's English Department for typing drafts of many of the articles; Rajiv Batra and Darlene Roth for drawing and coding our maps; John Burrison, Grady Clay, Peter Dowell, William H. Slavik, David Snyder, and Edward F. Sweat for sound advice when it was most needed; and Steven Wayne Grable for his research on other "Yankee visitors" to the South, particularly John R. Dennett. To that special world of Olmsted scholarship our special thanks: to Frederick Gutheim, who made it all happen when he organized the Olmsted sesquicentennial celebration in 1972; to Albert Fein, who always asked the tough questions and posed the right challenges; to Elizabeth Stevenson, who seemed always ready for one more "go" at Olmsted, particularly on matters that concerned the South; to Charles Capen McLaughlin, for somehow always finding the answers to our questions—both large and small—relating to the Olmsted Papers, as well as to his several assistants, especially Pamela Hoes Cohen; to Charles E. Beveridge, for his critical evaluations and shared insights into the complexities of Olmsted's Southern experience; and to Laura Wood Roper, who informed and encouraged us, evaluated our ideas and criticized our writings, and was ever gracious and generous in her sharing. From one of us, a few words of special thanks: to Leonard Gerson, whose findings on Olmsted's influence in Buffalo set the pattern for similar research in Atlanta; to Herbert G. Gutman, whose distinctive analyses of the historiography of the antebellum South helped suggest a framework for reevaluating the writings of the Connecticut Yankee; and to Thomas E. Norton, whose "communicativeness" (as FLO would have described it) led him to provide the hospitality and display the endurance during two critical summers to listen to "just one more" story, one more problem, or still another attribution to "that man" Olmsted. From the other, an expression of thanks for guidance and advice from a multidisciplinary view, both to Gordon Mills, who first provided encouragement, and still does so, and to Robert D. Jacobs. From both of us, a concluding expression of appreciation: to Dewey Weiss Kramer, who made many good and useful suggestions about the book; and to Darlene Roth, veteran of NHPRC's "Camp Edit," whose blue pencil ranged over a half dozen of these articles and whose own scholarly interests have now turned to that special world of Olmsted scholarship; and finally, and most important, to the contributors, for their hard work, patience, and goodwill, a hearty and sincere "Well done and thank you" from—

The Editors

Victor A. Kramer and Dana F. White

INTRODUCTION:
Yankee Visitor

The South has always had its Yankee visitors; some of them have
been carpetbaggers and some not. I hope you keep writing about
us. We need some friendly but critical outsiders.
—letter from a South Carolina lawyer to Robert Coles upon
the publication of Coles' first essay on the South[1]

OLMSTED SOUTH had its beginnings in April 1972 at the Southeastern
American Studies Association (SEASA) meetings in Atlanta, with the
presentation of a set of papers under the title "Frederick Law Olmsted, A
Southern Exposure," as part of the sesquicentennial celebration of
Olmsted's birth. These essays on Olmsted's work in and influence on the
design and building of turn-of-the-century Atlanta were considerably
expanded and suitably revised, and open the second half of the present
volume.

Part One ("Old South") focuses upon the "other" Olmsted—author of
the "Cotton Kingdom" or "Our Slave States" series, and extravagantly
praised, ardently challenged critic of antebellum Southern life and culture. This section was conceived after the presentation of the original set
of articles that comprised "Frederick Law Olmsted, A Southern Exposure"; its editors and authors had that earlier text before them and,
consequently, were ever aware that their Old South critic would reappear, nearly forty years later, as a New South planner. The record of what
Olmsted achieved *and* failed to achieve in the Atlanta of the 1890s, the
implications thereof, and questions raised—all served to draw together
the two parts of this book, the seemingly disparate "careers" of Olmsted,
Old South and New South. Throughout OLMSTED SOUTH, then, we
have attempted to achieve unity from duality.

"Old South" opens with Victor A. Kramer's "Olmsted as Observer,"
which examines the traits that contributed to Olmsted's success as travel
writer. Kramer's analysis begins with emphasis upon Olmsted's interest
in precise observation and suggests that this interest may have been

influenced by a knowledge of the travel writings of Timothy Dwight, but even more so by ideas about civilized taste propounded by Andrew Jackson Downing. The essay shows that Olmsted's method allowed him to write his first travel book, *Walks and Talks of an American Farmer in England* (1852), in a considerably different manner from those written by many of his contemporaries. Contrasts with Emerson, Melville, and Hawthorne demonstrate Olmsted's concern with the "dignity of actuality" of what he saw. Still other comparisons with slave narratives, and popular fiction, as well as with contemporary travel accounts further emphasize the singular success of Olmsted's early method, a way of writing which led to the success of his articles and books.

The observant Olmsted—careful, prudent, and skillful in adapting to a given environment (natural and/or social), as portrayed by Kramer—has been a figure of considerable controversy in Southern studies since the initial publication of his observations. For a century and a quarter, Olmsted has been attacked with remarkable vehemence and defended with equal vigor. The historiography of this debate—with Olmsted pictured as a "damyankee" on the one side and a "prince of observers" on the other—is the subject of the next contribution, "A Connecticut Yankee in Cotton's Kingdom." Here, Dana F. White surveys the range of FLO's Southern activities, beginning with Olmsted's composition of the "Cotton Kingdom" series, and continuing with his activities and writings relevant to the South during the Civil War and its immediate aftermath. Throughout he attempts to strike a balance between those dominant images of the Connecticut Yankee as "damyankee" and "prince of observers."

The next pair of articles introduce contemporary scholarly approaches to Olmsted's Southern writings. In "'Old' Sources for a 'New' History: Frederick Law Olmsted's Journeys in the Slave South," Karla J. Spurlock-Evans concentrates upon Olmsted's observations of slave life and demonstrates how his method of describing scenes and transcribing conversations is of special value to the student of black studies. According to her analysis, traditional or "old" sources may be examined from another or "an-other"[2] perspective, namely, the Afro-American, to produce a fresh or "new" interpretation of the history of American slavery: one drawing upon Olmsted's—and other reliable travel writers' as well—observations of a "range of living portraits of slave character types." Similarly, in "Olmsted's Contributions to Folklife Research," Kay Cothran examines the "Cotton Kingdom" writings as a source for the study of folklore or folklife. She notes Olmsted's constant concern about detail; for example, she analyzes his reporting of the processes of "lining out" in group singing, his recording of "memorates" in storytelling, his general skill and accuracy in reproducing the spoken word. In addition, she outlines his descriptions of Southern households, assorted occupations, cuisine, and patterns of social interaction. Here, as in Spurlock-Evans' "'Old' Sources for a 'New' History," Olmsted's writings are viewed from a fresh perspective—a developing field of sociocultural analysis of the past, in light of the present. Both Cothran and Spurlock-Evans are critical of Olmsted's own perspective—his "biased eye," in Cothran's words. Still, both demonstrate effectively how his observations, as distinguished from his criticisms, can be applied to new and developing areas of scholarly endeavor.

Robert Detweiler's "Transcending Journalism: Olmsted's Style in *The Cotton Kingdom*" brings close textual analysis to the summary volume of "Our Slave States," in order to demonstrate that the stylistic procedures which Olmsted relied upon were conscious and systematic. Detweiler argues that critics who have labeled Olmsted a "bad writer" have failed to recognize the types of discourse that function within *The Cotton Kingdom*. Moreover, the special powers of observation which characterize Olmsted's writings provide an approach which can be related to the "new journalism" of this century. Olmsted's style, we now see, was successful because his literary strategy was a very carefully controlled one. Detweiler demonstrates that Olmsted "when he wished to, could be a competent and sensitive literary artist."

The next set of articles shifts attention to the environment. In "The Landscape Observed: Olmsted's View of the Antebellum South," William Lake Douglas, a practicing landscape architect, examines Olmsted's Cotton Kingdom writings in order to arrive at "a clearer understanding of the rationale for his approach to environmental planning and a comprehension of the success of his designs." "The significance of his Southern experience," Douglas suggests, "was derived from the observation of diverse elements that were later synthesized into a rationale for his designs." "The Landscape Observed" details the diversity of Olmsted's observations, the many and varied scenes, structures, views, sights, and sites that he recorded, described, and criticized. Here, in these accounts of a "professional observer" of the American South, Douglas explains, is prefigured the "strong philosophical approach to landscape architecture" of the founder of that profession—one that was to be "based on social conscience and on dedication to design of the total environment."

In "Knickerbocker Illustrator of the Old South: John William Orr," the "image" of the environment, rather than the "total" environment, is the subject for analysis. Howard L. Preston and Dana F. White single out from among the tight band of New York engravers of books and magazines the illustrator-engraver of Olmsted's first book (*Walks and Talks*), John W. Orr. They examine Orr as one of those "absentee observers of the Old South" who played so large a part in "the formation of the image of the antebellum South in the mind of the North." The examination of Orr as a representative figure among illustrators and engravers also marks a new departure in this study. Here Olmsted stands as a pivotal figure, rather than the central character—a pattern that describes other succeeding chapters of OLMSTED SOUTH.

The concluding articles of "Old South" introduce other social critics and other identifiable critical stances. In "Harriet Beecher Stowe's Imagination and Frederick Law Olmsted's Travels: The Literary Presentation of Fact," Victor A. Kramer is concerned with types of "literary presentation of fact." Specifically, Kramer suggests that the conventions of romance were much too limited to portray the overpowering realities of slavery. Conversely, the almost "documentary" approach which Olmsted developed offered a "new method for looking at the culture of the South at precisely the time when fanciful pictures of romance were becoming less trustworthy, and less capable of mirroring reality."

The article which follows—"Free-Soil Advocacy and the New England Emigrant Aid Society: Five 1857 Letters by Olmsted"—introduces a group of five recently discovered letters by Olmsted. Written in 1857, at a high point of his recognition as travel writer, and before he had settled into his life's work in landscape architecture, these letters show Olmsted's powers of observation in still another way. He had been active in the free-soil movement in both Kansas and Texas, and events in 1857 seemed to be drawing him to the Southwest as an agent for the New England Emigrant Aid Society. For a myriad of reasons, he chose not to pursue that option, but these letters provide a valuable glimpse of some of the options which the Olmsted of 1857 did entertain.

The final article in Part One, by Timothy J. Crimmins, is also concerned with methods of cultural analysis. "Frederick Law Olmsted and Jonathan Baxter Harrison: Two Generations of Social Critics of the American South" examines the "consciousness of the early, nonspecialized social scientists," observers who saw themselves as "disinterested" and able to "discern and record the internal workings of society," with a view toward "developing procedures to control human action." Here again, Olmsted stands not as the central character, but as a pivotal figure in the development of the social-scientific method. By tracing the influence of both Olmsted and his disinterested approach to the antebellum South upon late-century Northern observers of the late-century South, this article bridges the apparent gap between the two periods and demonstrates convincingly that the Old South critic lived on in the person of the New South planner.

Part Two is concerned with the "other" Olmsted, the founder of the profession of landscape architecture in America, prophetic voice of city planning, and patron saint of the design professions. Its initial focus is Atlanta, self-proclaimed capital of the New South.

Dana F. White's ". . . the old South under new conditions" provides a brief overview of Olmsted's Southern projects during the quarter century following the Civil War. White takes Henry W. Grady's description of the region as a starting point in comparing the environmental *and* the social realities that FLO encountered in Atlanta during the 1890s. Elizabeth A. Lyon's "Frederick Law Olmsted and Joel Hurt: Planning for Atlanta," documents Olmsted's professional work in the Georgia capital, specifically his design of suburban Druid Hills and his consultation on the Cotton States and International Exposition of 1895. Once more, Olmsted serves to introduce another key figure—this time Joel Hurt, entrepreneur and land developer, who is also the main actor in Rick Beard's "Hurt's Deserted Village: Atlanta's Inman Park, 1885–1911." Beard's main concern here is less with Olmsted than with the influence of his ideas and example on the design and development of Atlanta's earliest planned suburb. In like manner, Howard L. Preston approaches "Parkways, Parks, and 'New South' Progressivism: Planning Practice in Atlanta, 1880–1917" by emphasizing FLO's direct influence and, more significantly, that of the profession that he (and later his sons) seemed to embody—"The Landscape Priesthood," as Elbert Peets described it.[3]

More than locale ties these three chapters together. Even in their earlier form as contributions to the "Frederick Law Olmsted, A Southern Exposure" program, these essays differed from what was being done in other cities during the Olmsted sesquicentennial year. Every other city which participated in that celebration of Olmsted's birth memorialized, in one fashion or another, the landscape architect. In Atlanta, we attempted to confront both the environment—physical and cultural—and the whole man—designer and social critic—within a sharply defined historical frame of reference. All of the studies in this book are an extension of that aim.

In Frederick Gutheim's "Olmsted at Biltmore," the Vanderbilt Estate at Asheville, FLO's "last great creative effort," is viewed against the backdrop of "regionalism . . . the great and challenging theme at Biltmore." It provides a final perspective on the Olmsted sesquicentennial year. It is fitting that Gutheim, who initiated and guided the sesquicentennial celebration, has the final word.

The one hundred and fiftieth anniversary of Frederick Law Olmsted's birth was celebrated across the nation in 1972. There were two major exhibitions, at the National Gallery and at the Whitney; plans for parks and open spaces in Atlanta, Boston, Buffalo, Louisville, and San Francisco; and a variety of seminars, conferences, happenings, scholarly articles, reviews, editings, and monographs. During the six years since that celebration, the first biography of Olmsted in nearly fifty years was published in 1973, a second in 1977, with two additional ones nearing completion; and perhaps most important, the first of the seven-volume *Papers of Frederick Law Olmsted* was released in June 1977. Despite all of this activity and an impressive record of accomplishment, much remains to be done. It is time for a new beginning, a new level of sophistication, a new generation of Olmsted scholarship. OLMSTED SOUTH is offered as one beginning, an interdisciplinary effort that addresses itself to the following areas of study: intellectual history, literary history, bibliographical studies, the study of the visual arts, the history of city planning, urban history, literary criticism, the study of landscape architecture, popular culture, the history of the South, Afro-American studies, folklife research—in short, that broad spectrum of scholarship known as American studies.

NOTES

1. Quoted in Robert Coles, *Farewell to the South* (Boston and Toronto, 1972), p. 9.

2. "An-other reality" is the term coined by Charles Long to describe the uniqueness of the Afro-American experience in "Perspectives for a Study of Afro-American Religion in the United States," *History of Religions* (August 1971): 54–66.

3. "The Landscape Priesthood," pp. 186–93, in Paul D. Spreiregen, ed., *On the Art of Designing Cities: Selected Essays of Elbert Peets* (Cambridge, Mass., 1968).

PART ONE

Old South

Victor A. Kramer

OLMSTED AS OBSERVER

When Frederick Law Olmsted took time from his experiment in scientific farming for a walking tour of England in 1850, he had no way of knowing how that tour would provide insights for his later work as landscape architect and as writer of travel literature about the South. Both of these activities were nurtured by his visit to England. Olmsted's conviction about the civilizing force of parks was strengthened by what he observed in England, and his confidence as an observer of everyday life developed through encounters with the day-to-day living conditions there. Subsequently, he transformed what he experienced during this ramble into his first book, *Walks and Talks of an American Farmer in England* (1852). Olmsted's experience in England was, then, a fundamental step toward his later work as observer, critic, and planner.

Within American letters, and especially within the region which Olmsted knew best, New England, there was ample precedent for travel literature which sought to record the facts of American civilization as it expanded into the frontier. Perhaps best known among travel writers was Timothy Dwight who, even while he was president of Yale College, spent his leisure time traveling in the back regions of New England, meticulously noting the conditions of an emerging civilization, in an attempt to correct untruths initiated by ignorant reporters, some of them foreigners.[1] Dwight loved his native New England and felt its admirable characteristics should be documented. His *Travels in New England and New York* stands both as a verification of the variety of life and as proof that the forces of civilization were gradually spreading westward. It is significant that among the books which Olmsted's father enjoyed reading to the assembled family were Dwight's travels.[2] Olmsted's own "documentary" procedure, especially in his books about the South, incorporates methods similar to Dwight's.

An even more immediate basic influence which contributed to Olmsted's method of observing and, then, writing about both England and the South was his familiarity with the magazine *The Horticulturist*, a publication which sought to cultivate "rural taste" among farmers. Its editor, Andrew Jackson Downing, was convinced that a cultivated rural gentry might provide stability, order, and taste,[3] and that systematic farming procedures could improve the efficiency of Yankee agriculture. (Olmsted's early interest in agricultural reform was related to the problem of rural emigration from New England to the western frontier.) Downing, who also possessed strong convictions about the settings for individual farms and the laying out of towns, was convinced that good houses and pleasant grounds were not just a matter of aesthetics, but a reflection of the level of civilization. Indeed, Charles Beveridge has suggested that for Downing such things as tasteful settings "were only the external sign by which we would have the country's health and beauty known. . .," and that Downing's ideas were finally echoed in all of Olmsted's writings.[4]

Dwight, Downing, and Olmsted all provide observations which emphasize the social implications of a civilized taste. For instance, the early traveler Dwight noted that in the North shabby houses would invariably be accompanied by bad manners; Olmsted often makes similar observations about the South. For related reasons, and without a doubt absorbed by Olmsted, Downing urged in issue after issue of *The Horticulturist* that New York City should have a large park; Olmsted helped to create it. All three of these observers, then, were finally concerned with communal needs.

Olmsted had been familiar with Downing's writings for several years before he went to England. After Olmsted's trip to Europe, Downing asked him to write a series of articles about rural Germany. While these articles never materialized, what Olmsted had observed in Germany and rural England was a lesson not forgotten. Although he did not feel he had spent enough time in Germany to write informed articles, he nevertheless urged his friend Charles Loring Brace to write the series. Significantly, a letter to Brace reveals his own convictions on the art of travel writing: "The character of a country is to be found in its rural life. . . . Cities are alike in much of their character the world over."[5] Olmsted felt that Brace's travel articles reported merely the standard, general views of German society and he scolded his friend: "Why not tell us what you *did, saw,* and *said,* and what was said by others? . . . What's the use of mysteriousizing about and giving us a dim idea."[6] These comments reveal Olmsted's own developing method of reporting and, significantly, he soon decided to write on another subject. Almost immediately after his arrival in England he had noted its public parks, and the consequent value of rural qualities blended into a city. He decided to do an article about Birkenhead Park near Liverpool, and with that as impetus he proceeded to compose *Walks and Talks*. That book follows the traditional patterns of travel accounts—some letters, some narrative, some anecdotes—but it is distinctly Olmsted's own manner of observation. In it, he combines detailed accounts of farming procedures along with the particulars of what he observed about the English countryside.[7]

Olmsted's book is considerably different from ordinary travel documents in that it is so much concerned with specific detail. If we compare his book with Emerson's *English Traits* (1856), we find that Emerson's usual procedure is to provide a framework of abstractions through which to present views. Not so with Olmsted. He reports exactly what he sees. He is barely ashore before he is comparing "the neat, firm, solid masonwork of the dock [with the] shabby log wharves we had stumbled over as we left New York."[8] His observation of the poverty of Liverpool is similarly precise. New York, were it to experience the same level of poverty, would be ten times as "stinking" and ten times as lively; but he also notes that among the general stupor of the masses of the poor observed in Liverpool, he occasionally perceived a flash of womanly beauty "so strangely out of place, that if they had been cleaned and put in frames, so the surroundings would not appear, you would have taken them for those of delicate, refined, and intellectual ladies."[9] This way of looking carefully at particularities is basic to Olmsted's method, and indeed, to his life's work. He was always seeking the potential within the large framework, consistently preoccupied about details. Liverpool, the normal port of arrival for Americans in England, was observed by many visiting Americans. Only a few years earlier, Melville had wandered the streets of Liverpool and later fictionalized his visit in *Redburn*. It is valuable to compare the literal-minded Olmsted's account with the philosophizing of Melville's narrator. What Melville's Redburn sees provides occasions for questions about the nature of the universe. Olmsted remains much more down to earth, and what he observes provides the occasion for asking how the English people have maintained a continuity of civilizing forces over centuries.

Coincidence though it may be, Nathaniel Hawthorne's *Our Old Home*, published in 1863, contains many passages similar to *Walks and Talks*. Hawthorne, who was United States consul in Liverpool a few years after Olmsted's visit there, shared his fellow American's delight in English parks. In his essay "Leamington Spa," Hawthorne speaks approvingly of the landscape gardener's "pleasure-grounds."[10] For Hawthorne, the elaborately contrived hedges of the park were a symbol of the intricate moral mazes which man builds for himself. For Olmsted, the promise of parks for the recreation of ordinary citizens was an ideal for which America might hope.

Some of Olmsted's book about England is difficult to categorize, but its qualities of clarity, directness, and observation of detail provide a hint of what will follow in his later travel writings and, indeed, in his life's work. It is significant that Olmsted began his writing in this way. The fact that his literary career began "by espousing English institutions" points to much of what he later accomplished.[11]

As a result of the success of *Walks and Talks*, Olmsted was asked to do a series of articles for the *New-York Daily Times* about the South. The fact that he had proved himself a relatively objective observer of England promised to make him a valuable observer of the South as well. *Walks and Talks* was only the most immediate preparation; another had been his own wanderings which, in turn, led to experiments as farmer. His ability to observe and to make judgments about an agricultural situation on his own land, backed by the generosity of a father who provided funds, also helped to provide a foundation for the task of observation for which he assumed responsibility when he traveled south.

Olmsted was by nature a questioning person. His father had allowed him to come of age in a way that allowed a good deal of freedom. His mind matured so that his habitual way of looking at any situation was to ask what its surroundings were, and how resources could be adapted to the best use of existing conditions. This is what any good critic or planner does, and this is what Olmsted as journalist and observer did so well. Later in life, his ability to plan and to stand back and make the proper judgments would prove indispensable in his shaping of subsequent land-use plans throughout the country, whether in cities, or at Niagara Falls, in Yosemite, or at Biltmore. Olmsted is best remembered for park planning and for his insightful ideas with regard to land use, but his documentation of the South during the period preceding the Civil War is finally cut of the same cloth as the later Olmsted.

Travel literature had always been an important part of the writing which grew out of the American experience. For Europeans, news about the New World was provided through documentary accounts early in the period of colonization. Similarly, as Americans became separated from each other by hundreds, and even thousands of miles, they became dependent on travelers for information about the farflung areas of their republic. Olmsted's visit to England was fortuitous because it prepared him for his travels in the South. This was at a time when, for the North, the Southern states seemed isolated. As the Civil War approached, it must have seemed more and more to the North that the states south of the Mason-Dixon line were in some ways like a foreign country. Bridging an emotional as well as physical distance had become vital.

During the years immediately before Olmsted went south, no doubt many observers had provided fairly accurate accounts about Southern culture. But much rhetoric, and perhaps overreaction, clouded the facts actually reported by partisans of both sides. The rhetoric of the South's defenders revealed attempts to provide favorable accounts of the way slaves were treated, and obviously the more unfavorable aspects of slavery were usually ignored. Just as serious a problem of distortion was reflected in some of the narratives published by the abolitionists. In fact, the manner in which many slave narratives were heavily documented to verify authenticity stands as an example of the problem which existed in providing truth.[12]

To learn about slavery from slave narratives or fiction frequently raised questions about the facts supporting such documents. The sheer weight of reports during the years preceding the Civil War was strong indication of the seriousness of the conditions produced by the "peculiar institution." Some narratives read like fiction, and many slavery novels were written to appear as true accounts. Often, narratives purported to be factual but were embellished so that the facts reported would seem most distasteful. Sometimes, through an editorial intermediary, facts were exaggerated. Thus, the facts about the complexity of slavery, like the institution itself, became a tangled web (an image which is recurrent in slave narratives). Imprecise observation entangled slaveholder and slaves, as well as abolitionists and those seeking the truth about the reality of Southern culture. Basic to Olmsted's desires was how to untangle the web and get at the truth. He did not consider himself an abolitionist. He sought only to find out the facts. Extreme varieties of reporting were available both pro and con; Olmsted's accounts aimed at providing a balance.

One extreme, but not unusual, example of partisan reporting about the South is the travel writing by Joseph H. Ingraham. A prolific writer of some eighty novels, he went south in 1835, and the book which resulted (published anonymously), *The Southwest*, "by a Yankee," overflows with romantic notions. Ingraham's report presents the South in the very best light. Apparently, he was truly impressed with the developing genteel life which he observed on Mississippi plantations. When Ingraham compared Mississippi planter life with New England, he announced: "every village can draw around it a polished circle of its own; for refinement and wealth do not always diminish here, as in New-England, in the inverse ration of distance from a metropolis—and elegant women may often be found blooming in the depths of forest far in the interior."[13] The fact is, however, as was true of many such accounts, he saw only a very small part of the South. Ingraham's accounts are of some value because he did actually observe rural activities, but on the whole he was pleased with what he saw, and he saw very little.

One might compare the views of John S.C. Abbott, polemical and partisan in spirit, which were published in 1859, with those of Ingraham. Abbott, who went on to become an active Unionist writer during the Civil War, traveled into Louisiana and Mississippi, apparently to glean information which would substantiate his own views about slavery. Because of his preconceptions, he finds it impossible to observe any slave dwelling or a mansion without passing judgment as to whether he would want to live there. He even writes that "no one can pass through our Southern States, and not be saddened by the aspect of forlorn and decaying villages; wretched cabins, where a degraded race, of more than four millions, live a mere animal existence, in homes which it seems a mockery to call a home."[14] The reader finally feels overwhelmed by Abbott's polemicism. Such extremes of reportage were common.

For Olmsted, who possessed a temperament for doing and did not rely on the theoretical, the task of verifying the conditions of slavery must surely have seemed a challenge. Written as newspaper articles, and then re-edited into book form, his writings were quickly noted for their objectivity of observation, and it is that accuracy which is the most important single fact about them. Olmsted sought to provide information about the conditions of the South on its many cultural levels. While many of his abolitionist friends might have hoped that Olmsted would find all kinds of horrors to report in the slave states, they were more than likely surprised at the objectivity of the accounts which he recorded. His careful eye observed many peculiarities which he chose only to report, but not to embellish. Reported in the proper context, absence of regard for slaves as persons stands like an indictment. Similarly, stereotyped ideas, such as those about the grandeur of the South, tended to be dispelled by Olmsted's cumulative record of farms and villages that he visited which did not in any way support the popular myth. He observed that towns in central Mississippi "were forlorn, poverty-stricken collections of shops, groggeries, and lawyers' offices, mingled with unsightly and usually dilapidated dwelling houses."[15] By contrast, he was impressed with the character of German settlements in Texas because, to him, they stood as proof of the productivity of free labor. Neu Braunfels was an example of what democracy and efficiency might accomplish together. (What he saw in Texas, no doubt, reminded him of what he had earlier observed in rural Germany.) The communal nature of these settlements contrasted favorably with what Olmsted observed in much of the South. Indeed, the many pages Olmsted provided to report favorable conditions in Texas reveal his feelings about those emerging communities as contrasted with (to his mind) the backward, isolated, and poorly planned ways of living which he had otherwise witnessed throughout the South.

That Olmsted's observations remain of value down to the present is demonstrated by the range of papers included in the first part of this volume. His concern with concentrating on fact allowed him to amass data which continue to serve as source material for students within many disciplines. Olmsted the traveler had an eye for detail which allowed him to write travel accounts which today can be seen as forerunners of the documentary, a genre which we sometimes assume was invented in the 1930s. Many later observers followed in Olmsted's path. In fact, one cannot read the middle essays of Du Bois's *The Souls of Black Folk* without realizing that the careful method which Du Bois uses in those essays about rural Georgia is not different in kind from the attentive and listening Frederick Law Olmsted.

Olmsted prided himself upon blending into the region in which he happened to be visiting. He stated that those he interviewed did not suspect that he was a traveler at all. Such care and prudence and skill in adapting to an environment make his travel writings (just like his parks) valuable in their continued use.

NOTES

1. See the introductory note in Lyon N. Richardson, ed., *The Heritage of American Literature* (New York, 1951), p. 311.

2. Laura Wood Roper, *FLO: A Biography of Frederick Law Olmsted* (Baltimore, 1973), pp. 11, 40.

3. Charles Eliot Beveridge, "Frederick Law Olmsted, The Formative Years 1822–1865," Ph.D. dissertation, University of Wisconsin, 1966, p. 143.

4. Ibid., p. 147.

5. Ibid., p. 150.

6. Broadus Mitchell, *Frederick Law Olmsted: A Critic of the Old South* (Baltimore, 1924), p. 46.

7. See Roper, *FLO*, pp. 77–85, for a detailed consideration of this point.

8. *Walks and Talks of an American Farmer in England* (Ann Arbor, 1967), p. 29.

9. Ibid., p. 47.

10. Nathaniel Hawthorne, *Our Old Home and English Note-Books* (Boston, 1891), p. 62.

11. Beveridge, "Frederick Law Olmsted, The Formative Years," p. 156.

12. See Gilbert Osofsky, Introduction to *Puttin' On Ole Massa* (New York, 1969), pp. 9–48.

13. In *A Mirror for Americans, Life and Manners in the United States, 1790–1870, as Recorded by American Travelers*, Vol. 2, *The Cotton Kingdom*, ed. by Warren S. Tryon (Chicago, 1952), p. 327.

14. Ibid., p. 412.

15. *A Journey in the Back Country in the Winter of 1853–54* (New York, 1970), p. 159.

Dana F. White

A CONNECTICUT YANKEE IN COTTON'S KINGDOM

In his recent analysis of Southern travel literature on the pre-Civil War North, *A Southern Odyssey*, John Hope Franklin opens with the question: "'Who was Olmsted's southern counterpart who wrote about the North?' The answer," he suggests, "is a simple one: 'There was no southerner who wrote so comprehensively about the North.'" This, for Franklin's purposes, is a fortunate situation,

for the report of one outstanding observer such as Olmsted would have been so singular in its character and influence as to diminish all other comments about the section. Few persons bother—if, indeed, they know—about the reports of the travels in the South of such luminaries as Ralph Waldo Emerson, William C. Bryant, Bronson Alcott, Walt Whitman, and Thomas Wentworth Higginson. They need not have gone at all for all the influence they wielded in shaping opinions about the South in their section; and in any case their comments reflected their quite limited experiences in only a few places for short periods of time. Olmsted's reports were simply too unique and, indeed, too overpowering for his day and ours to share the spotlight with someone else.[1]

Had there existed, in fact, some "Southern Olmsted," Franklin concludes that his own study would have been unnecessary, perhaps unworkable.

Praise of such magnitude may seem overstated—even extravagant; nonetheless, it is fully representative of one school of opinion concerning Olmsted's writings on the slave South. In the second volume of *The Americans*, for example, Daniel Boorstin, Professor Franklin's long-time colleague at the University of Chicago, strongly commends Olmsted's "full-bodied travel books, which are judicious without being dull, colorful without being lurid; they restore the reader's faith in the human capacity for precise and reliable observation, when few others seemed capable of it. . . . There is no better introduction to Southern life on the brink of the War, and there are few comparable travel books in all American history."[2] In similar fashion, Clement Eaton has described Olmsted as the authority "who is generally regarded as a star witness against the Southern slave system." In the Preface to another of his many studies of the region, Eaton explains that "I have preferred to follow the method of the Northern traveler, Frederick Law Olmsted, of writing concretely, of recording observations instead of excessive generalizing, and of paying attention to significant details that reveal the humanity and the inner thoughts and emotions of the people of the ante-bellum period."[3] Once again, this invocation of the patron saint of travel writing seems less extravagant when set beside the judgment of J. Saunders Redding in his classic *They Came in Chains* that Olmsted was "as objective an observer as ever took a journey."[4]

Acclaim for Olmsted's travel accounts is not limited to recent historical evaluations, for his contemporaries were equally lavish in their praise. James Russell Lowell, for example, described him as "no ordinary traveller for amusement or adventure." In fact, "so cool-headed is he, . . . [so] self-possessed and wary, almost provokingly unsympathetic in his report of what he saw, pronouncing no judgment on isolated facts, and drawing no undue inferences from them" that it could be said of his writings that "no more important contributions to contemporary American history have been made" and that, compliment of compliments, "We know of no book that offers a parallel to them, except Arthur Young's 'Travels in France.'"[5] Another influential New England man of letters, Charles Eliot Norton, advised his English counterpart, Arthur Hugh Clough: "I regard Olmsted's three volumes of travels in the Slave States as the most important contributions to an exact acquaintance with the conditions and result of slavery in this country that have ever been published. They have a permanent value, and will be chief materials for our social history whenever it is written."[6] This judgment was hardly novel in a Victorian market place of ideas in which John Stuart Mill "acknowledged his reliance on 'the calm and dispassionate Mr. Olmsted'" and before which Charles Darwin praised his work as "'an admirable picture of man and slavery in the Southern States'" and "described himself as a close student of Olmsted."[7]

It is little wonder then that seventy-five years later, historian J. Franklin Jameson could advise Senator Albert J. Beveridge on a draft of the latter's biography of Olmsted's greatest contemporary, Abraham Lincoln: "In your picture of Southern ante bellum society, you rely greatly on the word of travellers. I think that this is an insecure reliance in respect to such matters." However, Jameson continued:

There have been a few travellers, such as Arthur Young and F.L. Olmsted, who, intent on disinterested social observation, go everywhere, see all sorts of places, and strike an average that one can rely upon. Olmsted was a prince of observers, and he went through the back country as well as the seaboard slave states, and observed the small slaveholders and the non-slaveholders quite as much as the less numerous great planters. . . .[8]

The sovereignty of our "prince of observers" is usually measured only in *qualitative* terms—how honest or unbiased he seemed, how carefully he observed, how well he recorded those observations. Here, it might prove instructive to introduce some *quantitative* measures—the length of time Olmsted devoted to his studies of the region, the extent of the area he traversed, and the bulk of materials he produced. For, all too frequently, reference is made to Olmsted's "book," "books," "writings," or "travel accounts," and the context in which he worked, observed, wrote, and edited is largely ignored.

Olmsted's writings on the slave South span an entire decade, beginning with his first trip below Mason and Dixon's Line in 1852 and concluding with the publication of the second edition of *The Cotton Kingdom* in 1862. The details of the various phases of his career as critic of the American South have been described elsewhere.[9] Here, they will be presented in outline only, so that Olmsted's critics—admirers, detractors, and the disinterested alike—may be viewed in proper historical perspective.

On December 11, 1852, Frederick Law Olmsted "set forth," as his biographer records it, "on his classic tour of observation."[10] (See Map 1.) After first visiting Washington, he proceeded to Richmond and Petersburg, turned coastward to Norfolk, and then south to Raleigh and Fayetteville. "Reaching the coast at Wilmington," Roper tells us, "he made a detour inland and came to it again at Charleston. From there his journey took him to Savannah and westward across Georgia through Macon and Columbus to Montgomery, Alabama, and south to Mobile and New Orleans," and from the Crescent City north and west for "a short excursion up the Red River," then back again.[11] The first leg of his initial trip south was later to become the basis for *A Journey in the Seaboard Slave States.* With the possible exception of the summary volume for the series—*The Cotton Kingdom*—this opening volume of the trilogy "Our Slave States" became the most frequently cited of Olmsted's travel accounts. It also suggested an itinerary that would be adopted as a model by some later noteworthy travelers; sparked historical debate over just how "representative" of the Old South this area was—and therefore, by extension, Olmsted's and others' accounts thereof; and served to mislead, among others, Olmsted's first modern biographer, Broadus Mitchell, as to the route that the Connecticut Yankee actually followed on his return north.[12] For after his Red River sojourn, he did not sail home from New Orleans; instead, as Roper describes it, "he returned to the Mississippi and ascended it to Vicksburg and Memphis. Following the eastern

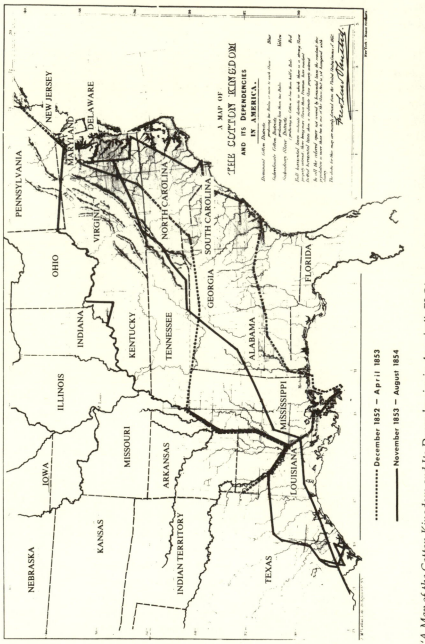

1. *"A Map of the Cotton Kingdom and Its Dependencies in America": FLO's two major journeys through the South are approximated.*

face of the Appalachians through upper Mississippi, Alabama, and Georgia, he finally made his way home through Virginia, arriving on April 6, 1853."[13]

Because he had traveled south as a correspondent for the *New-York Daily Times*, Olmsted's initial reports on the slave states were first published in Henry J. Raymond's year-old newspaper in "a series of fifty articles (misnumbered forty-eight) signed 'Yeoman'. . . . They ran, prominently displayed, from February 16, 1853, to February 13, 1854, and totaled about 120,000 words."[14] So pleased was Raymond with both their intrinsic merit and their critical reception that he soon commissioned Olmsted to undertake a second trip south as *Times* correspondent.

On November 10, 1853, "Yeoman," accompanied by his brother John, once again turned south. Starting from Baltimore, the brothers boarded the Baltimore and Ohio Railroad for Wheeling, which at that time still marked the northwestern border of an undivided Virginia. There, they transferred to a steamboat for a southwesterly trip along the Ohio River to its confluence with the Mississippi at Cairo, Illinois; and from there, down the Great Muddy to New Orleans. Along the way, they stopped over at such major river ports as Cincinnati and Memphis and, on two occasions, ventured inland for visits to Lexington-Frankfort-Louisville and, later in the trip, to Nashville (Map 1). Yet, all of this was but a prelude to, as the title of the resulting book described it, *A Journey Through Texas or, A Saddle-Trip on the Southwestern Frontier*.

The journey began when the brothers turned north and west from the Crescent City, crossing the state of Louisiana to its western entrepôt of Natchitoches. From there, they traveled due west to Nacogdoches and then dipped south to Bastrop, Austin, and San Antonio. With the Alamo City as their base, they explored the free German settlements to the north and west; the frontier outposts to the south and west, down to the Mexican border which they crossed for visits to Nava, San Juan, San Fernando, and Piedras Negras; and, to the south and east, the Gulf ports of Indianola and Port Lavaca. It was also from San Antonio that the brothers began their return journey home on April 24, 1854, by way of Houston and Beaumont to the Mississippi River.[15] Here they parted company. John, who had determined upon this trip with true Victorian kill-or-cure logic, found that his congenital tubercular condition had worsened; consequently, he sailed directly from New Orleans to New York City, arriving there in early June. Fred continued overland by horseback, traveled north and east across Mississippi and Alabama, followed the Georgia-Tennessee border in an eastward direction, and then turned north and east again to cut across North Carolina and Virginia, where he concluded his journey with a last visit to Richmond. When, in August 1854, he finally arrived at his Staten Island farm, he was concluding not only his second trip through the slave states, but also the action phase of his career as observer of the Old South. The travels were over. What remained was completing the record.

A second series of letters, thirteen numbered and two extras, had already been published in the *New-York Daily Times* between March 6 and June 7, 1854, "ending," Laura Roper notes, "abruptly and without editorial comment." For both series in the *Times*—a total of sixty-five letters, plus other reports used in editorials—our prince of observers received the regal sum of $720. [16]

During the summer of 1854, almost immediately upon his return to New York, Olmsted began the first of the three volumes (he may have projected a total of four) that eventually comprised the series "Our Slave States." [17] Although he was able to draw fully upon his initial series of letters for the *Times*, the book consumed much of his time and energy throughout the remainder of the year and for most of 1855. Not only was Olmsted a "painstaking writer" and "subject to spells of discouragement" that resulted in delays, but also he had decided to include at the beginning of the book—some two hundred of its first three hundred pages—a detailed historical account of Virginia (described by his brother John as "'a work of supererogation'"), which necessitated extensive research on his own part. Finally, on January 16, 1856, the firm of Dix and Edwards published in "one fat volume" of over seven hundred pages *A Journey in the Seaboard Slave States, with Remarks on Their Economy*. [18]

Even before this opening volume of the series was in print, the second was under way. "*Texas*," Laura Roper has observed, "was a far less difficult accomplishment than *Slave States*—for Frederick: his brother John wrote it." [19] From December 1855 through the autumn of 1856, John Hull Olmsted edited his brother's notes and letters to produce the five hundred-page text—portions of it reworked, in turn, by Fred—that appeared in mid-January 1857, again under the imprint of Dix and Edwards, as *A Journey Through Texas; or A Saddle-Trip on the Southwestern Frontier; with a Statistical Appendix*.

Once more, scarcely before the ink in the second book had dried, the third was in progress. In February 1857, this time without the aid of brother John, Fred began what would prove to be the concluding volume of "Our Slave States." Between June 3 and September 25, 1857, it was previewed in Horace Greeley's *New-York Daily Tribune* under the banner "The Southerner at Home." The first ten of the eleven articles were reprinted, this time under the imprint of the Mason Brothers—successor firm to Dix and Edwards—in the nearly five hundred-page volume *A Journey in the Back Country*, which finally appeared in April 1860.

Fully convinced by the end of that same year that war between the sections was "inescapable," Olmsted contracted with the London firm of

Sampson Low, Son and Company to produce a condensation of "Our Slave States." He was too busy himself to undertake its editing, and so, early in 1861, he contracted with the North Carolina-born, abolitionist editor of the *National Era*, Daniel Reaves Goodloe, to assume these burdens for 50 percent of the royalties. In their joint venture, "Goodloe made a number of editorial suggestions, no material one of which Olmsted accepted." In the judgment of Olmsted's biographer, the manuscript that was submitted to its London publishers in June 1861 evidenced "no change in tone or temper" in the body of the work to distinguish it "from its three sources." The Introduction, by contrast, indicated just how radically Olmsted's disposition toward the South had changed.[20] The American edition, *The Cotton Kingdom: A Traveller's Observations on Cotton and Slavery in the American Slave States*, and the English edition, *Journeys and Explorations in the Cotton Kingdom*, both appeared in November 1861. The nearly eight hundred-page, two-volume first edition sold out immediately and was quickly followed by a second, slightly revised edition in 1862. The travel record was complete.

The period between Olmsted's first trip south in 1852 and the publication of the second edition of *The Cotton Kingdom* in 1862 was not given over entirely to Southern matters. During these years, his actual travel time south was limited: he traveled between December 1852 and April 1853 and, again, between November 1853 and August 1854. His writing time stretched from the summer of 1854 to June 1857 and, thereafter, in fits and starts till 1862. In typical Olmsted fashion, there were many other activities, some of them related to the South, others not.

Most of these same activities may be dated from the spring of 1855 when Olmsted left his Staten Island farm to enter what he would describe to his father as "'a sort of literary republic.'"[21] As a partner in the New York publishing firm of Dix and Edwards and as an editor of the antislavery *Putnam's Monthly Magazine*, he came into frequent contact with many of the nation's leading abolitionist and Free-Soil thinkers. What is more, his second trip to England early in 1856, this time as a representative for Dix and Edwards, enabled him to extend his personal ties with the "Millite" persuasion of British intellectuals who, together with America's emerging "gentlemanly cosmopolitan elite," formed what has been termed recently the "Victorian connection."[22] The transatlantic link suggests itself further in Olmsted's being asked to write an introduction to T. H. Gladstone's 1857 account, *The Englishman in Kansas*.[23] During the same period, his unbroken connection with the free-soil movement is manifest in his continuing commitment to introducing its principles (and people) into Kansas, Texas, and finally the Neosho Territory. There seemed always to be new travel books in Olmsted's future: Henry Raymond was suggesting Kansas, Charles A. Dana was recommending Utah, and Olmsted himself was contemplating the recently emancipated Jamaica, as well as London, for a return visit.[24] But a series of shocks in late 1857 would dictate new directions.

The first shock was national, as the Panic of 1857 forced Dix and Edwards into bankruptcy and Olmsted out of his new career; the second was personal, as Fred learned of his brother's death (on November 24) in Europe. In addition to a deep personal loss, John's death also meant new responsibilities, for Fred would soon act upon the closing sentence of John's final letter—"'Don't let Mary suffer while you are alive'"—by marrying his brother's widow and raising her children as his own.[25] The year 1857 also promised another beginning and a new career (what would turn out to be *the* career), with Olmsted's appointment on September 11 as superintendent of New York's Central Park.[26] At this point, the man of letters gave way to the administrator—later, artist-administrator—but never again fully committed citizen of the literary republic.

The Civil War forced more changes in his life, but it also provided for important continuities. As secretary general of the United States Sanitary Commission from 1861 to 1863, Olmsted's primary responsibility was toward safeguarding the health and morale of the Union forces.[27] Typically, however, he managed to find time for a wide range of other interests. On the one hand, planning productive futures for the newly freed slaves or "contrabands" involved Olmsted as both adviser to the innovative Port Royal experiment and as on-again/off-again candidate for the directorship of what would develop at war's end as the Bureau of Refugees, Freedmen and Abandoned Lands or, more popularly, the Freedmen's Bureau.[28] Promoting the Union cause, on the other hand, made him a supporter of the Loyal Publication Society and an early member of the Union League Club of New York.[29] A breakdown in his health, caused in part by overwork, forced his resignation from the Sanitary Commission and contributed to his accepting, during the final two years of the war, the managership of the Mariposa Mining Estate in California. Here, his pro-Union loyalties remained firm as he campaigned for the National Union party in 1864. Among a plethora of other projects and plans, he even contemplated establishing "a nationwide book marketing concern" for the distribution of "the kind of literature that people really needed to read"—including Harriet Beecher Stowe's *Uncle Tom's Cabin* and the works of John Stuart Mill.[30]

The Civil War and its immediate aftermath also witnessed Olmsted's final ventures into the world of letters, with the publication of *Hospital Transports* in 1863 and his assuming the co-editorship of the *Nation* in December 1865. However, the book was more a memorial than an act of creation, and his active association with the journal lasted less than a year.[31] Within a year after Appomattox, Olmsted had resumed his career as park planner. He would, thereafter, devote most of his considerable energies to the development and promotion of the profession of landscape architecture. Not for another twenty-two years would he again turn south.[32]

The century and a quarter following Olmsted's introduction to the American South has witnessed his establishment as an authority, a "standard source" on the condition of that region prior to the Civil War. *The Cotton Kingdom*, for example, is included in Robert B. Downs' recent list of twenty-five *Books That Changed the South*, a work based on the "proposition . . . that the culture and civilization of the Southern region of the United States have been deeply affected by the printed word, or, more specifically, that certain seminal books have played key roles in shaping the South as it exists in the twentieth century."[33] Downs' "proposition" might be challenged, but that Olmsted's have been "seminal books" is beyond question. Moreover, they have exhibited a rare vitality in that, a century after their publication, they remain controversial.

Robert W. Fogel and Stanley L. Engerman's *Time on the Cross*, which itself epitomizes the controversial, provides, in its very exaggeration, a convenient beginning point for a summary perspective on one set of criticisms of Olmsted and his work.[34] In Fogel and Engerman's analysis, Olmsted figures prominently as one of the "architects of the economic indictment" of slavery, a school, they suggest, that dominated scholarship in the century before the "appearance of the cliometricians."[35] The other key "architects" of this school were Cassius M. Clay, to whom they pay minimal attention; John Elliott Cairnes, whose *Slave Power* (1862) they characterize "as largely a pithy and elegant restatement of the main themes enumerated by Olmsted";[36] and Hinton Rowan Helper, a major source for the contemporary "macro evidence" (as opposed to FLO's "micro evidence") on slavery.[37] Of the four, Helper and Olmsted were the "most influential," and judging from the attention given to each of them in *Time on the Cross*, Olmsted stands as the more important of the two.[38]

Their first criticism is of Olmsted the observer. "Despite appearances to the contrary," Fogel and Engerman explain, "the main elements of Olmsted's economic critique did not stem from firsthand observation of the actual operation of slave agriculture. For, as Olmsted noted, he reached the conclusion that slave labor was far less efficient, and more costly, in agricultural production than northern free labor during his first visit to Virginia." And, they continue with Sherlockian rigor, "his first visit to Virginia took place during the slack season." Consequently, "he could not possibly have seen, to any significant extent, the actual operation of slaves in plantation agriculture." They conclude that this first impression was confirmed throughout the rest of his travels.

Approximately 50 percent of his journey in the South took place after the completion of the harvest but before the onset of the period of intense cultivation. Much of the remainder of his time was spent in cities or in transit. Even when he visited plantations, he spent more time in the homes of planters or overseers than in the fields. Consequently, what he had to report were not mainly his own observations but the opinions of others.[39]

Having called into question the reliability of Olmsted's witness, Fogel and Engerman turn to a second major criticism of his writings[40]—their "racist foundations." "Racism," they suggest, "runs through the words of the architects of the [economic] indictment like a red line."[41] "Olmsted's view of Negroes," they caution, "should not be confused with those of Helper and Clay," for he was "a man of intense goodwill toward Negroes"; in fact, "in his sympathy for Negroes and optimism about them, Olmsted was obviously well ahead of his time."[42] But, "ironically, Olmsted's obvious goodwill toward Negroes has served to distract attention from the extent to which his biases led him to belittle the quality of black labor."[43] The Connecticut Yankee, as was true of even the most enlightened of his contemporaries, held a "low opinion of the quality of the black masses."[44] Simply stated, he underestimated them.

Nor did he comprehend the inner workings of the plantation economy of the South: his "northern chauvinism"—Fogel and Engerman's third and final indictment—precluded such an understanding.[45] One special "feature of plantation life—the organization of slaves into highly disciplined, interdependent teams capable of maintaining a steady and intense rhythm of work—[which] appears to be the crux of the superior efficiency of large-scale operations on plantations" seemed to be beyond his grasp. "Even on those few occasions when Olmsted actually witnessed gangs working in the field, he failed to appreciate the significance of slave teamwork, coordination, and intensity of effort, although he faithfully recorded these features of their work."[46]

It was not the slaves but men like Olmsted who retained a "pre-industrial peasant mentality," who viewed the teamwork, coordination, and intensity of effort achieved by black field hands as "stupid, plodding, machine-like," and "painful to witness." While Olmsted's revulsion is quite understandable, he was nevertheless wrong in concluding that the gang system was inefficient, and his belittling of the quality of slave labor was unwarranted.[47]

In short, his "northern chauvinism" blinded him to advances in agribusiness—as measured in cliometric terms, that is!

The analysis of Olmsted as set forth in *Time on the Cross*—concerning his techniques of observation, his racist biases, and his Northern chauvinism—forms one set of criticisms of the man and his work. Although often exaggerated by Fogel and Engerman, each of these points has a basis in fact, as is demonstrated later in this essay (concerning his techniques of recording observation), in Karla Spurlock-Evans' " 'Old' Sources for a 'New' History" (about his racial attitudes), and Kay Cothran's "Olmsted's Contributions to Folklife Research" (about his self-limiting regional perspective). Another set of criticisms—more specifically "Sothron"—while drawing upon these same general criticisms (particularly the first and third), tends to be more localized, more case-oriented in its indictment. In this second set, our Connecticut Yankee is transformed into a "damyankee."

The South's most formidable critic of Olmsted was Ulrich B. Phillips.[48] Phillips has been so closely identified with a Southern "loyal opposition" that there soon developed—and still persists—a scholarly debate over the comparative reliability of the Yankee traveler and this first "modern," native-son historian of the region. Its most notable expression is found in "U. B. Phillips and the Plantation Legend," published during 1944 in, significantly, the *Journal of Negro History*. In this article, Richard Hofstadter said: "I believe that a fuller and more accurate knowledge of the late antebellum South can be obtained from the volumes of Olmsted than from Professor Phillips' own writings."[49] To this "neoabolitionist" notion, Wendell Holmes Stephenson, the dean of "Southern revisionism," responded that Phillips used such sources "to good effect," that he ranked Olmsted among " 'expert observers,' " and "quoted, paraphrased, and cited him two dozen times in *American Negro Slavery*, less often in *Life and Labor in the Old South*. With few exceptions," Stephenson continued, "Phillips used the traveler's books approvingly, although his dissent was considerably more pronounced than his selections would indicate. The historian knew the South more accurately and more thoroughly than Olmsted; hence he rejected many statements in his travel accounts."[50] Another respondent to Hofstadter's claim, Bennett H. Wall, classified it as being, "perhaps as he intended, startling. But few scholars who have worked in the sources would agree. . . . Valid generalizations for the antebellum period cannot be made from what any traveler in the South saw on a given day. Even Olmsted erred."[51]

Perhaps, as Bennett Wall has suggested, it was Hofstadter's intention to "startle." Certainly, his setting up of "sides"—*either* Olmsted *or* Phillips—has had an unfortunate effect on scholarly analysis ever since. It has tended to obscure the real issue, which was not simply between the two men or even between their value systems, but, rather, in Phillips' implicit judgment that only a Southerner could comprehend the complexities of the region's social order. This same conviction unites a considera-

ble body of regional scholarship, as well as sheer propaganda, to constitute the second major set of criticisms of Olmsted and his work.

An examination of the workings of the Olmsted-Phillips debate should
serve to illuminate the underlying sectional bias of Phillips' perspective.
In the first place, while there is no denying Wendell Stephenson's statement that Phillips "quoted, paraphrased, and cited" Olmsted extensively, his contention that the historian used the travel writer "to good
effect" is open to question.[52] It is more accurate to say that Phillips
"used"—in the manipulative sense—Olmsted's witness to suit his own
purposes. Of the nearly two dozen references to the Yankee Visitor in
American Negro Slavery, published in 1918, some half dozen include qual-
ifying, condescending, or niggling comments by Phillips. Thus, for example, Phillips sketches out a cartoon version of abolitionist propaganda
in which "the master might be expected perhaps to expend the minimum
possible to keep his slaves in strength, to discard the weaklings and the
aged, to drive his gang early and late, to scourge the laggards hourly, to
secure the whole with fetters by day and with bolts by night, and to keep
them in perpetual terror of his wrath." This purposely exaggerated viewpoint is immediately identified with "Olmsted, who seems to have gone
South with the thought of finding some such theory in application." Or,
concerning the Connecticut Yankee's favorable report on the task system,
Phillips quips that "Olmsted's view was for once rose colored"; or, yet
again, following his description of a Savannah plantation, a gloating
postscript is attached to suggest that "Olmsted was in a mellow mood
that day."[53] Throughout, then, Phillips editorializes on Olmsted's observations, carefully containing them within his own prescribed framework
for Southern history.

Not until 1929, with publication of his *Life and Labor in the Old South*, did
Phillips include Olmsted among those "few to be classed as expert observers." This work is generally regarded as a "maturer" or "mellower"
book, and was recently characterized as his "least explicitly racist
work."[54] Regardless of this late concession and despite his shifting from
"negro" in 1918 to "Negro" in 1929, Phillips' framework for Southern
history remained essentially unchanged. "Southern history" meant
"white history." *American Negro Slavery*, as W.E.B. Du Bois judged it
upon its publication, was "not a history of American slavery but an
economic study of American slaveholders and their land and crops." In it,
"the Negro as a responsible human being has no place"; "by innuendo
and assumption," Du Bois continued, Phillips establishes slaves as "sub-
human," and, "by a similar method, evokes the slaveholding superman"
to create "a defense of American slavery."[55] For Phillips, the South
was—and must always remain—" 'a white man's country,' " and the
enlightened leadership that had sustained its racial order could only be

fully understood by the native Southerner—the native *white* Southerner.[56] This avowedly defensive posture branded the outsider—Northern white, any black—however "expert," as a hostile witness.[57] Such, for Ulrich Bonnell Phillips, was Frederick Law Olmsted.

A defensive alignment of a different order informed the writings of the founding generation of modern Southern studies, which established itself between the two world wars. It was sociologist Howard W. Odum who provided an innovative theoretical framework for his contemporaries with his formulation of the concept of "regionalism," a comparative-analytical approach "from the regional-national instead of the local-sectional point of view."[58] As applied to earlier critics of the South, Odum's comparative regional perspective evidenced less concern with the historical past than with the present and, even more, the future. Thus, Odum redrew that "old picture of Frederick Law Olmsted, wending his tedious and painful way through the slave states of the antebellum South," so that it "stood in vivid contrast to the picture of the swift-moving northern tourist of 1930 speeding from the national Capital to the deep South, by train or automobile or airplane in a single sweeping trip." Odum's "Olmsted complained vigorously of too plain hospitality and too meagre civilization. . . ."

Granting that this visit to the "Back Country" failed to reveal the best of the Old South, nevertheless had he visited every great southern place and been welcomed into every southern gentlemen's [sic] home, he would still have found but a fraction of the measure and range of the South's picture in 1930. . . . Whether he appraised the southern picture in measures of money and material things, in numbers and quantity, in aggregates or individual excellence; or whether he measured it in terms of the higher culture and form, . . . he would still have found southern wealth and resources far beyond the limits of any ante-bellum dream. . . . And he would also have beheld, mile after mile, area upon area, pictures of the same limited and sordid conditions of which he complained. For the South of 1930 was a kingdom of wealth and it was a kingdom of waste.[59]

Thus did Odum adapt Olmsted to the purposes of regionalism. On the one hand, he employed Olmsted's testimony to put to rest, for once and for all, a dead and often stifling past—with the goal of shaping a better future. On the other, somewhat in the manner of U. B. Phillips, Odum carefully qualified the record so as to maintain control over his witness—as with "granting that this visit to the 'Back Country' failed to reveal the best of the Old South," a judgment which, at best, begs the question.

Regionalism, in the Odum tradition, has been central to Olmsted scholarship. It found its most comprehensive expression with the publication in 1924 of Broadus Mitchell's *Frederick Law Olmsted: A Critic of the*

Old South, the first modern analytical study of FLO, which is examined later in this essay. But there were other important critical analyses of our Yankee Visitor during these same formative years of Southern studies that were more readily identifiable with "sectionalism" than regionalism.

Most notable among the sectional critics of Olmsted during this period was historian-folklorist Frank L. Owsley, one of the "Twelve Southerners" to declare in 1930 that *I'll Take My Stand*.[60] In his classic *Plain Folk of the Old South*, this Agrarian asserted that it was "Olmsted, perhaps, [who] contributed more than any other writer to the [generally accepted] version of Southern society" as having been composed exclusively of three groups—plantation slaveholders, their chattel, and poor whites. "For he was possessed of unusual skill in the art of reporting detail and of completely wiping out the validity of such detail by subjective comments and generalizations."[61] Thus, in the "back country":

A few systematic travelers, especially naturalists and those who became sojourners and studied the character and resources of a region and its people in the preparation of "geographies" and emigrant "guides," give a picture of the people of the pine barrens and mountains vastly different from writers such as Olmsted. . . . . So do the local historians, biographers, genealogists, and writers of autobiography and reminiscences (particularly lawyers, preachers, small-town newspaper editors, and doctors) who have lived in and near the pine belt and mountains, and who possessed intimate knowledge and understanding of the life and character of the folk in these regions.[62]

And yet the testimony of these "insiders" was largely ignored by "outsiders": namely, "other writers, who had little or no firsthand knowledge of the South, [and who] quite naturally relied on the writings of travelers, and particularly Olmsted, who was regarded as dispassionate and authoritative."[63] Lost in the process, Owsley concluded, was not only the insider's picture of the system, but also any recognition of the presence in the antebellum South of another important class of free whites, the plain folk.

That the *New-York Daily Times'* correspondent "Yeoman" could overlook the yeoman class of the South was accounted for in still another seminal work in early Southern studies, W. T. Couch's *Culture in the South*. In "The Tradition of 'Poor Whites,' " A. N. J. Den Hollander, who was highly critical of the state of the art of travel writing, singled out in Southern accounts a built-in set of biases in approach and attitude that contributed to misunderstanding of the plain folk.

The itinerary most commonly followed by travellers brought them in contact with the lower piney woods people and "poor-whites" to be found in the neighborhood of plantations. On the other hand, regions like the upper piedmont, eastern

Tennessee and eastern Mississippi, where a vigorous yeomanry lived, lay outside the tourist route. Besides the generally crude and poor aspect of the farmsteads, the tumbledown fences, ramshackle outhouses, razor-back hogs rooting under the porches, and the coarse "hoecake" or "hog and hominy" of the common people impressed northerners as unfavorably as their ignorance, rough-and-ready easy-going manners, and willingness to be satisfied with little. Frederick Law Olmsted wrote elaborately on this point.[64]

In sum, most travelers never saw Southern yeomen; many who did failed to recognize them; and still others, like Olmsted, let their Yankee preconceptions warp their observations of these plain folk.

The condition that unites these disparate approaches to Southern studies—regionalism and sectionalism: the works of Odum, Owsley, Den Hollander, and even Phillips—in their shaping of a critical perspective on Olmsted was perhaps best expressed at the beginning of the century by the "literary historian and essayist" William Garrott Brown.[65] Although he credited such analysts of the region as Cairnes and Olmsted, the latter especially for the "mass of interesting, accurate, and intelligent observations" that he "supplied," Brown finally discredited the picture of the South that emerged from their writings:

. . . it is quite possible that Mr. Cairnes's close reasoning, Mr. Olmsted's intelligent observation, and all similar attempts from outside, or at least from outsiders, have failed to paint for us the true form and hue of that vanished life. . . . We admit the facts, perhaps, and we admire the reasoning, but we do not recognize the picture. A perfectly faithful picture of the civilization of the lower South would show at work there the forces and tendencies which Mr. Cairnes discussed, but it would show others also. It would belie none of Mr. Olmsted's observations, but it would correlate them with other facts, not, perhaps, less important, and throw upon them a light not quite so pitiless and distorting.[66]

That "light" of truth would be filtered *not* through "the outside view of that society," *but* from within.[67] A Southern perspective was thus in order. This is what united Phillips, Odum, Owsley, and Den Hollander, despite their assorted attitudes about method, focus, race, class, and the like. For the founding generation of Southern studies, Olmsted's was "the outside view of that society."

This self-conscious exclusionary thrust, which seems almost endemic to area studies in their developmental stage, is certainly familiar to our own scholarly generation, which has observed similar tendencies in black, chicano, women's, and assorted ethnic and minority studies. For Southern studies, there was an important difference: among the "outsiders" excluded were the section's indigenous African Americans. An extreme statement of this view was offered by Edward Ingle in his 1896

Southern Sidelights: A Picture of Social and Economic Life in the South a Generation Before the War. "By Southerners," Ingle explained, "are meant the white people of the South, without regard to classes. If it had been possible to do so," he continued, "the subjects of slavery and the influences leading to the crisis of 1860 would have been disregarded." When their significance mitigated against his adopting this option, Ingle explained, he treated them "as secondary topics rather than as leading ones."[68] Admittedly, this represents an exaggerated expression of Southern white scholarship in the first half of the present century. Nevertheless, it was fully representative in its purposeful exclusion of a black perspective.[69]

A black scholarly perspective on Southern studies, for which Olmsted served as a major source, was to be found in the publications of the Association for the Study of Negro Life and History. For example, in the first sixty volumes of its *Journal of Negro History*, published from 1917 to 1975, there were some thirty-odd separate references to Olmsted, all dealing with his Southern writings or activities. In contrast, in the first eighty volumes of the *American Historical Review*, published from 1895 to 1975, there were fewer than ten, about half of them dealing with Olmsted's career in landscape architecture.[70] More important than mere numbers, however, was focus. The *Journal of Negro History* not only published Hofstadter's important "U. B. Phillips and the Plantation Legend," but also the Bauers' innovative "Day to Day Resistance to Slavery," which drew heavily upon Olmsted, and Arthur M. Schlesinger's "Was Olmsted an Unbiased Critic of the Old South?" which was later incorporated into the Editor's Introduction to the 1953 edition of *The Cotton Kingdom*.[71] Again by way of contrast, the forty volumes of the *Journal of Southern History* published from 1936 to 1975 contained only sixteen separate references to Olmsted, many of them basically critical in tone. Thus, three of the four presidential addresses to the Southern Historical Association that made references to him were skeptical (and sectional) in emphasis; the fourth, by the Association's first black president, John Hope Franklin, was not.[72]

Abundant reference to Frederick Law Olmsted will be found in the works of major black scholars of this century, from Carter G. Woodson and Bertram W. Doyle to J. Saunders Redding and John Hope Franklin.[73] This in no way indicates that scholarly sides have been drawn—with blacks for and whites against Olmsted. It does suggest, however, that in the area of Southern studies there has been no consensus about "the outside view"—on this point, at least, no solid South.

In his recent Introduction to the monumental *Slave Testimony*, John W. Blassingame addresses a number of questions concerning bias and verification in the documents for his edition that are similar in kind to those raised by Olmsted's critics.[74] Blassingame prefaces his own answers to these questions by repeating Stanley Elkins' judgment on the travel accounts of Fanny Kemble, Sir Charles Lyell, Olmsted, and others, that they "were men and women of character, and the things they wrote had character also; much is gained and not much lost on the provisional operating principle that they were all telling the truth."[75] "Yet," Blassingame offers,

there is considerable controversy about these and other eyewitness accounts traditionally accepted by historians. The best example of this is that ubiquitous traveler in the Old South, Frederick Law Olmsted. Although Elkins trusts what he says because of his character, U.B. Phillips, Stephen B. Weeks, James C. Bonner, Stanley Engerman, Robert Fogel, and Frank L. Owsley charge him with an antislavery bias. According to Bonner, Olmsted "saw only what he came to see. . . . and recorded his observations in terms of preconceived ideas, prejudice and subjectivity." Weeks feels that, because of Olmsted's "remarkable faculty for seeing the worst side of southern society," his work is full of "bitterness, prejudice, misrepresentation and contradiction."

"If, in spite of the bias charged against him, scholars can still trust Olmsted because he had character," Blassingame concludes, a similar trust ought to be placed in slave testimony.[76]

"Character" alone could never justify either Olmsted's witness or, for that matter, the reliability of slave testimony.[77] Far more is needed to place the observations and judgments of the prince of observers/damyankee in true perspective: specifically, a return to the written record and an overview of Olmsted scholarship of the past seventy-five years.

Olmsted's three travel accounts, Laura Wood Roper has estimated, "all together sold, probably, less than 25,000 [copies] from 1856 to the start of the Civil War."[78] His publisher, Mason Brothers, reissued *A Journey in the Seaboard Slave States* in 1859, 1861, and 1863; *A Journey Through Texas* in 1859 and 1860; and *A Journey in the Back Country* in 1861 and 1863 (with English editions also appearing in both years). The Texas volume was translated into German and released as *Wanderungen durch Texas und im mexicanischen Grenzlande* in 1857, 1865, and 1874. Not until early in the next century would there be further reissues, with a new edition of *Seaboard Slave States* published in 1904 and of *Back Country* in 1907. Modern editions of the travel books were not reissued until recently: *Seaboard Slave States* by the Negro Universities Press in 1968, *Texas* for Burt Franklin's "American Classics in History & Social Science" in 1969 and by the University of Texas Press in 1978, and *Back Country* for Schocken's "Sourcebooks in Negro History" in 1970. (James Howard's 1962 edition of *Texas* omits those sections of the original which did not apply directly to the Lone Star State.) *The Cotton Kingdom*, the summary volume of "Our Slave States," was not republished until 1953, with the Schlesinger edition.[79] Thus, in the century following their initial publication, Olmsted's became "rare books," literally as well as figuratively.

Part of the responsibility for the publishing industry's neglect of the "Cotton Kingdom" series must be attributed to Olmsted himself. During the immediate post-Civil War years, his biographer relates that "he was fully committed to the profession of landscape architecture, and no longer thought of himself as a writer." In 1891, for example, when Olmsted was again involved in Southern matters, John Murray Forbes, "on reading *Cotton Kingdom*, was so impressed and delighted that he proposed reissuing it, but Olmsted dissuaded him." While admitting that the book might "somewhat counteract the mischievous tendency in recent literature to romanticize falsely" the antebellum South, Olmsted insisted that "no commercial demand existed to justify its republication. There was no turning back for Olmsted," Roper concludes, "to his youthful career as man of letters."[80] Three subsequent generations of Olmsted scholars would also, for the most part, avoid "turning back" to the author "Yeoman," except as he prefigured the designer of "Greensward."[81]

Three clusters of dates form the first generation of Olmsted scholarship: *the early 1890s*, when FLO had achieved his greatest recognition as a landscape architect; *the early 1900s*, the year of his death, in 1903, when he was memorialized in numerous obituaries, and the publication date, in 1904, of the first new edition of his opening travel journal; and *the early 1920s*, the centennial of his birth, in 1922, which marked the occasion for the release of the first of two volumes of his professional papers and the appearance, in 1924, of Broadus Mitchell's account of "A Critic of the Old South." By this last date, Mitchell reported, he was "known to the public more for his later activity as a landscape architect than for his earlier work as a writer on society. A good deal of effort has been used, some of it by Olmsted himself," Mitchell suggested, "to show that his success in an aesthetic field was all along preparing, however, unconsciously."[82] The phrasing is not the best, but the message is clear: Olmsted's early life was being projected as a preparation for his later "life's work"—namely, landscape architecture.

In a recent dissertation about "Frederick Law Olmsted's Later Years," Leonard J. Simutis asserts rather forcefully that FLO "did everything he could late in life to reinforce the image of himself as a Romantic artist. In his autobiographical writings he altered factual material and chronology to make the events of his life more closely conform to actions, attitudes and beliefs attributed to the Romantic."[83] Whether, in fact, Olmsted went that far in his attempts to create a professional identity for himself and his fledgling profession is subject to debate and is challenged in Albert Fein's forthcoming critical analysis of FLO's design philosophy.[84] However, the progression of biographical materials about him from the early 1890s to the late 1920s would have made any such "creative biography" unnecessary.

The 1892 entry for him in the *National Cyclopaedia of American Biography*, for example, gives due weight to the "two Olmsteds"—author and landscape architect. However, in this one-column sketch, Olmsted's travels through "France, Italy and Germany, giving special attention to the study of parks and rural arts" in 1859, are related (at least according to their placement in the text) to his first visit to England in 1850 and his Southern journeys in 1852–1854.[85] Mariana Griswold van Rensselaer's influential eight-page portrait for the *Century* in 1893, which was written in close consultation with its subject, devotes only three paragraphs to Olmsted's Southern travels. After granting that "their picture of the rural communities of the South just before the war has great historical value," Mrs. van Rensselaer cautions that

their incidental autobiographical value should not be overlooked. They show that, despite the day-dreaming of his boyhood, Mr. Olmstead was an eminently practical person; and no one needs to be practical more than the landscape-gardener. They prove great breadth and strength of human sympathy, and this trait must afterward have inspired him to work enthusiastically and lovingly upon his pleasure-grounds for the poor of our great cities. They are marked by a simplicity, a lack of self-consciousness, which although the Philistine may not think so, almost always characterizes a true artist. Even more than the "Walks and Talks" they reveal a power of perception keen and catholic enough to excite the envy of a professional reporter; and this faculty is, of course, a needful part of an artist's equipment.[86]

The travel writer's role was thus redefined. Henceforth, he would often be presented as an *artiste manqué* in search of a fitting *milieu*, as in Daniel Burnham's tribute of 1893: "An artist, he paints with lakes and wooded slopes; with lawns and banks and forest-covered hills; with mountainsides and ocean view."[87] "Yeoman" was thus subsumed into "Greensward."

The *Nation* mourned his passing in 1903 with the observation that: "By a happy circumstance, his name has been actively perpetuated in the profession of landscape gardening and architecture, which . . . he brought to an unparalleled pitch of achievement and propaganda." At the same time, unfortunately, "the civil engineer and scientific farmer, the American Arthur Young travelling and observing in both hemispheres, will be forgotten in the creator of the pleasure-grounds of our teeming population, the promoter of civic embellishment. . . . Forgotten too much—but they are time-proof—are Mr. Olmsted's classic reports of his journeys in the Southern States before the war."[88] *World's Work*, in its obituary notice, called these "the best books of observation in the South that exist in the whole great volume of literature about ante-bellum conditions there," but otherwise concentrated upon his achievements as landscape architect.[89] The *American Historical Review* praised him as "the leading authority to whom historical students must always refer for contemporaneous and first-hand accounts of the agricultural resources of the south on the eve of the Civil War, and for the effects of slavery in the agricultural system," but granted that "he is most generally known for his remarkable achievements in beautifying the landscape of many parts of our country."[90] The theme was constant in obituary after obituary: the great landscape architect had, in his youth, written important works about the South. But there was mention only, not analysis, the implication being that Olmsted's travel accounts—all of which had been published last (in this country) before the end of the Civil War—were of antiquarian or, at best, historical interest. Only Godkin's weekly, now edited by Wendell Phillips Garrison, which continued to pride itself on "Mr. Olmsted's connection with the incipiency of the *Nation*," suggested that his Southern writings merited serious attention: "In them may now be read, and should be read by every one alarmed at present Southern conditions, the underlying causes of post-bellum backwardness and reaction."[91] Nevertheless, in its insistence on the contemporary relevance of "Our Slave States," as has so often been the case with this "Weekly Journal Devoted to Politics, Literature, Science, and Art," the *Nation* constituted a majority of one.

The publication of two works in 1904 provided a potential starting point for a reevaluation of the "Cotton Kingdom" series, as suggested by the *Nation*, in light of the transformation of the South in the half century after their initial publication. In the January issue of the *South Atlantic Quarterly*, Thomas H. Clark released a previously unpublished letter to him that was written by Olmsted in 1889, in which the Connecticut Yankee related "how I look upon the after troubles of slavery." For all practical purposes, this was a random piece that received little attention at that time or later.[92] Putnam's new edition of *Seaboard Slave States* in the same year was another matter.

The Biographical Sketch by Frederick Law Olmsted, Jr., which opens this volume, is, as might be expected, a sympathetic, one-sided account of the great man by his dutiful son: it contains no surprises. The same cannot be said of the Introduction. That it was written by William P. Trent, a native Southerner, was the first surprise.[93] Trent, the founding editor of the *Sewanee Review*, biographer of William Gilmore Simms and, at the time, professor of English at Columbia University, seemed a curious choice, in some quarters, to introduce Olmsted's travel account to a new generation of readers.[94] A reviewer for the *Nation* suggested that "the calling in of Professor Trent as a sort of sponsor seems calculated to propitiate Southern readers and bookbuyers."[95] But Trent was no spokesman for the Old South, the Lost Cause: his was a voice of careful moderation, one representing what Paul Gaston has termed the "New South creed."[96] From his perspective, "the vast good wrought to the South by the abolition of slavery, even at the cost of the war, of Reconstruction, and of the present agitation of the race question, can be brought home in no better way than by a journey through the New South after a careful study of this [Olmsted's] book dealing with the Old."[97] That Trent's own journey along what Paul H. Buck was to call the "road to reunion"[98] was not universally appreciated by Southerners is evidenced in historian Walter L. Fleming's review of *Seaboard Slave States* in *The Dial*. According to Fleming, Olmsted was "a hostile critic who paid slight attention to the ameliorations of the institution" of slavery and who "did not see what forty years of freedom have shown, that it was the negro, not slavery, that injured the economic system of the South." For Fleming, despite these criticisms, Olmsted's book was a valuable, if biased source; Trent's Introduction he dismissed as adding "nothing to the value of the work."[99] Again, there was no solid South when it came to interpreting the record of the past.

A third and final publication about Olmsted that appeared in 1904, again by a native Southerner, merits attention: William Garrott Brown's "The South at Work," a series of twenty articles for the *Boston Evening Transcript*. According to Wendell Holmes Stephenson,

as 1904 was the fiftieth anniversary of Frederick L. Olmsted's journey, Brown desired to make "pretty constant reference" to the New Yorker's observations by way of contrasts and comparisons, but this approach was discouraged. "That is going rather too far back," the editor wrote. "What we want to know is how the South is picking up now and how it has improved in the last ten years."[100]

"Brown adjusted his method to meet the desires of his employers," Stephenson concludes, "although conformity to a journalistic pattern sacrificed historical perspective. . . ." Nevertheless, "like Olmsted, Brown began his itinerary at Washington, D.C., and . . . traversed the seaboard states from Virginia to Texas."[101] That Brown, who had been so critical of Olmsted two years earlier in *The Lower South in American History*, was unable to carry out his initial plans is doubly unfortunate: perhaps Brown's New South (and secular) version of *In His Steps* would have elicited a Northern response, quite possibly from the *Nation*. And, one final surmise, the resulting exchange might have brought about a serious reconsideration of the entire "Cotton Kingdom" series.

The "Centenary of Frederick Law Olmsted, Sr." was proclaimed in the December 1922 issue of the *American City* by Theodora Kimball, "Editor of the Olmsted Papers," without mention of his Southern writings.[102] This brief note announced the start of publication that same year of FLO's "Professional Papers." The first volume of *Forty Years of Landscape Architecture*, edited by Olmsted, Jr. and Kimball, was divided into three parts: "Biographical Notes 1822–1903"; "Early Experiences: Their Contribution to His Later Career"; and "American Landscape Gardening in 1857." These miscellaneous letters, autobiographical jottings, and excerpts from the published works—tied together with a running commentary by the editors—were intended, according to the Preface of the second volume published in 1928, "to serve as a background for a projected series of volumes containing his most important professional papers." Thus, for example, the selections in Chapter 8, "Southern Trips, 1852–1854," are all of the landscape or cityscape. Their statement of editorial policy is mirrored in the weight of the two volumes: the first is a mere 131 pages; the second, "Central Park as a Work of Art and as a Great Municipal Enterprise 1853–1895," is a thick 575 pages.[103] Mariana van Rensselaer or, for that matter, Olmsted, Sr., himself could scarcely have done more to spotlight "Greensward."

The final major work of the first generation of Olmsted scholarship was Broadus Mitchell's analysis of the "Critic of the Old South." Ever since its publication in 1924, it has been a difficult book to come to grips with. A reviewer for the *American Historical Review* judged it "a remarkably good book about a most remarkable man," but another contemporary, reviewing it for the *Mississippi Valley Historical Review*, found Mitchell's "account sketchy, random, and loosely narrated."[104] Charles Beveridge has provided the most lucid and telling criticism of Mitchell's book, which he describes as "a convenient compendium of information about Olmsted's life and southern travels." He then qualifyies this praise by adding that "Mitchell does not understand Olmsted the man and this leads him into errors of organization and interpretation."[105] According to Beveridge, the essential shortcomings of Mitchell's work were "his misinterpretation of Olmsted at crucial points because of clear misuse of sources" and his failure to "indicate the development that took place over the years in the way that Olmsted viewed the South and the purposes for which he wrote about it." The second deficiency was based largely on "his inexplicable failure to use the original newspaper articles" in the *Times* and *Tribune*.[106] Still, Mitchell's has been an influential work. For nearly half a century it was the only book available on Olmsted's Southern travels, but now that other and more scholarly studies are at hand, it seems time to examine *Frederick Law Olmsted: A Critic of the Old South* in a new light.

Broadus Mitchell's analysis is best understood in relationship to the founding generation of Southern studies, particularly Howard W. Odum and Frank L. Owsley. Like Odum's, Mitchell's method was comparative-analytical, his focus not only on the historical past, but also on the present, with an eye to planning the future; like Owsley's, his commitment was to the plain folk. For Mitchell, slavery constituted an enduring "system of colonization": "Evidences of this system marked the whole face of the country, as they will continue to do for generations yet to come."[107] Mitchell's version of regionalism, a response to this colonialism, called for economic development and social change or, more simply, modernization.[108] But change must be evolutionary, not revolutionary: the South had to maintain its distinctiveness. Here is where Olmsted came in, for Mitchell judged him a reasonable critic of the South, one who, unlike many of his contemporaries and followers, had approached it in a spirit of conciliation.[109] And finally, Olmsted's witness was itself still of value, for many of the conditions that he described as "obtaining seventy-five years ago, are exactly matched all over the South to-day."[110]

Relevance, that catchword of the 1960s, gave Olmsted's Southern writings special significance for Broadus Mitchell. Relevance would come to have a new meaning for the second generation of Olmsted scholarship, as both contemporary events and historical commemorations during the 1950s and 1960s served to create a new reading public for the "Cotton Kingdom" series. The civil rights revolution of the 1950s, the opening of a new phase in the debate over slavery, the Civil War Centennial, and the one hundredth anniversary of Olmsted's travels south combined to provide the occasion for a reassessment of the work of the Connecticut Yankee.

A convenient starting point for this second generation of Olmsted scholarship is the publication in 1953 of a new edition of *The Cotton Kingdom*. It was under the editorship, as Charles Beveridge described him over a decade later, "of the historian who has written about Olmsted with the most accuracy, intelligence and understanding—Arthur Schlesinger, Sr."[111] Schlesinger's editing was, in fact, meticulous and superlative, and his analysis, informed and challenging. He defended the historical significance of Olmsted's book by suggesting that it was "a uniquely candid and realistic picture of the pre-Civil War South. *The Cotton Kingdom*," in Schlesinger's judgment, ". . . is the nearest thing posterity has to an exact transcription of a civilization which time has tinted with hues of romantic legend. Olmsted's account," he concluded, ". . . is an indispensable work in the process of recapturing the American past."[112] Some responses to

Schlesinger's edition were predictable. A reviewer for the *Journal of Negro History*, for example, suggested that the book's "resurrection . . . at this time may well be one of the most outstanding contributions to social history in recent years."[113] Some reactions had to come as surprises, however, particularly those from England.

The *Times Literary Supplement* gave a front-page review to this reprint of a hundred-year-old work because it "is a beautiful and timely piece of bookmaking and editing. . . [W]hy timely?" The *TLS* answered its own question: "Because the social strains to which the whole of the United States and, above all, the slave states were being subjected in the decade before the outbreak of the war are strains that other 'plural' societies are undergoing to-day, and in *The Cotton Kingdom* are warnings and hopes for societies that, in no very long time, must choose their way."[114] D. W. Brogan, in *The Spectator*, maintained that "all in all this is a first-class piece of reporting. It deserves to be widely read here, and still more in South Africa."[115] Again, relevance: this time not just to the contemporary South or even the United States, but to the world.

The most important review of the Schlesinger edition appeared in the *New York Times Book Review*, under a heading that only a professional banner-writer could dream up: "The South Called Him a Liar."[116] Laura Wood Roper's favorable review of Schlesinger's editing was especially significant, for in the decade of the 1950s, she would not only establish herself as the foremost authority on the Connecticut Yankee, but would also begin to right the imbalance between "Yeoman" and "Greensward" that was created by the previous generation of Olmsted scholars.[117] Her comprehensive and gracefully written *FLO*, the culmination of over two decades of work on Olmsted, is as close to an authorized biography as we are ever likely to see: it is *the* standard source.

Other potential standard sources may be found in the dissertations of three young scholars of the period: Charles McLaughlin, Charles Beveridge, and Albert Fein. Charles McLaughlin, who had begun work on FLO's papers as an undergraduate at Yale in 1950, completed the "Selected Letters of Frederick Law Olmsted" at Harvard in 1960; Charles Beveridge wrote about "The Formative Years 1822–1865" in his Wisconsin dissertation of 1966; and Albert Fein concentrated on "His Development as a Theorist and Designer of the American City" at Columbia in 1969. The long-term impact of their work is still to be felt.

As editor-in-chief of *The Papers of Frederick Law Olmsted*, Charles McLaughlin's work over the past twenty years has been both scholarly and entrepreneurial. On the one hand, it has involved the gathering, organizing, and interpreting of enormous amounts of information about Olmsted and his times. On the other, it has necessitated his training a staff, establishing a permanent office, and, most important, raising the funds needed to support this major publications project. The superb opening volume, *The Formative Years 1822–1852*, fully justifies his labors for the project. Charles Beveridge, an associate editor of the Papers and co-editor of the initial volume, is preparing an analysis of FLO's professional life and work. His imaginative "Frederick Law Olmsted's Theory of Landscape Design" suggests that Beveridge's forthcoming book will probably surpass even the excellence of his dissertation.[118] Albert Fein's innovative interpretations of the man and his times have been widely distributed, most notably in his admirable synthesis, *Frederick Law Olmsted and the American Environmental Tradition*.[119] His forthcoming study of the cultural and social forces that helped shape FLO's theory of design promises to extend the Fein trademark: the ability to connect Olmsted with a wide range of contemporaries and ideas and movements, and provide, thereby, a valuable historical synthesis.

There were other and lesser interpreters of Olmsted following Schlesinger. Harvey Wish, for example, compiled selections from all four of the Cotton Kingdom books in *The Slave States*.[120] Charles Beveridge, the most discerning critic on the subject, dismissed Wish's Introduction to this edition as having "no important insights to offer," and he applied the same judgment to F. Garvin Davenport's "The South in Sectional Crisis, 1852–1860."[121] Davenport's bibliographical summaries on the *Back Country* and *Seaboard Slave States* are fully as testy about Olmsted as Davenport accuses Olmsted of being about the South. Nevertheless, since they are part of Thomas D. Clark's five-volume bibliography of Southern travel accounts, their importance must be recognized.[122] In addition to these lesser interpreters, there was one major American man of letters who reassessed *The Cotton Kingdom* in the spirit of the Civil War Centennial. To literary critic Edmund Wilson, "Olmsted, in the literary sense, was a very bad writer."[123] To most postwar critics of American society—whether of its present state or its history—this judgment, if indeed valid, would have been of little interest. (Robert Detweiler's "Transcending Journalism," which appears later in this volume, challenges Wilson's judgment.)

The central interest during this period was in Olmsted's testimony as it might apply to current social questions, as well as to long-standing historical debates. In the spate of books on the so-called civil rights question, for example, selections from his travel accounts were often incorporated into anthologies or "readers." Nor was Olmsted's witness absent from imaginative works on the race issue. In his "documentary play" *In White America*, Martin Duberman included Olmsted—together with Jefferson, Nat Turner, John Brown, and others—among his "narrators."[124] The renewal of the so-called debate over slavery, an academic manifestation of the national confrontation over a redrawing of racial lines—first in the South and then nationwide—also lent new significance to Olmsted's testimony. Thus, Kenneth Stampp's *The Peculiar Institution*, the first major revisionist work on slavery by a white historian of U. B. Phillips' synthesis on slavery, opened with a scene from *Back Country* and relied, throughout, on the observations and many of the judgments of Frederick Law Olmsted.[125]

The primacy of *The Peculiar Institution* in what Fogel and Engerman have called the "neoabolitionist resurgence" seems to have led them into making Kenneth Stampp their special target. Part of their attack on Stampp results from what F+E judged to be his excessive reliance on Olmsted.[126] In fact, their portrait of FLO in *Time on the Cross* as a kind of cliometric version of Milton's Satan, the publishing industry's opening barrage in the most recent scholarly conflict over slavery, may be identified as one key factor in the generation of a third phase of Olmsted scholarship. Another generator, far removed from the smoke of battle (as well as of Milton's Hell), was the singularly successful celebration in 1972 of the sesquicentennial of Olmsted's birth, a carefully orchestrated national happening that was designed to coincide with the "environmental awakening" of the early 1970s. This second side of Olmsted—"Greensward," not "Yeoman"—has, by and large, dominated most recent scholarship.

Many of the questions raised in *Time on the Cross* about FLO's witness remain unanswered, but as Bennett H. Wall has observed, "Fogel and Engerman have done historians a service needed for more than a century—they criticize Frederick Law Olmsted's reliability as an observer." Thus, while other historians involved in the current phase of the debate over slavery—including Eugene Genovese and Herbert Gutman, who have written two of the major studies in the field for the 1970s—continue to draw upon Olmsted's testimony, the methodological problems of reliability and verification remain.[127] These problems are addressed in the final section of this essay.

One final and recent work that deals extensively with Olmsted's travels through the South is that of my colleague, Elizabeth Stevenson.[128] *Park Maker*, her fourth biography, is in the tradition of life writing described by Catherine Drinker Bowen as "The Craft and the Calling." That is, it combines historical recreation with artistic sensibility to create a distinct *genre* called biography.[129] Consequently, *Park Maker* stands outside the limits set for the debate over slavery and, in fact, most of the scholarly categories included in this essay. All the same, it incorporates two elements that merit special consideration here. The first is the biographer's attempt to internalize her subject's experience by trying to see things through his eyes and tell the story, essentially, from his perspective. The second is Stevenson's own perspective, that of a native Southerner attempting to balance the good and the bad of the Old South, so as to draw a believable picture of the slave states. At times, her insider's view is certain to strike the outsider as overly defensive: there are echoes of *I'll Take My Stand* here. Still, her biography is an interesting one and always good reading.

Interesting, too, especially from the design perspective, are the plenitude of studies that clustered around the Olmsted sesquicentennial celebration. Many of these efforts were simply local history projects, intended to complete the official record of a suburb, town, or city; others were essentially preservation plans—"save" an Olmsted park here, a parkway there. As history, most of these studies were unsophisticated: the political, economic, and social realities confronting the man and his times were often masked by glittering generalities and pious platitudes. The portrait of Olmsted that usually emerged from such efforts was of the patron saint of the design professions or a Santa Claus for the urban masses. Two particular studies that resulted from the sesquicentennial celebration which do reflect historical sophistication and which also relate to Olmsted's Southern experiences are worthy of note: Victoria Post Ranney's *Olmsted in Chicago* and Elizabeth Barlow and William Alex's *Frederick Law Olmsted's New York*.[130] Finally, two dissertations of the 1970s, Leonard Simutis's "Frederick Law Olmsted's Later Years" and Thomas Bender's "Discovery of the City in America," also merit attention. The former, as indicated above, challenges any unquestioning acceptance of the "facts" of Olmsted's life, and the latter suggests that his Southern journeys raised in Olmsted the "first doubts about the superiority of rural life." "In the rural (and slave) South," Bender hypothesizes, "these doubts ripened into a firm conviction that the city, not the country, offered the greatest possibilities for social democracy."[131] This is a challenging idea, but like so much else in Bender's work, it is an unconvincing one. Still, speculation along such lines—with, it must be added, more concern for hard evidence—suggests the possibility of relating the two Olmsted's, "Greensward" and "Yeoman"—which might, perhaps, be the challenge of yet another scholarly generation.

Three generations of Olmsted scholarship have established a basis for addressing critics of the Connecticut Yankee, but many questions remain unanswered. At this point, it seems best to suggest an agenda for further research and analysis. To begin with, a larger historical perspective is required—one that transcends the narrow limits of biography and institutional (i.e., design) history. Next, more attention must be paid to the craft of travel writing, particularly in comparative terms. Finally, a reassessment must be made concerning the evolution of Olmsted's viewpoint over time—his ten years in the South.

In the first instance, Olmsted has, too often, been described in narrow biographical or landscape architecture terms. Here, again, we have the case of the two Olmsteds.[132] One, the author of the "Cotton Kingdom" series and critic of the slave South, has been assigned to the "Middle Period" or "South and Civil War" niches in American historical scholarship. The second, the founder of the profession of landscape architecture in America and precursor to modern city planning, has been adopted as culture hero for the design professions. It is not surprising that the two Olmsteds seldom come together in the same place—whether it be in a field of study, an academic course, or between the covers of a book. It is in the American South that the two Olmsteds meet: here, synthesis is possible. But, first, a broader perspective is required, one that will fit Olmsted into his milieu and utilize the findings of the new social history, the study of elites, the Victorian connection, modernization theory, and the like. The works of Eric Foner identifying Olmsted with the Free-Soil movement and of George Frederickson relating him to the Sanitary Commission are suggestive and might serve as take-off points.

Second, much remains to be done with Olmsted's travel accounts. A comparative perspective suggests itself: with other travel writers, such as Arthur Young, whose tone was so similar to Olmsted's, but who, by contrast, deliberately and carefully separated observation from generalization; and with the host of travelers south who were directly influenced by the Connecticut Yankee—from his contemporary E. L. Godkin to such later writers as John R. Dennett, Charles Nordhoff, Jonathan Baxter Harrison, and William Garrott Brown.[133] Then, too, there is the problem of verification. Here, only localized studies will suffice: investigations of verifiable records, drawn from state, county, and local documents, wherever and whenever available. Throughout, the question must be not how convincing is Olmsted's witness, but in what instances can it be verified from other sources?

Finally, there remains the question of how Olmsted's ideas evolved over time. In this instance, his Cotton Kingdom writings must be compared closely with his newspaper accounts in the *Times* and *Tribune*. What is more, his other contemporary works must be reexamined for clues as to his changing perspective on the slave states: the revisions in the second edition of *Walks and Talks* concerning slavery; the contents of *Putnam's* during his tenure there; and, of course, his private correspondence for the entire decade and, very likely, into the Civil War and early Reconstruction years. Olmsted's writings should cease to be merely a data bank of observations of a "reliable" or "standard" source: their internal history itself ought to become a subject for analysis.

OLMSTED SOUTH addresses each of these issues and questions. Still, much remains to be done before a balance can be struck between the conflicting perceptions of the Connecticut Yankee as prince of observers and damyankee. Perhaps, at this juncture, Olmsted would have suggested, along with an even more famous contemporary, that his critics shift their attention from the abstract to the concrete and look at what he was looking at instead of trying to outguess him: "'I am not thinking at all,' [Sherlock] Holmes replied coldly. 'I am observing, as you evidently, have failed to do.'"[134]

Observation is the starting point of the essays to follow.

NOTES

1. John Hope Franklin, *A Southern Odyssey: Travelers in the Antebellum North* (Baton Rouge, La., 1975), p. xiii.

2. Daniel J. Boorstin, *The Americans: The National Experience* (New York, 1965), p. 466. More recently, as Librarian of the Congress, Boorstin reversed the decision of his predecessor concerning the acquisition of the records of the Olmsted firm still housed at Brookline. Whereas L. Quincy Mumford had reported that the Library would be unable to accept custody of the Brookline records on the basis of its existing (and anticipated) space limitations, Boorstin not only promised the allocation of future room for them, but he also testified before the Senate Subcommittee on Parks and Recreation during the summer of 1976 in behalf of the so-called "Kennedy Bill" (*S*. 1750. A bill to establish the Frederick Law Olmsted Home and Office in Brookline, Mass., as a national historic site).

3. Clement Eaton, *The Mind of the Old South*, rev. ed. (Baton Rouge, La., 1967), p. 197; *The Growth of Southern Civilization, 1790–1860*, "New American Nation" series, ed. by Henry Steele Commager and Richard B. Morris (New York, 1961), p. xiii.

4. J. Saunders Redding, *They Came in Chains: Americans from Africa*, ed. by Louis Adamic (Philadelphia and New York, 1950), p. 55.

5. [James Russell Lowell], review of *A Journey in the Back Country*, *Atlantic Monthly* 6 (November 1860): 635. In *Frederick Law Olmsted: A Critic of the Old South* (Baltimore, 1924), Broadus Mitchell has noted that, in addition to Lowell, Gladstone's biographer John Morley and "others" (not specified) among his contemporaries compared Olmsted with Arthur Young (p. xv). This comparison, which is examined at the conclusion of this article, is a constant, if understated, theme of Mitchell's study (cf. pp. 83, 92, 95, and 142–43).

6. Charles Eliot Norton to A. H. Clough, September 24, 1860, in Sara Norton and M. A. DeWolfe Howe, eds., *Letters of Charles Eliot Norton, with Biographical Comment* (Boston, 1913), 1: 211.

7. Laura Wood Roper, "Frederick Law Olmsted in the 'Literary Republic,'" *Mississippi Valley Historical Review* 39 (December 1952): 481, 478.

8. J. Franklin Jameson to Albert J. Beveridge, May 24, 1926, in Elizabeth Donnan and Leo F. Stock, eds., "Notes and Documents: Senator Beveridge, J. Franklin Jameson, and Abraham Lincoln," *Mississippi Valley Historical Review* 35 (March 1949): 659. The remainder of Jameson's counsel on the reliability of travel literature merits attention: ". . . but your ordinary traveller goes where he has

letters of introduction, and sees the show places, and if he is a writer, writes of that which gives a glow to the reader rather than that which is drab and usual." Then, almost prefiguring *the* major historical debate of the 1970s: "If we had no statistical facts respecting Southern society, and were forced to base our judgments on the statements of travellers, no one could complain of us, but, on the contrary, there are plenty of available facts that discount the praises of many of your travellers. The statistics, for instance, are harder to study, but they are more solid."

9. The most convenient summary of his Southern involvement remains Laura Wood Roper's "Olmsted in the 'Literary Republic,'" but reference should also be made to her *FLO: A Biography of Frederick Law Olmsted* (Baltimore, 1973), especially Chaps. 8-10. Charles Eliot Beveridge's "Frederick Law Olmsted, The Formative Years 1822–1865," Ph.D. dissertation, University of Wisconsin, 1966, on the other hand, is still the most thorough treatment of Olmsted's journeys in and writings about the South. Arthur M. Schlesinger's Editor's Introduction to the Knopf edition of *The Cotton Kingdom: A Traveller's Observation on Cotton and Slavery in the American Slave States* (New York, 1953) is yet another indispensable source. The outline of events sketched out here draws essentially upon the work of these three scholars.

10. Roper, "Olmsted in the 'Literary Republic,'" p. 461.

11. Roper, *FLO*, p. 86.

12. The influence of the route traveled by Olmsted on post-Civil War observers is examined later in this essay, as well as in Timothy J. Crimmins' " Frederick Law Olmsted and Jonathan Baxter Harrison: Two Generations of Social Critics of the American South," below. The map provided as frontispiece to Broadus Mitchell's *Olmsted: Critic of the Old South* had remained virtually unchallenged since the publication of that influential biographical study in 1924. Compare it with Map 1 here.

13. Roper, *FLO*, p. 86.

14. Roper, "Olmsted in the 'Literary Republic,'" p. 462.

15. The After-Word, maps, and bibliography provided by James Howard in his modern edition of the *Journey Through Texas* (Austin, 1962) are especially noteworthy, in that Howard's is the first "localized" or local history approach to any of Olmsted's travel accounts. Although this edition is generally more reliable about the details of Texas history than about the facts of Olmsted's biography, it still merits more attention than it has received thus far.

16. Roper, "Olmsted in the 'Literary Republic,'" p. 466.

17. In "Olmsted's Texas Journey," an essay review that was published in the March 1857 number of *Putnam's Monthly Magazine* (9: 274–82), his "plan" for the series was described in the following terms: "The entire subject divides itself into the *sea-board, cotton-growing, border,* and *hill-country,* [sic] regions of the slave states, and will be completed in two more volumes" (p. 274). Since Olmsted had been associated with *Putnam's* since April 1855 and he was not to sever his connections, officially, with that journal until June 1857, this projection carries extra weight. Indeed, given the editorial policies of contemporary periodicals, it is possible that Olmsted himself wrote the essay.

18. Roper, "Olmsted in the 'Literary Republic,'" pp. 466, 467, 469.

19. Ibid., p. 473. "Frederick and John were not only brothers but such devoted friends that each seems to have regarded his own interests and duties as practically interchangeable with his brother's" (p. 473, n. 102). The same may be said for their collaboration on *A Journey Through Texas*, in that it is all but impossible to separate out from that volume the contributions of either brother. See also Schlesinger, Editor's Introduction, pp. xxii–xxiii.

20. Ibid., p. 480. A page-by-page accounting of the editing is neatly summarized on pp. xxxii–xxxiii of Arthur Schlesinger's Editor's Introduction to the 1953 Knopf edition of *The Cotton Kingdom*. The "tone and temper" of the book are analyzed below in Robert Detweiler's "Transcending Journalism: Olmsted's Style in *The Cotton Kingdom*."

21. Roper, "Olmsted in the 'Literary Republic,'" p. 469.

22. The New York circle is described in ibid.; the influence of antislavery intellectuals on Olmsted is highlighted in Albert Fein's account of FLO's frequent visits to the Raritan Bay Union, a utopian colony also known as Eagleswood, in "Frederick Law Olmsted: His Development as a Theorist and Designer of the American City," Ph.D. dissertation, Columbia University, 1969, pp. 104–09. The term "gentlemanly cosmopolitan elite" is from Geoffrey Blodgett's "Frederick Law Olmsted: Landscape Architecture as Conservative Reform," *Journal of American History* 62 (March 1976).

David Hall's "The Victorian Connection," *American Quarterly* 27 (December 1975), is a valuable summary article of recent scholarship on the transatlantic exchange of ideas and individuals (see especially pp. 566–67, 569–70, and 572 for references to FLO).

23. Thomas H. Gladstone, *The Englishman in Kansas, or Squatter Life and Border Warfare*, Introduction by Frederick Law Olmsted, Foreword by James A. Rawley (Lincoln, Nebr., 1971). In "Olmsted in the 'Literary Republic,' " Roper suggests that brother John might have written the Introduction (p. 474, n. 105). However, in her more recent biography, she attributes it solely to Frederick (*FLO*, p. 120).

24. Eric Foner's excellent *Free Soil, Free Labor, Free Men: The Ideology of the Republican Party Below the Civil War* (New York, 1970) is the best introduction to the movement. Olmsted's interest in the Neosho Territory was uncovered with the discovery of five of his previously "lost" letters to Samuel Cabot, all the subject of "Free Soil Advocacy and the New England Emigrant Aid Society," below. The projected Kansas, Utah, Jamaica, and London ventures are included in Roper, "Olmsted in the 'Literary Republic,' " p. 474.

25. Roper, *FLO*, p. 133.

26. Ibid., pp. 124–29. Significantly, Olmsted secured the superintendency with the backing of the "gentlemanly cosmopolitan elite" represented, as Roper describes it, on a petition of support, with "a list of almost two hundred signatures" that constituted a who's who of New York influentials (p. 128).

27. The most thorough history of the Sanitary Commission is William Quentin Maxwell's *Lincoln's Fifth Wheel: The Political History of the United States Sanitary Commission* (New York, London, Toronto, 1956); George M. Frederickson's *The Inner Civil War: Northern Intellectuals and the Crisis of the Union* (New York, 1965),

especially Chap. 7: "The Sanitary Elite: The Organized Response to Suffering" (p. 98–112) is critical of the Commission and of its impact on Olmsted's generation of reformers.

In "The Great Transatlantic Workshop," pp. 307–25, in *A More Perfect Union: The Impact of the Civil War and Reconstruction on the Constitution* (New York, 1973), Harold M. Hyman has examined the "Victorian connection" between "sanitarians" on both sides of the Atlantic.

28. Roper, *FLO*, pp. 184–85, 264. See also Willie Lee Rose's *Rehearsal for Reconstruction: The Port Royal Experiment* (New York, 1964), especially pp. 101, 204, and 226, for the influence of Olmsted's writings on the project. George W. Curtis's letter to Secretary of the Treasury Salmon P. Chase suggesting that Olmsted be appointed to head up "a sub-department or bureau" responsible for the welfare of freedmen (February 1862) is found in Gordon Milne, *George William Curtis and the Genteel Tradition* (Bloomington, Ind., 1956), pp. 112–13.

29. Beveridge, "Frederick Law Olmsted, The Formative Years," p. 427; Roper, *FLO*, p. 215.

30. Beveridge, "Frederick Law Olmsted, The Formative Years," p. 468; the words quoted are Beveridge's, not Olmsted's. For the significance of Mill's inclusion , see David Hall's "The Victorian Connection," cited in note 22 above.

31. William M. Armstrong, "The Freedmen's Movement and the Founding of the Nation," *Journal of American History* 53 (March 1967): 708–26; Roper, *FLO*, pp. 294–301.

32. Olmsted's "second career" in the South is the subject of " . . . the old South under new conditions," which introduces Part Two of the present work.

33. Robert B. Downs, *Books That Changed the South* (Chapel Hill, N.C., 1977), p. 13. Only four of the twenty-five authors included were Northern-born, two were English, and the remaining nineteen Southerners; for the critical antebellum decade of the 1850s, only Olmsted and Hinton Helper are represented (p. xiv). In an earlier work of Downs' that examined fifty *Famous American Books* (New York, 1971), only five of the books (six of the authors) included in *Books That Changed the South* appear. The significance for Olmsted scholarship of such underrepresentation for the region—creating, in scholarly terms, a separate South—is examined later in this essay.

34. Robert W. Fogel and Stanley L. Engerman, *Time on the Cross: The Economics of American Negro Slavery*, 2 vols. (Boston, 1974). The debate over "F + E" is beyond the scope of the present essay; however, its implications cannot be ignored out of hand. Its dimensions are the subject of Charles Crowe's "Slavery, Ideology, and 'Cliometrics,' " *Technology and Culture* 16 (April 1976): 271–85, and his book in progress, "The Great Cliometric Controversy"; Herbert G. Gutman's *Slavery and the Numbers Game: A Critique of Time on the Cross* (Urbana, Ill., 1975) demolishes its scientific pretensions. My own views on the negative impact of the controversy on the "new urban history" are set forth in "The Underdeveloped Discipline: Interdisciplinary Directions in American Urban History," pp. 152-70, in Robert H. Walker, ed., *American Studies: Topics and Sources* (Westport, Conn., 1976), p. 165.

35. Fogel and Engerman, *Time on the Cross*, 1: 189.

36. Ibid., p. 182. Fifty years earlier, Broadus Mitchell made reference to Olmsted's "testimony as given indirectly through Cairnes" (p. xv), to the latter's

"largely relying upon Olmsted both for his point of view and his basis in fact" (p. 106), and to his "reasoning deductively upon Olmsted's induction," thereby carrying "the theory of slave economy further" (p. 143). Fogel and Engerman, while crediting Cairnes on this last point, fail to mention Mitchell's analysis.

37. Fogel and Engerman, on Clay, *Time on the Cross*, 1: 159–60; on Cairnes: 181–90; and Helper: 161–69.

38. Ibid., p. 160. "Among those whose conceptions of slavery were influenced by Olmsted," Fogel and Engerman include Karl Marx, W. E. B. Du Bois, U. B. Phillips, William E. Dodd, Lewis C. Gray, Charles Sydnor, E. Franklin Frazier, Avery O. Craven, Richard Hofstadter, John Hope Franklin, and Kenneth Stampp (p. 174).

39. Ibid., pp. 174, 175. It is not intended in these pages to engage Fogel and Engerman on a point-by-point basis. However, to place the reliability of their work in scholarly perspective, two points in the above analysis merit consideration. In the first place, since Olmsted was both a practicing farmer and published agricultural economist, he should certainly have been aware that "the slack season" had its own work rhythm. In the second, inasmuch as Olmsted's travel notebooks and manuscripts were destroyed in a fire in 1863, there is no way of determining how much of his time was spent "in cities or in transit," "in the homes of planters or overseers," or "in the fields."

40. A lesser criticism, and one not common to other analyses of Olmsted's writings, is their contention that his "attempt to make use of census data to evaluate the performance of the slave economy was deeply flawed" (ibid., p. 176).

41. Ibid., p. 179.

42. Ibid., p. 180. In the next sentence, Fogel and Engerman go so far as to suggest: "If our objective were to evaluate the man, his enlightenment would certainly deserve more emphasis than his biases."

43. Ibid., p. 181.

44. Ibid., p. 213.

45. Ibid., p. 218.

46. Ibid., pp. 204, 205.

47. Ibid., pp. 208–209. "There can be little doubt," Fogel and Engerman explain later, "that Olmsted's jaundiced views of black relative to white labor, and of southern relative to northern labor, were influenced by the racial presuppositions that he brought with him on his travels through the South" (p. 218).

48. The reactions of his Southern contemporaries, which are not included in these pages, are covered in Roper's "Olmsted in the 'Literary Republic.' " Other responses from Northerners of his day will be found in Howard R. Floan's *The South in Northern Eyes 1831 to 1861* (Austin, Tex., 1958), pp. 32, 48–49, 96–99, 104–05, 124.

49. Richard Hofstadter, "U. B. Phillips and the Plantation Legend," *Journal of Negro History* 29 (April 1944): 121.

50. Wendell Holmes Stephenson, *The South Lives in History: Southern Historians and Their Legacy* (Baton Rouge, La., 1955), pp. 78–79.

51. Bennett H. Wall, "African Slavery," pp. 175–97, in Arthur S. Link and Rembert W. Patrick, eds., *Writing Southern History: Essays in Historiography in Honor of Fletcher M. Green* (Baton Rouge, La., 1965), p. 187.

52. There is general agreement among scholars from all camps that Phillips was strongly influenced by Olmsted. See, for example, Harvey Wish, *The American Historian: A Social-Intellectual History of the Writing of the American Past* (New York, 1960), p. 243, and Fogel and Engerman, *Time on The Cross*, 1: 160, 189–90.

53. Ulrich Bonnell Phillips, *American Negro Slavery: A Survey of the Supply, Employment and Control of Negro Labor as Determined by the Plantation Regime*, Foreword by Eugene D. Genovese (Baton Rouge, La., 1966), pp. 293, 248, 253.

54. Ulrich Bonnell Phillips, *Life and Labor in the Old South* (Boston, 1929), p. 218; Charles Crowe, "Historians and 'Benign Neglect': Conservative Trends in Southern History and Black Studies," *Reviews in American History* 2 (June 1974): 166.

55. W.E.B. Du Bois, review of *American Negro Slavery* by Ulrich Bonnell Phillips, *American Political Science Review* 12 (November 1918): 722, 724, 725.

56. Wish, *The American Historian* especially pp. 252–53, 259–62.

57. Interestingly enough, Du Bois' criticisms of Phillips have been branded as extreme, while Phillips' racism has been portrayed as understandable—given his background. See, for example, Wood Gray's "Ulrich Bonnell Phillips," pp. 354–73, in William T. Hutchinson, ed., *The Marcus W. Jernegan Essays in American Historiography* (Chicago, 1937), especially pp. 370–71.

58. Downs, *Books That Changed the South*, p. 239. For an analysis of Southern studies during the interwar period, see James P. Hendrix, Jr., "From Romance to Scholarship: Southern History at the Take-Off Point," *Mississippi Quarterly* 30 (Spring 1977), especially 209–10. Regionalism, as described by Odum, contrasted sharply with "sectionalism," an approach defined as lacking in comparative perspective. In these pages, U. B. Phillips' works would approximate this definition. For an excellent analysis of regionalism, see George Brown Tindall, "Howard W. Odum: A Preliminary Estimate," pp. 88–115, in *The Ethnic Southerners* (Baton Rouge, La., 1976).

59. Howard W. Odum, *An American Epoch: Southern Portraiture in the National Picture* (New York, 1930). This became something of a set piece for Odum, who repeated it, for example, in *The Way of the South: Toward the Regional Balance of America* (New York, 1947), pp. 132–33. It was retold in Francis B. Simkins' influential text *A History of the South* (New York, 1953), p. 485, and somewhat recast in J. G. Randall and David Donald, *The Civil War and Reconstruction* (Boston, 1961), pp. 25–26: compare their juxtaposition of Olmsted and Odum with Odum's *Way of the South*, pp. 132–33.

60. Twelve Southerners, *I'll Take My Stand: The South and the Agrarian Tradition*; Introduction by Louis D. Rubin, Jr.; Biographical Essays by Virginia Rock (New York, 1962). Owsley's contribution was "The Irrepressible Conflict" (pp. 61–91).

61. Frank L. Owsley, *Plain Folk of the Old South* (Chicago, 1965), p. 2. See Charles Beveridge's thorough refutation of Owsley's argument in the Bibliographical Essay in his dissertation, pp. 488–90.

62. Owsley, *Plain Folk of the Old South*, pp. 36–37.

63. Ibid., p. 3.

64. A. N. J. Den Hollander, "The Tradition of 'Poor Whites,' " ' pp. 403–31, in W. T. Couch, ed., *Culture in the South* (Chapel Hill, N.C., 1934), p. 416. See above, pp. 13-15, for the controversy over FLO's route.

65. The designation is Wendell Holmes Stephenson's, from *Southern History in the Making: Pioneer Historians of the South* (Baton Rouge, La., 1964), pp. 27–51.

66. William Garrott Brown, *The Lower South in American History* (New York, 1902), pp. 27–28.

67. Ibid., p. 28.

68. Edward Ingle, *Southern Sidelights: A Picture of Social and Economic Life in the South a Generation Before the War* (New York, 1896).

69. For an introduction to the continuing debate over a black perspective, see Karla J. Spurlock-Evans' " 'Old' Sources for a 'New' History," below.

70. These approximations are in no way "scientific." They are based on a search of indexes (cumulative, when available), supplemented by the scanning of some individual volumes. All the same they do indicate some interesting patterns. For the *Journal of Negro History*, references to Olmsted are spread rather evenly throughout the period from 1917 to the end of the 1960s; conversely, in the *American Historical Review*, they appear in 1903, 1907, 1917, and 1925, with three references in the early 1950s and then nothing until 1973. This pattern approximates the three generations of Olmsted scholarship that are the subject of the next section of this essay.

71. Hofstadter, *Journal of Negro History* 29 (April 1944): 109–24; Raymond A. Bauer and Alice H. Bauer, "Day to Day Resistance to Slavery," *Journal of Negro History* 27 (October 1942): 388–419; and Arthur M. Schlesinger, "Was Olmsted an Unbiased Critic of the Old South?" *Journal of Negro History* 37 (April 1952): 173–87. The Bauers came in for heavy criticism from Fogel and Engerman for relying "largely" on "Olmsted, who was cited 27 times" (*Time on the Cross*, 2: 210).

As would be the case nearly thirty years later when practically a full issue of the *Journal* was turned over to Herbert Gutman's critique of *Time on the Cross* ("The World Two Cliometricians Made: A Review Essay of $F + E = \frac{T}{C}$," *Journal of Negro History* 60 [January 1975]: pp. 53–227), Fabian Linden responded to Frank L. Owsley's claims for the existence of a large Southern yeomanry in "Economic Democracy in the Slave South: An Appraisal of Some Recent Views," *Journal of Negro History* 31 (April 1946): 140–89. While Linden failed to mention Olmsted by name, Olmsted's views are supported in this article.

72. The speeches of A. B. Moore (1942), Francis Butler Simkins (1954), and James W. Patton (1956) are found in George Brown Tindall, ed., *The Pursuit of Southern History: Presidential Addresses of the Southern Historical Association 1935–1963* (Baton Rouge, La., 1964).

73. Carter G. Woodson, *The History of the Negro Church* (Washington, D.C. 1921), pp. 149–51, 212–13; Bertram Wilbur Doyle, *The Etiquette of Race Relations in the South: A Study in Social Control*, Introduction by Robert E. Park; New Introduction by Arthur Sheps (New York, 1937 and 1971), thirteen references in text, fifty-nine in notes. For Franklin and Redding, see notes 1 and 4 above.

74. John W. Blassingame, ed., *Slave Testimony: Two Centuries of Letters, Speeches, Interviews, and Autobiographies* (Baton Rouge, La., 1977), especially pp. xvii–xlii.

75. Stanley M. Elkins, *Slavery: A Problem in American Institutional and Intellectual Life*, with an Introduction by Nathan Glazer (New York, 1959 and 1963), p. 3. Elkins' original text, which is split in two sections by Blassingame, is given here.

76. Blassingame, *Slave Testimony*, pp. xxxi–xxxii.

77. Most of Blassingame's excellent Introduction is devoted to establishing this reliability, as it effectively addresses criticisms point by point.

78. Roper, "Olmsted in the 'Literary Republic' " p. 459.

79. Until quite recently, this volume was part of Random House's popularly priced "Modern Library" series. At this writing, it is available only in the handsome, but expensive, Knopf edition. The only textbook copy on the market is in the Bobbs-Merrill "American History Landmarks" series. David Freeman Hawke has edited the text to 208 pages, with no index or scholarly aids; the Schlesinger edition, by comparison, is 626 pages, with index. Any comparison between Hawke's Editor's Introduction and Schlesinger's would be invidious.

80. Roper, "Olmsted in the 'Literary Republic,' " p. 482. Olmsted's intention of getting "a footing" and having "an established 'good will' at the South" (FLO to John C. Olmsted, March 13, 1894) may also have some bearing on his not wanting *The Cotton Kingdom* reprinted. Social criticism seldom makes for good business advertising. See below, ". . . the old South under new conditions," for an examination of the "New South creed" that confronted FLO when he was attempting, as he wrote in the same letter to his stepson, "to make the firm favorably known at the South and 'extend its connections' as the merchants say."

81. "Greensward" was the Olmsted-Vaux title for their competition-winning plan for New York's Central Park in 1858. Here, and in the pages to follow, I use it as a signature, corresponding to "Yeoman."

82. Mitchell, *Olmsted: Critic of the Old South*, p. xiii.

83. Leonard J. Simutis, "Frederick Law Olmsted's Later Years: Landscape Architecture and the Spirit of Place," Ph.D. dissertation, University of Minnesota, 1971, p. 222; see also Simutis' "Frederick Law Olmsted, Sr.: A Reassessment," *Journal of the American Institute of Planners* 38 (September 1972): 283–84.

84. Cornell University Press.

85. "Frederick Law Olmsted," *National Cyclopaedia of American Biography* (New York, 1892), 2:298–99.

86. M. G. van Rensselaer, "Frederick Law Olmsted," *The Century Illustrated Monthly Magazine* 46 (October 1893): 862.

87. See, for example, Charles S. Sargent's "official" biography of Olmsted in M. A. De Wolfe Howe, ed., *Later Years of the Saturday Club 1870–1920* (Boston and New York, 1927), pp. 183–87. Much of Burnham's laudatory address is reprinted in Charles Moore, *Daniel H. Burnham: Architect Planner of Cities* (New York, 1921 and 1968), p. 74.

88. "Notes," *Nation* 76 (September 3, 1903): 191.

89 "Frederick Law Olmsted," *World's Work* 6 (October 1903): 3949.

90. "Notes and News," *American Historical Review* 9 (October 1903): 211. Not until 1917 would a major article on Olmsted appear in this, the organ of the historical profession.

91. "Notes," p. 191.

92. Thomas H. Clark, "Frederick Law Olmsted on the South, 1889," *South Atlantic Quarterly* 3 (January 1904): 11–15. See ". . . the old South under new conditions," especially pp. 162–163, for further analysis.

93. Frederick Law Olmsted, *A Journey in the Seaboard Slave States, with Remarks on Their Economy*, with a Biographical Sketch by Frederick Law Olmsted, Jr., and with an Introduction by William P. Trent, 2 vols. (New York, 1904).

94. For biographical information, see W. H. Stephenson, "William P. Trent: The 'Mountain Fastness' at Sewanee," *Southern History in the Making*, pp. 71–92.

95. "The South Before the War," *Nation* 79 (August 4, 1904): 102.

96. Paul M. Gaston, *The New South Creed: A Study in Southern Mythmaking* (New York, 1970). See also ". . . the old South under new conditions," passim.

97. Trent, *Introduction to Seaboard Slave States*, p. xxxvii.

98. Paul H. Buck, *The Road to Reunion, 1865–1900* (Boston, 1937).

99. Walter L. Fleming, "The Seaboard Slave States," *The Dial* 37 (October 1, 1904): 204, 205.

100. Stephenson, *Southern History in the Making*, p. 42. The year 1904, strictly speaking, marked the fiftieth anniversary of the conclusion of FLO's second trip to the South.

101. Ibid.

102. Theodora Kimball, "Centenary of Frederick Law Olmsted, Sr.," *American City* 27 (December 1922): 500.

103. I have used the reprint of this work: *Frederick Law Olmsted, Landscape Architect, 1822–1903; Two Volumes in One*, edited by Frederick Law Olmsted, Jr., and Theodora Kimball (New York, 1970).

104. C. S. Boucher, review of *Frederick Law Olmsted: A Critic of the Old South*, by Broadus Mitchell, *American Historical Review* 30 (January 1925): 402; Thomas Robson Hay, review of *Frederic [sic] Law Olmsted, a Critic of the Old South*, by Broadus Mitchell, *Mississippi Valley Historical Review* 12 (June 1925): 129.

105. Beveridge, "Frederick Law Olmsted, The Formative Years," pp. 490–92.

106. Ibid., pp. 491, 492.

107. Mitchell, *Olmsted: Critic of the Old South*, pp. 137, 145.

108. Ibid., pp. 79, 115–19.

109. Ibid., Preface, 56, 57, 65–66. By way of contrast, Mitchell questioned Tocqueville's abilities for "dealing in realities" (p. 148) and took U. B. Phillips to task for prejudging Olmsted's intentions for traveling south (p. 70, n. 5).

110. Ibid., pp. 132–33.

111. Beveridge, "Frederick Law Olmsted, The Formative Years," p. 492.

112. Schlesinger, Editor's Introduction, p. ix.

113. W. M. Brewer, review of *The Cotton Kingdom* . . . , by Frederick Law Olmsted, *Journal of Negro History* 38 (July 1953): 347. For a conflicting view, see Chase C. Mooney, review of *The Cotton Kingdom* . . . , by Frederick Law Olmsted, *Mississippi Valley Historical Review* 40 (December 1953): 536–37. According to this reviewer: "Editorial work on the volume has been minimal . . ." (p. 537).

114. "The Old South," *Times Literary Supplement* (May 28, 1954): 337.

115. D. W. Brogan, "The Old South," *The Spectator* (February 19, 1954): 212.

116. Laura Wood Roper, review of *The Cotton Kingdom* . . . , by Frederick Law Olmsted, *New York Times Book Review* (April 12, 1953): 6, 34.

117. Her major articles were: "Frederick Law Olmsted and the Western Texas Free-Soil Movement," *American Historical Review* 56 (October 1950): 58–64; "Olm-

sted and the 'Literary Republic,'" *Mississippi Valley Historical Review* (1952); "'Mr. Law' and *Putnam's Monthly Magazine*: A Note on a Phase in the Career of Frederick Law Olmsted," *American Literature* 26 (March 1954): 88–93; and "Frederick Law Olmsted and the Port Royal Experiment," *Journal of Southern History* 31 (August 1965): 272–84.

118. Charles Capen McLaughlin and Charles E. Beveridge, eds., *The Papers of Frederick Law Olmsted*, Vol. 1, *The Formative Years 1822–1852* (Baltimore, 1977); Charles E. Beveridge, "Frederick Law Olmsted's Theory of Landscape Design," *Nineteenth Century* 3, No. 2 (Summer 1977): 38–43.

119. Albert Fein, *Frederick Law Olmsted and the American Environmental Tradition* (New York, 1972), especially pp. 14–17, for the genesis of FLO's social outlook. See also Fein's seminal article, "Parks in a Democratic Society," *Landscape Architecture* 55 (October 1964): 24–31.

120. Frederick Law Olmsted, *The Slave States*, revised and enlarged edition; edited, with an Introduction, by Harvey Wish (New York, 1959). This is the paperback edition and is probably the most widely circulated recent edition of selections of FLO's writings.

121. Beveridge, "Frederick Law Olmsted, The Formative Years," p. 493.

122. F. Garvin Davenport, "The South in Sectional Crisis, 1852–1860," pp. 337–89, in Thomas D. Clark, ed., *Travels in the Old South: A Bibliography*, Vol. 3, *The Ante Bellum South, 1825–1860: Cotton, Slavery, and Conflict* (Norman, Okla., 1959), pp. 369–75.

123. Edmund Wilson, *Patriotic Gore: Studies in the Literature of the Civil War* (New York, 1962), pp. 219–31; the quote here is on page 221.

124. Martin B. Duberman, *In White America: A Documentary Play* (Boston, 1964), pp. 10–14.

125. Kenneth M. Stampp, *The Peculiar Institution: Slavery in the Ante-Bellum South* (New York, 1956). Black historians, since Du Bois and Woodson, had long rejected the "Phillips school."

126. Fogel and Engerman, *Time on the Cross*, 2: 217–46, especially 234–35 on FLO. See also Kenneth Stampp's measured response in "Introduction: A Humanistic Perspective," pp. 1–30, in Paul A. David, Herbert G. Gutman, Richard Sutch, Peter Temin, and Gavin Wright, *Reckoning with Slavery, A Critical Study in the Quantitative History of American Negro Slavery* (New York, 1970).

127. Bennett H. Wall, "An Epitaph for Slavery," *Louisiana History* 16 (Summer 1975): 249. Eugene D. Genovese, *Roll, Jordan, Roll: The World the Slaves Made* (New York, 1974); Herbert G. Gutman, *The Black Family in Slavery and Freedom, 1750–1925* (New York, 1976).

128. Elizabeth Stevenson, *Park Maker: A Life of Frederick Law Olmsted* (New York, 1977).

129. Catherine Drinker Bowen, *Biography: The Craft and the Calling* (Boston, 1968, 1969), especially pp. ix–xiv.

130. Victoria Post Ranney, *Olmsted in Chicago* (Chicago, 1972); *Frederick Law Olmsted's New York*, text by Elizabeth Barlow; illustrative portfolio by William Alex (New York, 1972).

131. Thomas Bender, "Discovery of the City in America: Development of

Urbanism in 19th-Century Social Thought," Ph.D. dissertation, University of California, Davis, 1971, p. 225. A revised version appeared as *Toward an Urban Vision: Ideas and Institutions in Nineteenth-Century America* (Lexington, Ky., 1975).

132. The "case of the two Olmsteds" is, of course, a scholarly and not a medical one. It does not suggest *dementia praecox*, some form of avocational *Doppelgänger* effect, or tweedledum and tweedledee. "There was *never* but one Olmsted," as Laura Wood Roper advised: "it's scholarly diplopia that saw two of him." To counter this academic double vision, Mrs. Roper lectured at SUNY/Syracuse on the subject "Olmsted Is Indivisible." Letter from Laura Wood Roper to the author, August 13, 1977.

133. I am presently engaged in relating each of the above travel writers to Olmsted.

134. From one of the most recently discovered "lost" manuscripts of Dr. John Watson: Nicholas Meyer, *The West End Horror* (New York, 1976), p. 33.

Karla J. Spurlock-Evans

"OLD" SOURCES FOR A "NEW" HISTORY:
Frederick Law Olmsted's Journeys in the Slave South

Historians of American slavery have never given serious enough attention to the study of the culture and life experiences of slaves. Volume after volume has chronicled the Southern planter's existence—his behavior and belief system, his social, economic, and political positions—but next to nothing has been written of the slave, who, on the eve of the Civil War, outnumbered the slave owner by ten to one. Only in recent years have scholars, to any significant degree, begun to appreciate the importance of the slave's story, both in illuminating more fully our understanding of that most troublesome of all American institutions and in lending historical dimension to the study of patterns in contemporary black life.

While it has become unfashionable to deny the relevance of slave activities and ideas, numerous scholars still excuse deficiencies in the historiography of American slavery on the grounds that valid primary source materials for the study of slave life are extremely rare. A number of those who argue this point fail to consider that respected historians have ruled inadmissible much of what slaves or former slaves themselves said about slavery. Traditionally, fugitive narratives and autobiographies have been dismissed categorically as biased, of questionable authenticity, or of doubtful veracity.

Increasingly, this position has come under fire from younger historians who, in seeking to re-focus the distorted image of slavery pictured in standard history texts, are applying interdisciplinary techniques to traditional as well as hitherto unacceptable historical sources. Their work has indicated not only the potentialities of original approaches to novel sources, but also the vast untapped wealth of the traditional primary record. "Old" facts from public annals, plantation journals, and travel narratives can, when placed in a different and more meaningful context, supply the substance of a "new" history. Thus, a clear imperative for those of us seriously intent on reshaping the contours of American history must be the close rereading of classic primary sources on slavery.[1]

The works of Frederick Law Olmsted, considered by many the best travel account of life in the antebellum South, are an excellent example of the kind of primary material that readily lends itself to the study of slave culture. *A Journey in the Seaboard Slave States* (1856), *A Journey through Texas* (1857), *A Journey in the Back Country* (1860), and *The Cotton Kingdom* (1861) grew out of observations made by the author during a two-part tour through the South as a correspondent for the *New-York Daily Times* from December 1852 to April 1853 and from November 1853 to August 1854.[2]

Frederick Law Olmsted was, by birth and temperament, a product of nineteenth-century upper-class New England. Typically nineteenth century were his references to the pseudo-science, phrenology; typically upper class were his prejudice against the Irish, his support of temperance reform, and his abhorrence of emotional religious display; typically Yankee were his insistence on efficiency and punctuality and his strong antifeudal bias. These traits and characteristics color his writings throughout and must not be ignored.

Despite his patrician upbringing, young Olmsted fancied himself a Northern yeoman at the time of his travels through the South—a true democrat—"not," as he put it, "in the technical and partisan but in the primary and essential sense of that term."[3] In truth, however, philosophically he was always more republican than democrat.

Favoring gradual emancipation for slaves, Olmsted opposed slavery on practical rather than moral grounds. His first journey through the South allowed him to test the hypothesis that slavery was the principal cause of economic inefficiency, social backwardness and degeneracy in the Southern people—slave and free.[4] Olmsted's stance is important, for, to some extent, it determines his choice and treatment of topics. Nevertheless, his writing is valuable to the modern student not because its theme is particularly brilliant or original, but because its description of people, places, and events is crisp and detailed. Unraveling Olmsted's remarkable descriptions and dialogues from the skeins of personal prejudice, preference, and intellectual dogma is a challenging task, but one well worth the undertaking.

In his narratives, our Northern traveler explores the observed and attributed behavior and potentialities of blacks, carefully weighing the influence of attendant environmental factors. His writings consider differences in color, in social, economic, and political status, as well as in occupation, food, housing, and clothing within one locale and from one region to another. In addition, such particulars of slave life as morality, health, family relations, marriage, and child-rearing fall under the writer's close scrutiny. Particularly interested in slave religion, music, and entertainments, Olmsted even goes so far as to dictate verbatim epitaphs from the headstones of the "colored" cemetery in Savannah, Georgia; in contrast, he makes only casual reference to the white cemetery through which he first passes.

Perhaps to reinforce the impact of his argument on the deleterious effects of slavery, Olmsted, at points, employs inordinately harsh criticism of the slave population: "The field hand negro is, on the average, a very poor and a very bad creature, much worse than I had supposed before I had seen him and grown familiar with his stupidity, indolence, duplicity and sensuality."[5] This kind of sweeping and impressionistic assessment of an entire group is only occasional in Olmsted's writing, but is all too characteristic of Southern travel literature of the period. Fortunately, his work can generally be distinguished from other contemporaneous accounts by its balance and relative reserve. In large measure, his writings are a subtle blend of hearsay (from both blacks and whites), observation, and library research.

Olmsted's material is rich enough in primary data to support profitably explorations into a number of themes and topics bearing on slave life and culture. Students interested in documenting the lore of the fugitive slave or the significance of the runaway as epic hero might, for instance, turn with success to Olmsted for numerous larger-than-life accounts of fugitive resistance. En route through eastern Texas, Olmsted stopped off at a cotton plantation where he overheard the following account:

We caught him once, but he got away from us again. We was just tying his feet together and he give me a kick in the face and broke. I had my six-shooter handy, and I tried to shoot him, but every barrel missed fire. Been loaded a week. We shot at him three times with rifles, but he'd got too far off, and we didn't hit but we must have shaved him close. We chased him, and my dog got close to him once. If he'd grip'd him, we should have got him; but he had a dog himself and just as my dog got within about a yard of him, his dog turned and fit my dog, and he hurt him so bad we couldn't get him to run him again. We run him close though, I tell you. Run him out of his coat, and his boots, and a pistol he'd got. But 'twas getting towards dark, and he got into them bayous, and kept swimming from one side to another.[6]

It is ironic that the slave-catcher, so absorbed by what he perceives as merely a bad run of luck, unwittingly bears eloquent testimony to the superhuman, almost supernatural, qualities of fortitude, determination, and strength exhibited by the runaway slave. In this instance, a lone slave, without support or sympathy—for there existed no "underground railroad" to smooth his passage through eastern Texas—by dint of sheer willpower, was able to elude the grasp of armed pursuers. Nor was this incident singular. Equally amazing accounts, as well as listings of advertisements for fugitives cited in Olmsted, suggest that the occurrence, if not routine, was not unusual. This fact offers a serious challenge to the prevailing image of the Negro slave as the prototype of docility.

A similar topic which might benefit from an examination of Olmsted's writing is that of slave maroon colonies. While the impact of such groups in South America and the West Indies has been documented, the occurrence of similar bands in the United States has gone virtually unnoticed. Olmsted's account of the escaped slaves in the Dismal Swamps of Virginia gives at least rudimentary documentation of the existence of fugitive colonies right up to the eve of the Civil War. The importance of these colonies may have been significantly greater than their numbers would ordinarily have warranted. Magnified by fear in the minds of the planters and by hope in the minds of the slaves, such colonies may well have assumed mythic stature.

The Dismal Swamps are noted places of refuge for runaway negroes. They were formerly peopled in this way much more than at present; a systematic hunting of them with dogs and guns having been made by individuals who took it up as a business about ten years ago. Children were born, bred, lived and died here. Joseph Church [a slave] told me he had seen skeletons, and had helped bury bodies recently dead. There were people in the swamps still, he thought, that were the children of runaways, and who had been runaways themselves all their lives.

• • •

Joseph said that they had huts in back places, hidden by bushes, and difficult of access; he had, apparently, been himself quite intimate with them.

• • •

I asked if they were ever shot. "Oh yes," he said. . . . "But some on 'em would rather be shot than be took, sir," he added, simply.[7]

This passage not only documents the presence of one slave colony but also reveals the degree to which blacks in bondage were acquainted with its existence. It indicates that channels of communication did exist between those in slavery and those outside of the law, and suggests that slaves understood the motives of those who sought liberty, even at a dear price.

The works of Frederick Law Olmsted are also an invaluable source for the study of occupational differentiation and variations in life-style among slaves. He observes, in fine detail, slaves working in an unexpectedly broad range of jobs, many with an equally surprising degree of autonomy: black men working in the coal mines of Virginia alongside Welsh miners; black fishermen and divers working off the North Carolina coast; black lumbermen and blacks in the turpentine industry, who labored in the swamps and forests. Olmsted postulated that the incentive

of virtual freedom or money encouraged in these workers the expression
of positive character traits. He further noted that the lumbermen who
registered each year were issued provisions and clothing and then were
sent into the swamps where they were allowed to govern their own time;
and that they "were more sprightly and straight-forward in . . . manner
and conversation than any field-hand plantation negroes that I saw at the
South."[8]

Of the black men working in the turpentine forest distilling pitch from
tar, he noted: "Negroes employed in this branch of industry seemed to
me unusually intelligent and cheerful. Decidedly they are superior in
every moral and intellectual respect to the great mass of the white people
inhabiting the turpentine forest."[9] And of the skillful divers in North
Carolina whose job it was to remove tree stumps from the bottom of
rivers, and who were rewarded for their efforts with whiskey and money,
Olmsted recorded: "the harder the work you give them to do, the better
they like it." Commenting on this phenomenon which contradicted
prevalent generalizations about the innate motivational capacity of
slaves, he wrote: "their ambition stimulated by wages—suddenly, they,
too, reveal sterling manhood and honor their Creator."[10]

Olmsted's reports offer preliminary evidence that, at least in the upper
South, slavery was no longer a monolithic institution, if, indeed, it ever
had been. Though slavery was unquestionably harsh and dehumanizing,
many of its intended victims were able to slip through faults in the
structure and thereby avert their own psychic devastation.

One decided advantage of Olmsted's writing is its occasional reference
to conversations with slaves themselves. While he is sometimes guilty of
generalizing without direct knowledge, Olmsted did at times solicit and
obtain straightforward responses from slave informants. Our Northern
traveler owes no small debt in this regard to his own impatient, slightly
abrupt Yankee manner. He probably had too much information to gather
and too little time to waste it adapting to the circumlocutions expected of
one caste when speaking with the other. Then, too, Olmsted quite likely
regarded slaves and free persons of color as men, albeit men of a lower
station in life. Thus, he was direct and to the point when addressing
them, a practice which, seemingly, elicited equal candor on the part of his
respondents. For example, while traveling through South Carolina, Olmsted came upon an old man and his young son.

> "Good evening, uncle," [he said]. . . . "Where are you going?"
> "Well, we ain't goin' nower, master; we's peddlin' tobacco roun'."
> "Oh! peddling tobacco. Where do you come from?"
> "From Rockingham County, Norf Car'lina, master . . ." responded the old
> man. "Twill be seven weeks tomorrow, sar, since we left home."

"Are you bound homeward, now?" [asked Olmsted].
"No, massa; wish we was . . . I likes my country better dan dis. . . . I'se a
   free nigger in my country, master."
"Oh, you are a free man, are you!" [responded Olmsted]. "North Carolina
   is a better country than this, for free men, I suppose."
"Yes, master, I likes my country de best . . ."[11]

Near the conclusion of *Journey in the Seaboard Slave States*, he recounts an
unusual interview with William, a household slave from Louisiana.
When asked what he thought would occur if all blacks were made free,
William readily replied that he felt they would go to work on the sugar
plantations once again, but this time for fair wages. Olmsted then asked,
"The black people talk among themselves about this, do they; and they
think so, generally?" Replied William, "Oh! yes, sir; day talk so; dat's wat
day tink." "Then," queried Olmsted, "they talk about being free a good
deal, do they?" "Yes, sir. Dey—dat is, dey say dey wish it was so; dat's all
dey talk, master—dat's all, sir."[12]

To the question of what he himself would do if he were freed, the slave
replied:

If I was free, massa; if I was free (with great animation) I would—well, sar, de fus
thing I would do, if I was free, I would go to work for a year, and get some money
for myself—den—den—den, massa, dis is what I do—I buy me, fus place, a little
house, and little lot land, and den—no; den—den—I would go to old Virginny,
and see my old mudder. Yes, sar, I would like to do dat fus thing; den, when I com
back, de fus thing I'd do, I'd get me a wife; den, I'd take her to my house, and I
would live with her dar; and I would raise things in my garden, and take 'em to
New Orleans, and sell'em dar, in de market. Dat's de way I would live, if I was
free.[13]

William's statement, which tells us as much about his values as about his
concept of freedom, reveals a keen awareness of the responsibilities as
well as the privileges bestowed with freedom. Is it not likely that the
majority of slaves shared William's sentiments on slavery?

Two images which prevail in thinking on slave personality are the
house servant—genial, loyal, pliant—totally dedicated to securing ease
and pleasure for his master, and the fieldhand—dull-witted, lazy, and
degraded—a creature seemingly incapable of managing his own affairs. If
these two prototypes were the only images applicable to the entire slave
population, then black people were most certainly dehumanized.
Nothing is more characteristically human than the probability of variation
and uniqueness in individuals. A careful reading of the Southern travel
narratives of Frederick Law Olmsted, however, restores our sense of the

humanity of the slaves. His work does not deny the existence of the prototypical house or field slave, but it does add a whole range of living portraits to the gallery of slave character types. If Frederick Law Olmsted had done nothing other than merely portray variability in slave behavior—if, for instance, he had not catalogued in great detail the habits and social customs of slaves—he would still have made an invaluable contribution to the scholarship of slave life and culture.

NOTES

1. One of the most recent of such works is John W. Blassingame's *The Slave Community: Plantation Life in the Ante-Bellum South* (New York, 1972). I consulted this work frequently while attempting to crystallize the thoughts expressed in this paper.

2. Laura Wood Roper, *FLO: A Biography of Frederick Law Olmsted* (Baltimore, 1973), pp. 86–99.

3. Frederick Law Olmsted, *A Journey in the Seaboard Slave States, with Remarks on Their Economy* (New York, 1856), p. x.

4. Broadus Mitchell, *Frederick Law Olmsted: A Critic of the Old South* (Baltimore, 1924), pp. 45, 47.

5. *The Cotton Kingdom: A Traveller's Observations on Cotton and Slavery in the American Slave States* (New York, 1861), 2: 339.

6. *Ibid.*, p. 20.

7. *Seaboard Slave States*, pp. 159, 160.

8. Ibid., p. 155.

9. Ibid., p. 348.

10. Ibid., p. 355.

11. Ibid., pp. 389–90.

12. Ibid., pp. 683, 684.

13. Ibid., pp. 679, 680.

Kay L. Cothran

OLMSTED'S CONTRIBUTIONS TO FOLKLIFE RESEARCH

Unlike many other travelers in the South before and after the Civil War, Olmsted looks for facts rather than for confirmation of preconceptions and examples of the bizarre. His purpose in traveling through the South, as stated in the preface to *A Journey in the Back Country* (1860),[1] is to make "a personal study of the ordinary condition and habits of the people of the South" (p. vi). Much the same purpose animates folklife studies today, now that some researchers choose to go beyond recounting the conspicuously quaint toward portraying and analyzing the traditional organization of everyday life. That he tries, despite frequent lapses, to assemble facts before engaging in polemic sets Olmsted apart from those travelers whose accounts of Southern folklife suffer from pretentious invocations of Social Darwinism and from naive inability even to try to see another way of life on its own terms. Of course, Olmsted was not a folklorist or an enthnographer in the modern sense of these terms. Indeed, in his day folklorists and anthropologists themselves did not go into the field at all. The very word "folklore" was coined only in 1846, and the word "folklife" did not come into English until relatively recently.

To see what Olmsted has to say about folklore, let us consider first *A Journey in the Back Country*. We find references to dancing by both blacks and whites; blacks, who are also good singers, dance to fiddle and banjo music (pp. 145–46). Olmsted finds that whites believe singing and dancing wear slaves out and thus inhibit work (p. 93). In New Orleans, he observes a black religious service and comments upon the body motion that accompanies singing by blacks—the significance of which has recently been demonstrated by Lomax[2]—and upon the lining out of hymns (pp. 187–96). "Lining out" refers to the song leader's speaking or chanting a line of a hymn stanza, which is then sung by the congregation, and so on for each line. This practice compensates for illiteracy or lack of hymnals. Olmsted finds a white family in the uplands lining out hymns in home singing (p. 241). In *Journey in the Seaboard Slave States* (1859),[3] Olmsted presents a few texts of black folksongs (pp. 607–10).

In the realm of traditional narrative, Olmsted gives us a wealth of anecdotal biography, the experience stories that folklorists sometimes call "memorates." Many folklorists do not consider personal anecdotes to be folklore, strictly speaking, because one person's anecdotes rarely come to be repeated by others, but some now tend to think in terms of traditional activities rather than in terms of traditional items. Whether folklore properly so called or oral history germane to folklore, these stories appear in abundance in Olmsted's accounts. Through them, we apprehend character and learn about the tradition of telling stories, of death, disaster, and hunting. One conversationalist "told a good many stories of his experiences in life, about a white man's 'dying hard' in the neighborhood, and of a tree falling on a team with which one of his negroes was plowing cotton, 'which was lucky'—that is, that it did not kill the negro—and a good deal about 'hunting' when he was younger and lighter" (JBC, p. 157).

Olmsted reproduces these stories in something like paraphrase; obviously, he did not have the advantage of videotape recording to capture exact performance, but he had an ear for dialogue. In the letters he sent home as a youth, Olmsted included passages set in dialogue.[4] While traveling, he kept careful and copious notes which no doubt aided in his reconstruction of linguistic qualities. We can be grateful for Olmsted's temperamental inclination toward great detail and for his insistence that one must talk with everyday people about everyday life.[5]

It is in the area of folklife information, rather than oral literature and music, that Olmsted's work is most valuable to modern folklorists. As he travels, Olmsted visits households belonging to many social levels in the Southern class system, a system that, as he recognizes, is not easily understood by outsiders.[6]

We see through him the wretched "white trash," who are socially inferior to blacks because they belie the notion that whites are naturally superior beings; honest poor whites; and self-styled aristocrats, themselves insufficiently civilized by Northern standards. Later, W. J. Cash would document the fiction of Southern aristocracy and gentility in *The Mind of the South* (New York, 1941). As Woodward points out, poverty, or at least relative poverty, has been woven into the fiber of Southern life and mind for a very long time.[7] With respect to the refined peacefulness one might attribute to "aristocrats," Olmsted remarks upon the violence that characterizes the Southerner's presentation of self; present-day research shows that he does not engage in facile stereotyping.

Olmsted describes, for example, a homestead and the house's interior in Mississippi:

The house was half a dozen rods from the high road, with a square yard all about it, in one corner of which was a small enclosure for stock, and a log stable and corn-crib. . . . The house was a neat building of logs, boarded over and painted on the outside. On the inside, the logs were neatly hewn to a plane face, and exposed (JBC, p. 140).

He continues with considerable detail useful to folklife research. Differences in use of land and division of space constitute important historical information and valuable insight into structural symbolisms. The manipulation of space is silent speech that tells us much about the tradition in which a family participates. Thus, from Olmsted's details we can derive possible patterns.

In *Journey in the Seaboard Slave States*, we find not only verbal descriptions but illustrative plates as well. Olmsted made sketches, unfortunately now destroyed, to complement his written notes.[8] *Journey in the Seaboard Slave States* is particularly valuable for its treatment of traditional occupations, such as tapping pines for gum to be made into pitch, naval stores, and turpentine near the Great Dismal Swamp (pp. 338–51.) Olmsted notes technical terms: "box" (the shelf chopped by "hackers" to catch flowing gum), "dippers" (who collect gum from boxes), and "scrape" (the poor quality residue left on the raw tree face). Though changed, this industry still exists, and its year-cycle rhythm affects the temporal perceptions of employees.[9] Other references to crafts such as spinning and weaving appear throughout Omsted's accounts (e.g., JBC, pp. 140–41). Many of these references lack detail. We must realize that much of what we now consider valuable folklife data, Olmsted himself saw as evidence of the South's cultural and economic backwardness. It was enough simply to note the existence of home crafts as a major form of production.

In a poor white household Olmsted remarks upon food, child-rearing practices, and such aspects of technology as "smokes" (here, tin pans filled with hot coals and corncobs) used to discourage gnats from entirely devouring sleeping people (JBC, pp. 197–204). Olmsted refers to the craft of capturing honeybees and cites the belief that to prevent stings in this undertaking one ought to carry leaves from three (the Indo-European magical number) different kinds of trees (JBC, p. 211). Again without going into much detail, Olmsted refers to group corn shucking, one of the important social occasions in backwoods life, and in the mountains he finds a craftsman who turns maple bedposts (JBC, pp. 225, 247). He describes the clothing of cracker men, lists the crops that coastal crackers supply to market towns, and mentions the uses of cash proceeds from these sales.[10]

We read a great deal about traditional cuisine, partly because Olmsted cares little for it. Few writers of travel accounts feel otherwise.[11] Olmsted does not like Southern biscuits and cornbread, nor does he relish the custom of soaking everything in grease. He reproduces a hotel menu from Memphis that tells us what fine people ate, including bear sausages (JBC, p. 127). At this establishment Olmsted has to settle for "grimy bacon and greasy cabbage" because all the dubious delicacies have been exhausted by other diners. One has to smile at Olmsted's expressions of distaste as well as at the Southerners' naive attempts at grandeur through giving French names to the homeliest dishes; but our appreciation of the data does not diminish.

Olmsted gives us information about the roles of women in old Southern folklife. In the Piedmont cotton district, he finds white women working "half naked" at shoveling bits of iron out of the earth (JBC, p. 208). Elsewhere, he notes that rural women do the heaviest kind of work and smoke pipes while driving their oxcarts (TCK, pp. 180–81). A fieldworker can still find two ideals for women in the South. Backwoods women work hard and present themselves as hardy, while town women act out the ideal of the plantation lady. Olmsted tells us, further, that liquor stills abound among the crackers (TCK, pp. 180–81). In showing us these less refined sides of Southern life, Olmsted is inadvertently laying groundwork for later stereotypes, but through it all he presents good data on bygone norms of which many modern Southerners are unaware. Southern Protestantism did not always oppose liquor and tobacco, nor were all Southern women in favor of the aristocratic lady image.

Having begun on the Kentucky frontier around 1800, camp meetings, those frolicsome combinations of piety, socializing, flamobyant preaching, and vigorous singing, were well-established institutions by the time Olmsted traveled. This "effervescing mixture of impiety and theology" (JBC, p. 132) perplexes Olmsted and strikes him as droll, as he hears camp meeting anecdotes.

In relating his encounters with Southerners, Olmsted portrays some scenes that convey character through action rather than words. Let us look at the first scene in A Journey in the Back Country, one of these portraits that tells us more today than Olmsted suspected.

One from among the gloomy, staring loungers at the door, as I pass, throws himself upon a horse, and overtaking me, checks his pace to keep by my side. I turn toward him, and full of aversion for the companionship of a stranger, nod, in such a manner as to say, "Your equality is acknowledged; go on." Not a nod; not the slightest deflection of a single line in the austere countenance; not a ripple of radiance in the sullen eyes, which wander slowly over, and, at distinct intervals, examine my horse, my saddle-bags, my spurs, lariat, gloves, finally my face, with such stern deliberation that at last I should not be sorry if he would speak. But he does not; does not make the smallest response to a further turning of my head, which acknowledges the reflex interest excited in my own mind; his eyes remain

fixed upon me, as if they were dead. I can no longer endure it in silence, so I ask, in a voice attuned to his apparent humor,
   "How far to Woodville?"
   The only reply is a slight grunt, with an elevation of the chin.
   "You don't know?"
   "No."

What have we here? Principally, that which present-day students of social interaction call "facework," a term coined by Erving Goffman.[12] Olmsted acts to acknowledge the other's existence with a nod, which ought to end matters in Olmsted's opinion. The two ought to continue their ways, politely inattentive to one another. But the cultures of these two men have different facework rules. Again Olmsted tries to terminate the encounter; again he fails. Finally, Olmsted is driven to speak aloud. The other replies nonlexically until Olmsted gives him another request for talk. For the other, there has not been and was never supposed to be a conversation. For Northerners, especially urban ones, "bold" use of the eyes *is* conversation. Southerners, especially rural ones, rule the eyes differently; a "stare" is not a conversational opening. Even the urban Southerner of today is surprised at having initiated talk just by looking at a Northerner in a way that would not cause another Southerner to speak. Many times he sees people squirm, until he learns to keep eyes politely focused on a plane just behind the other's body. Olmsted's grouchy companion did not know that when one looks directly at a Northerner one changes a passing encounter into an unintended conversation that nobody knows how to terminate without offense. At some time or another, every modern fieldworker gets himself into just such a facework predicament; today, we consider these problems important data on patterns of traditional communication.

The difference between Olmsted's treatment of Southern folklife and that of most other travelers lies partly in attitude but more in method. Few other travelers frankly state their purposes and make clear the assumptions conditioning their observations. Olmsted likes Southern folklife no more than other travelers and less than some, but unlike most others he does not allow his values to get in the way of his reporting. Nothing in ethnographic method, though much in ethnographic myth, obliges the observer to like everything and everyone he studies. Olmsted's is a biased eye; repeatedly, he compares Southern culture unfavorably to that of the North, not so much because it is less moral, but rather because it is less efficient and generally less sane than that of the North. Southerners are "notoriously careless, makeshift, impersistent people" (JSSS, p. ix). Nineteenth-century observers, travelers and anthropologists alike, assume that there is civilization and then there are defective versions of it.[13] Today we argue that each culture is a system and that comparisons are difficult, especially in terms of "good" and "bad." The alternative assumption made in the last century is that folk and primitives are better than civilized people because the former are closer to nature and God; today, most scholars also reject this assumption.

Olmsted offers a blistering comparison of Cape Cod and Georgia folk-life styles. "In both," he writes, "there is frankness, boldness, and simplicity; but in the one it is associated with intelligence, discretion, and an expansion of mind, resulting from considerable education; in the other with ignorance, improvidence, laziness, and the prejudices of narrow minds" (JSSS, p. 538). He goes on to say that Georgia folk "are still coarse and irrestrainable in appetite and temper; with perverted, eccentric and intemperate spiritual impulses; faithless in the value of their own labor, and almost imbecile for personal elevation" (JSSS, p. 540).

Thus, a present-day researcher has to separate Olmsted's facts from his interpretations, the latter colored by considerable ethnocentrism, a quality that Olmsted's time did not find particularly objectionable. The fact remains that Olmsted's are among the most useful travel accounts because we seldom have to infer his biases, if we are properly trained. Social historians, however, who are innocent of anthropological sophistication may fall into much error by depending upon the interpretations of Olmsted and other travelers.

What of the Southern folklife of the future, as Olmsted envisions it? In Chapter VIII of *A Journey in the Back Country*, Olmsted presents portions of a decidedly self-congratulatory annual report of a South Carolina manufacturing company (pp. 303–306). According to this report, putting the poor whites in the mills has had great uplifting effect. Olmsted does not quarrel with this report, although he later observes that setting up mills may prove more than Southern capital can manage on any large scale and that it takes a long time for the poor whites to become good workers (JBC, pp. 355–59).

Olmsted undoubtedly never imagines that servitude of whites in the mills will prove as vicious a social evil, North and South, as servitude of blacks in the fields. Understandably, Olmsted cannot foresee the baneful effects of the modern technology which was making the North industrially powerful; he finds in it only progress far beyond the level of backward Southern folklife. Here Olmsted's thinking resembles that of other travelers, most of whom hold that the Northerner's duty is to go south and uplift his retarded brothers: missionaries with carpetbags. The difference is that Olmsted's is a socioeconomic, not a moralistic, version of the solution. It is good to read Olmsted's professions of faith in progress via modern technology along with Cash's documentation of the sad, ironic outcome of the measures Olmsted sees as beneficial (though perhaps infeasible). Of course, Olmsted is not responsible for these future abuses, but his faith in technological progress seems to have clouded his vision.

All who have done research into Southern folklife with any concern for human welfare have asked what, if anything, can be done to improve matters. The problem has presented many faces, from the "Peculiar Institution" and its successor racial segregation, to tenant farming, to rapacious industry, to the revival of the plantation through agribusiness. In this sense, Olmsted's folklife reporting falls into natural sequence with that of Agee and Evans, Cash, the University of Chicago sociologists, and some of us in folklife studies today.

Consequently, Olmsted as folklife researcher has more for us than a descriptive catalogue of customs and habits. If he gave only that, his contribution would still have been great. His tables of contents read like indexes to Southern folklife precisely because they are, and unlike some later folklorists, he does not restrict his reporting to just "the folk," narrowly conceived. More than that, he gives us an interpretation of folklife and plans for social change. That an observer so percipient as Olmsted thinks that making poor whites into millhands might improve society ought to temper the enthusiasm some now feel for "applied" folklore and folklife. *All* folklore is applied folklore; the differences lie only in who applies what to whom toward what ends. Tradition may be malevolent as well as benign, as we see in the anecdotes Olmsted reproduces. Evil may be as innocent as the assumption that one's own folklife is *the* way, as we see in those same anecdotes and in Olmsted's trust in the beneficence of Yankee technology. Only now are we discovering just how dangerous our progress can be. We may have better training than Olmsted, but are we better prophets?

Olmsted is one of those who concludes that Southern ways of life are not just different but also inferior. We cannot logically condemn him for this conclusion, so common in his time, but we cannot commend him for it either. The conclusion is too common today, and too many thinkers have believed Olmsted and other travelers implicitly. Today, the Southern white belongs to the only American ethnic group of which it is still generally acceptable to utter the most extreme vilifications, with or without observations as evidence. Some folklorists now believe the time has come to stop this practice.[14]

However much of his interpretation of Southern folklife as demonstrably inferior may wound the sensibilities of postliberal Southerners today, it is unjust to belittle Olmsted's contribution to our knowledge of Southern, and indeed American, folklife because he cannot have our retrospective view. On the other hand, it is also unwise to make hagiography of discussions of his work. Olmsted tells us more than those who traveled to record the queer and outlandish, and more than many who study folklore and folklife today to extract the quaint and romanticize the grim. He shows us people, including himself, using tradition as a way and as a means of life, and that is no mean accomplishment.

NOTES

1. Henceforth abbreviated as JBC.
2. Alan Lomax, *Folk Song Style and Culture* (Washington, D.C., 1968).
3. Henceforth abbreviated as JSSS.
4. Broadus Mitchell, *Frederick Law Olmsted: A Critic of the Old South* (Baltimore, 1924), p. 92.
5. Ibid., p. 46.
6. See Allison Davis, Burleigh B. Gardner, and Mary R. Gardner, *Deep South: A Social Anthropological Study of Caste and Class* (Chicago and London, 1941); John Dollard, *Caste and Class in a Southern Town*, 3d ed. (Garden City, N.Y., 1957).
7. C. Vann Woodward, *The Burden of Southern History*, enlarged ed. (Baton Rouge, La., 1970), p. 17.
8. Mitchell, *Olmsted: Critic of the Old South*, p. 90. The history and significance of such illustrations is the subject of "Knickerbocker Illustrator of the Old South: John William Orr," below.
9. For another early account of this industry, see "Porte Crayon" (David Hunter Strother), "North Carolina Illustrated, II, the Piny Woods," *Harper's* 14 (1857): 741–55.
10. Frederick Law Olmsted, *The Cotton Kingdom: A Traveller's Observations on Cotton and Slavery in the American Slave States*, Arthur M. Schlesinger, ed. (New York, 1953), p. 180. Hereafter abbreviated as TCK.
11. Mitchell remarks upon Olmsted's repeated, fussy complaints about discomforts, especially culinary ones (p. 84).
12. See *Relations in Public: Microstudies of the Public Order* (New York, 1971).
13. For a short comparison of Olmsted's views and those of European travelers, see Victoria Post Ranney, *Olmsted in Chicago* (Chicago, 1972), pp. 9–11.
14. See F. N. Boney, "The Redneck," *Georgia Review* 25 (1971): 333–42; Edgar Z. Friedenberg, "Southern Discomfort," *New York Review of Books* (September 2, 1971). A major work on stereotyping written by a folklorist is Roger D. Abrahams, *Positively Black* (Englewood Cliffs, N.J., 1970).

Robert Detweiler

TRANSCENDING JOURNALISM:
Olmsted's Style in *The Cotton Kingdom*

Most of the critical commentary on Frederick Law Olmsted's travel writing emphasizes his message rather than his method, the content of what he wrote rather than the art of writing it. This relative lack of attention to his style should be corrected, for Olmsted himself aspired toward recognition as a man of letters, and indeed, the skill with which he composed and assembled his extensive commentary accounts for a good part of its high quality.[1] We shall focus on *The Cotton Kingdom* as a representative Olmsted text (even though it was not edited by Olmsted alone) in order to show that its overall structure is more carefully and strategically designed than the overtly casual format would suggest and contributes strongly to the impact of the book as a social-historical document.[2] We shall see also that the texture of the book—the elements of image, diction, syntax, and the like, that shape an individual style—amounts to a composition that transcends the level of journalism. The book therefore deserves to be examined as a literary work that can stand by itself as an aesthetic object. Another reason for choosing *The Cotton Kingdom* as a text that exhibits Olmsted's accomplished style is to counteract the opinion of negative modern critics such as Edmund Wilson. Although Wilson acknowledged the historical and political significance of *The Cotton Kingdom*, he thought little of Olmsted's literary talents. In *Patriotic Gore*, Wilson writes: "Olmsted, in the literary sense, was a very bad writer; when he is generalizing, he often has difficulty on account of the clumsiness of his syntax, in expressing what he wants to say, and he is always entirely pedestrian."[3] Our study should demonstrate the inaccuracy of Wilson's own generalizing and pedestrian judgment.[4]

Four kinds of discourse function in *The Cotton Kingdom*: the argumentative, the narrative, the dramatic, and the lyrical. None of these exists in isolation from the others, of course. They are interwoven throughout the whole work, but we shall separate them and discuss them individually in order to expose their components and show how Olmsted joins them to fashion his distinctive style. Argumentative discourse functions in two ways in *The Cotton Kingdom*: as the rhetorical framework that surrounds the other three elements and as a device used inside of the narrative discourse. Narrative discourse, the kind that predominates in *The Cotton Kingdom*, consists of two elements: reportage and storytelling. Dramatic discourse appears in *The Cotton Kingdom* as dialogue and in certain particularly intense descriptive scenes. Lyrical discourse, the rarest kind in the book, is employed effectively in occasional metaphorical constructs and in a few depictions of nature and natural landscapes.

Olmsted's strategy was to surround the narrative body of *The Cotton Kingdom* text with a framework of argument. That framework consists of a polemical first chapter (Introductory. The Present Crisis) and a final four chapters (XV–XVIII) that return to the vigorous disputatious tone of the first chapter and conclude on that note. The argument is single-minded but versatile. It is an effort to destroy the Southern contention that slavery is necessary to the economic well-being of the South and that the black slaves are much better off in bondage than they would be as free men. The nature of Olmsted's challenge has been explained often enough, but the technique bears analysis. His argument is a veritable arsenal of persuasive devices. He offers first-hand observation, statistics, supporting quotations, common sense logic, sarcasm; he even makes his opponents' objections work for him.

Regarding personal observation, for example, he reminds his readers in Chapter I that he has been on the cotton plantations "on the Mississippi, the Red River, and the Brazos Bottoms" and has seen the efforts of the slaveholding planters to become wealthy, against odds, through concentration on cotton and the neglect of responsible husbandry of the land and the culture.[5] He supplies statistics from respectable sources (the United States Census, for instance) on matters such as the number of slaves and slaveholders in the slave states and on the yearly expenses for operation as reported by representative plantations. Among the scores of supporting quotations is a striking one by the "Georgia Scenes" author, A. B. Longstreet, on the deterioration of once productive Georgia soil as a result of the cotton and slave economy:

The sun poured his whole strength upon the bald hill which once supported the sequestered school-house; many a deep-washed gully met at a sickly bog, where had gushed the limpid fountain; a dying willow rose from the soil which had nourished the venerable beech; flocks wandered among the dwarf pines, and cropped a scanty meal from the vale where the rich cane had bowed and rustled to every breeze, and all around was barren, dreary, and cheerless (p. 529).

Commonsense logic is the earmark of the argumentative discourse. For example, if it can be proven, quite apart from morality and in economic terms alone, that it actually costs more to produce cotton through slave labor than by the labor of remunerated free men, why persist in maintaining the wasteful system?[6] Sarcasm appears in Olmsted's response to the rumination of the well-known statistician James D. B. De Bow on the limited mental capacity of blacks; after quoting a passage in which De Bow compares the brain power of blacks to that of asses, Olmsted asks, "Are there laws on our statute-books to prevent asses from being taught to read" (p. 569)? An instance of Olmsted turning an opponent's argument against its author occurs in his answer to a racist article from the *Richmond Examiner* in which blacks are described as brutish and criminal creatures. If this is how blacks really are, Olmsted inquires, if they are truly so intellectually irredeemable, why then the great effort to prevent them from opportunities for education (p. 570)?

The net result of Olmsted's polemical exercises, such as those just illustrated, that surround the body of narrative is to situate the relatively relaxed and meandering story of Olmsted's travels in a context of aggressive, rational, and disciplined purpose. An interplay between argument and story is thus established that is mutually enhancing. The argument provides the episodic, rambling, casually composed travel narrative with a superimposed (but not forced) unity, a sense of direction, a rationale, while the narrative, as we shall see, gives the argument a great wealth of varied and powerful illustrative support.

Olmsted also employs argument adeptly and to great advantage *within* the narrative body of the text. Often it is a dialectical interchange in which Olmsted seems interested in demolishing an opponent's logic not with forensic flair but rather by calm and persistent questioning, causing him to reveal—at least to a Northerner—a fallacious and intolerable opinion. A conversation that Olmsted holds with a fellow passenger, a slave-owning merchant, on the river steamer "St. Charles," illustrates the technique (pp. 276–77). The discussion begins with an exchange of comments on *Uncle Tom's Cabin* and turns immediately to the matter of brutal treatment of slaves. When the merchant introduces the analogy between slave-beating and wife-beating, Olmsted with near-socratic patience and finesse shows how faulty the comparison is because slavery is at last based on the unchecked power of the master over his human property.

Sometimes Olmsted presents a brief argument in the context of the narrative, not by locating it in a dramatized interchange, but rather by summarizing a commonly held erroneous Southern attitude and then, in a sentence or two, efficiently inverting and thus refuting it. In a late chapter, he does just this by explaining how wealthy white Southerners seek to have their children educated free of contamination from Negroes, but then he remarks that the very refusal to educate the slaves is bound to increase even more the dangers of such inevitable contamination: "if the slaves must not be elevated, it would seem to be a necessity that the citizens should steadily degenerate" (p. 475). If the argument of the beginning and final chapters surrounds the narrative and gives it unity and coherence by anticipating and concluding it, then the arguments within the narrative, and sometimes constituting it, interpret the narrative episodes and, in a sort of counter-rhythm to them, recall for the reader the underlying theses regarding slavery and its effects on the South.

Obviously, narrative constitutes, both qualitatively and quantitatively, the dominant form of discourse in *The Cotton Kingdom*. It is not always easy and sometimes not even possible to distinguish between the two components of narrative discourse as Olmsted employs them here, reportage and storytelling. Usually, however, the reportage consists of information gleaned and presented as the result of rigorous inquiry, while the storytelling is a more informal mode in which the narrator relates, with considerable anecdotal detail, what befell him on the way. It is not fiction but embellished personal observation. As reporter, Olmsted is a fairly objective mediator of the news about the South; as storyteller, he is his own protagonist—the one about whom he reports and hence the one through whom he forfeits objectifying distance. Comprehending how he succeeds in combining these disparate aspects of narrative is essential to appreciating the text's influence and staying power.

Olmsted's "new journalistic" powers of observation were recognized early in his career (the *New-York Daily Times* review of 1853 referred to his "looking at things through a pair of sharp Northern eyes"), and modern critics have reinforced that view. For example, Alex L. Murray says that Olmsted "had an eye for those special qualities which determine the style of a situation, a person, or an object, and this sensitivity was reinforced by a talent for vivid description."[7] These deserve to be called "new journalistic" powers—granted that "new journalism" has been a much overworked phrase—because they prefigure in important ways the insertion of a personal and subjective spirit into the objective reporter's stance characteristic of present-day new journalists such as Norman Mailer or Truman Capote. (Olmsted, however, is less the creative artist and more the recording craftsman than either of these two.) As a roving reporter in the South, Olmsted concentrates on the overview; he remarks many details, summarizes and generalizes from them. He is at pains to convey accurate information from a sympathetic distance. As a storyteller, on the other hand, instead of focusing on the overview he selects and elaborates incidents. Instead of generalizing from the details, he chooses and develops the typical. Instead of striving to convey accurate information, he offers, often through caricature and other purposeful distortion, an *experience* of the South from a self-conscious participant-observer's perspective.

The beginning of Chapter III, "Virginia," provides examples of Olmsted's technique of reportage (pp. 31–32). The first paragraph gives concentrated information on modes and costs of travel between Washington and Richmond. The second paragraph consists of generalizing details about the agricultural conditions observed en route. The third and fourth paragraphs continue in this manner, describing the houses and grounds of wealthy and poor whites and the slave quarters, and start presenting impressions ("Swine, hounds, and black and white children, are commonly lying promiscuously together on the ground about the doors"—p. 31). The fifth paragraph ventures into quasi-sociological commentary based on the previous observations: "I am struck with the close cohabitation and association of black and white—negro women are carrying black and white babies together in their arms; black and white children are playing together (not going to school together); black and white faces are constantly thrust together out of the doors, to see the train go by" (p. 31). The sixth paragraph, then, shifts focus and turns to Olmsted's travel companions, yet without losing the sense of a reporter's scrutiny. In these pages, Olmsted's manifest intention is to depict things through the long view, the overview, the accumulation of details susceptible to quick generalization, without intruding his presence.

A few pages later, Olmsted the raconteur supplants Olmsted the reporter. On a Sunday afternoon in Richmond, he comes upon a black funeral procession and follows it out of town to the rural cemetery. He portrays the types of mourners, the graveyard ceremony, and the burial itself, emphasizing the inadvertent humor of the illiterate speakers' attempts to use homiletic language, especially their malapropisms ("We do not see the end here! oh no, my friends! there will be a *putrification* of this body!"—p. 36). The caricature is skillfully done. Above all, Olmsted confesses his own emotional response in markedly nonjournalistic fashion: "I was deeply influenced myself by the unaffected feeling, in connection with the simplicity, natural, rude truthfulness, and absence of all attempt at formal decorum in the crowd" (p. 35). Most of the storytelling in *The Cotton Kingdom* is like this, a casual (but definitely not aimless) account of a particular incident with considerable dependence on unusual details (unusual for a Northerner, at least) that cohere to form the *typical* in the South and that include the narrator's personal reaction.

Of the literally hundreds of examples of Olmsted's storytelling in *The Cotton Kingdom*, three will demonstrate his ability to create vignettes, when he wants to, that have a more concentrated narrative power, based on a more efficiently organized plot than the one just presented. The first is a story within a story, a lengthy joke-anecdote which Olmsted overheard in the Red River Valley and retold. It concerns a man who in a dream meets the devil in hell and tells him that a revival is going on in the town (Alexandria) he has just departed. The devil shods himself to go there at once to frustrate the meeting, but when he learns that a notorious Elder Slocum is conducting the revival, the devil relaxes: " 'Why in hell couldn't you have said so before?' says he. 'Here, boy, take away these boots'; and he kicked 'em off, and laid down again" (p. 279). Here, aided by the regionalism and joke format, Olmsted tells a succinct bit of fiction that is genuinely funny and that characterizes both the moral flavor of the area he is visiting and his ability to sense quickly such an atmosphere as if from an insider's perspective. The second story, from a visit to Houston, concerns the brutal treatment of a captured runaway mulatto slave. In about one page Omlsted recounts how the captor, also a black man, found the runaway by stabbing into a hayloft with a pitchfork until he struck the fugitive in the face and brought him out to be returned to his master. It is a poignant account of a slave's mistreatment by another slave, made all the more shocking by the understated and laconic manner of Olmsted's retelling (pp. 309–10). The third story is a marvelously animated two-page rehearsal of a torturous and exhausting overnight which Olmsted spent at a house in central Mississippi. Olmsted is set upon by varieties of vermin throughout the night, and he finally flees the bedroom at four o'clock in the morning. The narration has appeal for anyon‐ who has ever spent a sleepless night fighting some sort of physical discomfort and arises in despair "with that feverish dryness of the eyes which indicates a determination to sleep no more" (p. 363).[8]

Still other aspects of Olmsted's narrative style that characterize both the reportage and the storytelling must be mentioned. One of these is what we have called his laconic manner. We know that his efforts at simplicity were self-conscious and serious (regarding his *Walks and Talks of an American Farmer*, he said, "the most simple parts are those I worked hardest at to make simple"), and sometimes so successful that a key observation is delivered in an off-handed way that diffuses its impact.[9] It may appear contradictory to the evidence, on the other hand, to refer to his laconic style, for the very bulk of *The Cotton Kingdom* (which is itself an abridgment) suggests that Olmsted was anything but given to few words. Nevertheless, as an illustration will show, part of Olmsted's distinctive stylistic accomplishment is to be both efficient in language usage and comprehensive in subject matter: pages 235–241 of *The Cotton Kingdom* seem at first glance to wander from the topic of racial intermingling in New Orleans through the subjects of white men and mulatto (or quadroon) mistresses, the beauty of the mixed-blood women, the comparative licentiousness of South and North, illegitimate children of black women and white men, and a black-white church service. A closer reading, however, reveals that these six pages in fact examine facets of the original single topic of racial intercourse—its sexual, domestic, economic, social, moral, pedagogical, even religious aspects. Olmsted does this largely by offering a sequence of aptly joined illustrations and commentary on the kept mulatto and quadroon girls, their children, their quasi-marriages with their white lovers, a contrast of this life-style to that of young white men in New York, the helplessness of the black women against white male exploitation, and an ethnically mixed New Orleans church service attended by a stunning mulatto woman. Each of these topics is treated concisely and evenly and leads smoothly to the next. Together, they contribute to a versatile overview of the subject that, if it is loquacious, is also balanced and most effective.

Lest Olmsted's studied simplicity should seem to be ingenuousness, one should mention the counterside: his surprising adeptness with literary allusions; his occasional deployment of an often mordant humor, especially to expose the lubricious proslavery arguments of his Southern hosts, and, above all, the art of developing a sober but utilitarian imagery that carries his overall intentions and concerns.

That he should use literary allusions so familiarly is surprising in light of his self-education, although not so much so when one considers this talent in the context of his many self-generated accomplishments. *The Cotton Kingdom* contains occasional evidence that Olmsted appreciated a sophisticated literary style and strove towards this style himself. Describing the sermon at the black church in New Orleans, he demonstrates a fine sense of discrimination:

Much of the language was highly metaphorical; the figures long, strange, and complicated, yet sometimes, however, beautiful. Words were frequently misplaced, and their meaning evidently misapprehended, while the grammar and pronunciation was sometimes such as to make the idea to be conveyed by the speaker incomprehensible to me. Vulgarisms and slang phrases occasionally occurred, but evidently without any consciousness of impropriety on the part of the speaker of his congregation (p. 241).

Olmsted's own literary sophistication appears in passages like the one treating the house of the Italian-French immigrant "Old Man Corse" in southwestern Louisiana. Olmsted says that the interior is reminiscent "of the Acadian fireside" and quotes, without identifying poet or text, eight lines from Longfellow's *Evangeline*. [10] In Chapter XIV, "Slavery in Its Property Aspect," Olmsted offers an appealingly apt classical allusion. Speaking of a plantation overseer's satisfaction with "the gang of toiling negroes" around him who are to him "as essential an element of the poetry of nature as flocks of peaceful sheep and herds of lowing kine," he toys further with the pastoral mood and concludes, "he [the overseer] would no more appreciate the aspect in which an Abolitionist would see them, than would Virgil have honoured the feelings of a vegetarian, sighing at the sight of flocks and herds destined to feed the depraved appetite of the carnivorous savage of modern civilization" (p. 446). It is a startling and even in some ways a clumsy trope, but withal an effective one. A third example will round out our demonstration of Olmsted's literary knowledgeability. Speculating on the existence of the vaunted Southern gentleman, Olmsted declares that he "is as rare a phenomenon in the South at the present day as is the old squire of Geoffrey Crayon in modern England."[11] This familiar reference to Washington Irving's pseudonym both confirms Olmsted's easy acquaintance with the American world of letters and suggests that he identifies with Irving's urbane social criticism and travel observations composed under the alias of Crayon.

Olmsted's humor is exercised most frequently in his display of good-natured exasperation over poor Southern hospitality.[12] He remarks comically and ruefully on inadequate conditions in his Washington boarding house ("I am humble, and I am short, and soon curried; but I am not satisfied with a quarter of a yard of towelling, having an irregular vacancy in its centre, where I am liable to insert my head"—p. 25). And he relishes the incongruity of the "polyglotic" speech of New Orleans, reporting the reply of an Irish taxi driver: "*Oui*, yer 'oner" (p. 227). But his humor is at its best when it becomes caustic. It is gently so at the spot where he gives verbatim an inane song sung by black steamboat hands on the Red River. After repeating ten lines, all of the quality of "*Oh, we is gwine up de Red River, oh!*" each followed by a chorus of "Oahoiohieu," he comments that "The wit introduced into these songs has, I suspect, been rather over estimated" (p. 271). Later, he becomes involved in conversation with a Mississippi farmer who assumes that Olmsted is in the market for slaves, and the conversation goes like this:

> "Expect you're going to buy a rice-farm, in the Carolinies, aint you? and I reckon you're up here speckylating arter nigger stock, aint you now?"
> "Well," said I, "I wouldn't mind getting that fat girl of yours, if we can make a trade. How much a pound will you sell her at?"
> "We don't sell niggers by the pound in this country."
> "Well, how much by the lump?" (p. 355)

Neither of these illustrations shows Olmsted ridiculing black mentality or belittling the worth of individual blacks. Rather, in both places his sarcasm is directed finally at the whites who denigrate blacks either by patronizing interest in black folk culture or by assuming bluntly their primary value as economic objects. In such instances, Olmsted's humor displays a cutting edge; even when it is only abrasive, it adds vigor and strength of personality to the narrative discourse. It is one of the elements that lifts Olmsted's account a healthy distance above the level of mere journalism.

Yet another element of his style that balances its practiced simplicity of expression is Olmsted's narrative imagery. It is characterized by two distinct but complementary tendencies: one toward caricature and the other toward the picturesque. The caricaturizing impulse is followed, naturally, in his descriptions of people, while the interest in the picturesque expends itself on architecture and the landscape. Caricature emerges in Olmsted's description of people through his habit of depicting mainly the facial expressions, clothing, and relative degree of cleanliness. That is to say, he does not often avail himself of the various possibilities for characterization that an author (even one, such as Olmsted, writing nonfiction) has at hand. Rather, he limits himself to the same few of these and hence produces a few predictable types such as the taciturn farmer, the voluble plantation owner, the rough fellow hotel guest, and the procrastinating house slave.[13] Olmsted's eye for the picturesque, on the other hand, focuses inventively on buildings and natural scenery. He has an appreciation for the varieties of architecture and landscapes in the South that sometimes seems to exceed what the South has to offer. At any rate, he does do justice to what is there. For example, Chapter V, on the Carolinas, has numerous passages on structures and natural features that are rich in technical and imaginative detail. Speaking of the swamps, he names and describes kinds of trees: "the white-shafted sycamore, the gray beech, and the shrubby blackjack oak, with broad leaves, brown and dead, yet glossy, and reflecting the sunbeams" (p. 159). And a few sentences further on a more fanciful effort:

The tylandria hung in festoons, sometimes several feet in length, and often completely clothed the trunks, and every branch of the trees in the low ground. It is like a fringe of tangled hair, of a light gray pearly colour, and sometimes produces exquisite effects when slightly veiling the dark green, purple, and scarlet of the cedar, and the holly with their berries. The mistletoe also grew in large, vivid, green tufts, on the ends of the branches of the oldest and largest trees (p. 159).

The fact that Olmsted often sketches people conventionally and as types but treats their surroundings lavishly does not imply a disinterest in humanity. If anything, it suggests a lingering romanticism (as do the literary references to the pastoral and to Irving and Longfellow) that wishes to see humans in an ideal natural environment. One might even conjecture that Olmsted's recurrent depictions of buildings and natural sites as sanctuaries are his own spiritual preparation for later practical accomplishments. The chapter on the Carolinas contains Olmsted's account of blacks taking refuge in the Dismal Swamps and of whole generations of runaway blacks living and dying in precarious fugitive freedom there (p. 121). This image of the wild place of refuge appears at other spots in the book. It obviously appeals to Olmsted and could well be a strong element in the landscape of his imagination that would be translated into real American sanctuaries like Manhattan's Central Park.[14]

Dramatic discourse, the third kind that informs *The Cotton Kingdom*, appears as dialogue, as the imitation of dialects that are part of the dialogue, and in certain very intense descriptive scenes. The frequent employment of direct dialogue is one of the major factors contributing to the vigor and strong sense of life that the text exudes. Since Olmsted obviously had no modern technological means of recording conversations at his disposal (and since it would have been nearly impossible to record the conversations verbatim when he did take notes), the interchanges must be read as approximations of actual talk and as fictions that sound like genuine conversation.[15] But one should not therefore consider the dialogue any the less authentic. Olmsted presents typical conversations, the distillations and reworkings of hundreds of dialogues in which he was involved. One can surmise that his composed dialogue preserves the flavor and spirit of what he actually engaged in, and hence it can be accepted, if not as history, certainly as a reliable way of conveying truth about the South as he experienced it.

His imitation of dialects within the dialogue is another instance of this subtle relationship of fact and fiction. Olmsted could not catch via tape recorder the distinctions of vocabulary, pronunciation, rhythm, pitch, and the ineffable personal presence that constitute dialects. Instead, in the manner of the creative writer, he had to select certain distinguishing words, idioms, and spellings and from these fashion not the simulation but the representation of regional and ethnic speech patterns. It would take a specialist in the history of Southern dialects to evaluate Olmsted's success in approximating the various vernaculars, but we can call attention to the ambitiousness and rigor of his effort. Although one notices first his imitation of black dialects, one should not overlook the others. He chooses terms and spellings to distinguish among the patois of native white Southerners such as Carolinians, Mississippians, and Texans but also among those of Creoles and the more recently immigrated Germans and Italians. Thus, the Germans say "ding" and "deenk" for "thing" and "think" (pp. 421-42) but the Italians "tzing" or "ting" and "tzink" (pp. 425-26) according to Olmsted's transliteration, and each betrays his origins by a Germanic or Romance syntax and word order. Such differentiation, whether or not it is linguistically reliable, accomplishes what the use of dialogue and dialect generally ought to: it creates the sense of immediacy, of individualizing presence, of action happening that is the genius of the dramatic and that both enlivens and intensifies Olmsted's argument and narration.

A few remarkable passages, composed of both dialogue and description, convey such intensity by the sheer power of Olmsted's dramatic sense. One of these is worth quoting in part, for it shows the author rising to unwonted creative heights. It is the scene in Chapter XIV, "Slavery in Its Property Aspects," in which a truant slave girl is discovered and viciously beaten by the overseer. Olmsted describes the actual beating as follows:

At every stroke the girl winced and exclaimed, "Yes, sir!" or "Ah, sir!" or "Please, sir!" not groaning or screaming. At length he stopped and said, "Now tell me the truth." The girl repeated the same story. "You have not got enough yet," said he; "pull up your clothes—lie down." The girl without any hesitation, without a word or look of remonstrance or entreaty, drew closely all her garments under her shoulders, and lay down upon the ground with her face toward the overseer, who continued to flog her with the raw-hide, across her naked loins and thighs, with as much strength as before. She now shrunk away from him, not rising, but writhing, grovelling, and screaming, "Oh, don't, sir! oh, please, stop, master! please, sir! please, sir! oh, that's enough, master! oh, Lord! oh, master, master! oh, God, master, do stop! oh, God, master! oh, God, master" (p. 455)!

The straightforward portrayal of impersonal cruelty combined with the girl's acute and helpless agony provides an emotional impact, late in the book, that relieves Olmsted's carefully maintained distance in most encounters.[16]

The fourth kind of discourse in *The Cotton Kingdom* is the lyrical discourse. This type is employed least and is therefore all the more effective when it does appear in supplementing the argumentative, narrative, and dramatic modes. Here one finds substantial evidence that Olmsted can be a literary craftsman when he so chooses. His metaphors, for instance, are artful and effective; through them he can initiate a mood or draw a deft analogy. He recalls a spring day in Louisiana with the lines, "A deep notch of sadness marks in my memory the morning of the May day on which I rode out of the chattering little town of Bayou Sara, and I recollect little of its immediate suburbs but the sympathetic cloud-shadows slowly going before me over the hill of St. Francis" (p. 405). Later in the same chapter, he writes, "I passed during the day four or five large plantations, the hillsides worn, cleft, and channelled like icebergs; stables and negro quarters all abandoned, and everything given up to nature and decay" (p. 410). Toward the end of the book, he speaks as follows of an old slave intimidated by a threat of whipping by a twelve-year-old white girl: "The man quailed like a spaniel, and she instantly resumed the manner of a lovely child with me . . ., no more conscious that she had increased the security of her life by strengthening the habit of the slave to the master race, than is the sleeping seaman that he tightens his clutch of the rigging as the ship meets each new billow'' (pp. 574-75).

This metaphoric flair is on occasion sustained through whole passages. One of them is an evocative depiction of a marshy area in southeastern Texas, a depiction that because of its contents we might call negative-lyrical:

The many pools, through which the usual track took us, were swarming with venomous water-snakes, four or five black moccasins often lifting at once their devilish heads above the dirty surface, and wriggling about our horses' heels. Beyond the Sabine, alligator holes are an additional excitement, the unsuspicious traveller suddenly sinking through the treacherous surface, and sometimes falling a victim, horse and all, to the hideous jaws of the reptile, while overwhelmed by the engulfing mire in which he lurks (p. 310).

Olmsted offers a positive-lyrical passage to celebrate a Mississippi River vista overlooking Natchez:

I suddenly found myself on the very edge of a great cliff, and before me an indescribably vast expanse of forest, extending on every hand to a hazy horizon, in which, directly in front of me, swung the round, red, setting sun. Through the otherwise unbroken forest, the Father of Waters had opened a passage for himself, forming a perfect arc, the hither shore of the middle of the curve being hidden under the crest of the cliff, and the two ends lost in the vast obscurity of the Great West. Overlooked from such an eminence, the size of the Mississippi can be realized—which is difficult under ordinary circumstances; but though the fret of a swelling torrent is not wanting, it is perceptible only as the most delicate chasing upon the broad, gleaming expanse of polished steel, which at once shamed all my previous conceptions of the appearance of the greatest of rivers (p. 424).

This study shows that Olmsted, when he wished to, could be a competent and sensitive literary artist and that, because he often chose the literary over the journalistic mode of expression, his book transcends the ephemeralness and unidimensionality of journalism. It deserves to take its place among those documents of American culture that, by virtue of the power of style that confirms an authenticity of message, have influenced the nation's course. The book itself is, in fact, metaphoric of the country's genius: sprawling, easy-going but always attending to its business, struggling to unite the general with the particular, seeking to reconcile ideal freedom with the hard political and economic realities, constantly arguing its rationale and retelling its story, and in the act clarifying its experience for itself and the world. *The Cotton Kingdom* embodies a typically and uniquely American style, and it is fitting that its author, so closely connected to the land, should also have the craft to shape its meaning.

NOTES

1. Laura Wood Roper in *FLÓ: A Biography of Frederick Law Olmsted* (Baltimore, 1973) discusses Olmsted's desire to make his mark in the world of letters. Cf. also Roper, "Frederick Law Olmsted in the 'Literary Republic,'" *Mississippi Valley Historical Reivew* 39 (December 1952): 459–82.

2. Frederick Law Olmsted, *The Cotton Kingdom: A Traveller's Observations on Cotton and Slavery in the American Slave States*, Arthur M. Schlesinger, ed. (New York, 1953). The text was originally published in 1861 as a condensation, with some new material, of three earlier volumes of travel writing on the South by Olmsted: *A Journey in the Seaboard Slave States with Remarks on Their Economy* (1856); *A Journey Through Texas* (1857); and *A Journey in the Back Country in the Winter of 1853 –54* (1860). *The Cotton Kingdom* was co-edited by the newspaper editor Daniel R. Goodloe. Since Goodloe's main task was, as Schlesinger states it in his Editor's Introduction, "The work of compression and consolidation" (p. xxxi), it might seem inaccurate to comment on the overall structure of the book as if it were Olmsted's own design, especially since Olmsted himself, as Schlesinger reports (p. xxxiv), "is said to have been dissatisfied with the abridgment." Nevertheless, we are justified in doing so because the structuring of the text ultimately remained Olmsted's responsibility (Goodloe was not even mentioned as co-editor in the 1861 edition) and because Goodloe contributed nothing of actual substance to the text. Further biographical information on Goodloe may be found in Stephen B. Weeks, "Anti-Slavery Sentiment in the South," *Southern History Association Publications* 2 (April 1898): 118–30; and in John Spencer Bassett, "Anti-Slavery Leaders of North Carolina," *Johns Hopkins University Studies in Historical and Political Science*, Series 16, No. 6 (June 1898): 306–16.

3. Edmund Wilson, *Patriotic Gore: Studies in the Literature of the American Civil War* (New York, 1962), p. 221. Daniel Aaron also slights Olmsted's style, at least by near omission of him altogether, in *The Unwritten War: American Writers and the Civil War* (New York, 1973). In that work, Aaron mentions Olmsted four times, once by quoting him (p. 333) in a way that makes Olmsted appear to be an unmitigated racist: "Frederick Law Olmsted, a member of the United States Sanitary Commission pronounced the Negro 'little better than a cunning idiot, and a cowed savage.' " As we shall see, such citations seriously distort Olmsted's attitude toward blacks and toward the South.

4. For a more sophisticated and comprehensive example of the approach I am using in this essay , cf. Steven Marcus, *Engels, Manchester, and the Working Class* (New York, 1974).

5. *The Cotton Kingdom*, p. 12. All further page numbers from *The Cotton Kingdom* will be given in parentheses in the text following the quotation or reference.

6. Robert William Fogel and Stanley L. Engerman in their highly controversial *Time on the Cross: The Economics of American Negro Slavery* (Boston and Toronto, 1974), 1: 171 ff., have attacked Olmsted's argument on this subject (and others). They have attempted to prove via "cliometrics" that, had Olmsted taken the proper factors into account, he would have seen that cotton production through the slavery system was indeed an efficient operation.

7. *The New-York Daily Times* quotation is given by Schlesinger (p. xvii). Alex L.

Murray's comment is made in his introduction to Olmsted's *Walks and Talks of an American Farmer in England* (originally published in two editions in 1852 and 1859; modern edition published by the University of Michigan Press, Ann Arbor, 1967), p. vii.

8. Roper, in *FLO: A Biography of Frederick Law Olmsted*, makes numerous references to Olmsted's chronic insomnia, e.g., pp. 13, 146, 430.

9. Quoted by Schlesinger, Editor's Introduction to *The Cotton Kingdom*, p. xii.

10. *The Cotton Kingdom*, p. 318. The lines from *Evangeline* are 199–206 of Part One.

11. *The Cotton Kingdom*, p. 476. Irving used the pseudonym in *The Sketch Book of Geoffrey Crayon, Gent.*, which was published in New York, 1819–1820, in seven installments.

12. For a discussion of Olmsted and Southern folkways, cf. Kay L. Cothran, "Olmsted's Contribution to Folklife Research," above.

13. Such characterization was not Olmsted's province alone. It was also employed by his famous contemporary "Porte Crayon" (David Hunter Strother) in *The Old South Illustrated: Profusely Illustrated by the Author*, edited with an Introduction by Cecil D. Eby, Jr. (Chapel Hill, N.C., 1959), 1857 and 1871 eds.: and by Jonathan Baxter Harrison, a later collaborator of Olmsted's. Cf. Timothy J. Crimmins, "Frederick Law Olmsted and Jonathan Baxter Harrison: Two Generations of Social Critics of the American South," below.

14. For a more thorough analysis of Olmsted's descriptive talents, cf. Lake Douglas, "The Landscape Observed: Olmsted's View of the Antebellum South," below.

15. Edmund Wilson writes in *Patriotic Gore*, p. 221, that "The conversations reported by Olmsted give the impression of all having been reproduced, without any art of selection, precisely as Olmsted remembered them, and he seems to have remembered everything." Wilson is either speaking facetiously or has not bothered to reflect on the physical impossibility of what he suggests is Olmsted's technique.

16. Olmsted does not merely observe in this situation. Although he does not intervene, he is sufficiently agitated by the beating to spur his horse and ride away. He writes, "it was a red-hot experience to me, and has ever since been a fearful hing in my memory" (p. 456).

William Lake Douglas

THE LANDSCAPE OBSERVED:
Olmsted's View
of the Antebellum South

Frederick Law Olmsted was an observant critic whose meticulously re-corded impressions of antebellum social conditions also included many references to the physical landscape, farming practices, general life, and customs of Southern society. The intention of his journeys in the South was "to make a personal study of the ordinary condition and habits of the people of the South" and to report on slavery from an economic rather than purely a humanistic point of view.[1] Olmsted's manner of examining the component of slavery against the general background of the Southern landscape gives added significance to his impressions.

In his Southern journals, Olmsted used techniques similar to those found in *Walks and Talks of an American Farmer in England*, his first pub-lished work, which he described as the product of his having "not merely seen the rural character, but lived in it, and made it a part" of himself.[2] This earlier experience was the first clear manifestation of Olmsted's social consciousness, which, after his journeys in the South, crystallized into a strong philosophical approach to landscape architecture, a new profession based on total environmental planning.

Olmsted's observations are primarily of an economic and social nature. Discussing a region that was strongly agrarian and economically depen-dent on that "Peculiar Institution," Olmsted illustrated the complexities of Southern life and presented his antislavery arguments through fre-quent references to environmental conditions. Therefore, a closer exami-nation of his observations of environmental phenomena—native flora, crop cultivation and farming techniques, soil types and drainage condi-tions, housing types and plantation spatial organization, conditions of transportation, urban open space, public health, welfare, and convenience—will bring a clearer understanding of the rationale for his approach to environmental planning and a comprehension of the success of his designs.

Frequently, Olmsted's landscape descriptions are expressions of the romantic ideas popularized in mid-nineteenth-century America by the landscape gardener and architectural critic Andrew Jackson Downing, whom Olmsted met in 1846, and the architectural examples of Downing's friend and the prime exponent of his philosophy, Alexander Jackson Davis, whom Olmsted met in 1847.[3] Downing, in his *Treatise on the Theory and Practice of Landscape Gardening Adapted to North America* (1841), wrote that all landscape design should be an abstract or an idealized imitation of nature. According to Downing, there were two expressions of landscape design: the *beautiful*, "characterized by simple and flowing lines" or the *picturesque*, "expressed by strikingly irregular, spirited forms."[4]

A careful reading of Olmsted's descriptions of Kentucky and east Texas reveals his understanding of Downing's ideas, and it also shows Olmsted's powers of observation, his recognition and sensitivity to natural environmental design, and how much better he understood the effects of these natural phenomena than did Downing. An awareness of such phenomena would later appear in the common vocabulary of Olmsted's profession and would find expression in all of his professional work. In Kentucky, his observations include recognition of the power and value of scale ("an immense natural park"), the function of open space ("delight and service of man"), and the effect of natural vistas ("oaks and beeches . . . arranged in vistas and masses").[5] In eastern Texas, he noticed the natural fertility of a flood plain ("the rich alluvial border of a creek"), native vegetation and the effects produced by their natural contrast ("grotesque cactus and dwarf palm, with dark, glossy evergreen shrubs, and thickets of verdant cane"), and the effects of shade through a vegetative canopy ("sunshine but feebly penetrating through the thick, waving canopy of dark gray moss"). The following passage illustrates how strongly Olmsted was impressed by a sequential experience, the effectiveness of a grade change, the sudden opening of a view, the contrast between open spaces and natural plantings, and the ability of vegetation to contain space:

Soon after fording the creek, we ascended a steep hill, the forest still continuing, till, reaching the brow, we came out suddenly, as if a curtain had risen, upon a broad prairie, reaching, in swells like the ocean after a great storm, to the horizon before us; a thick screen of wood edging it in the distance on the left, and an open grove of low, branching oaks breaking irregularly upon it, with spurs and scattered single trees, to the right. Our path, turning before us, continued along this broken edge, crossing capes and islands of the grove, and bays of the prairie.

The romanticism of his observation is made complete by his noting "horses and gray and red cattle dotting the waving brown surface" and six deer "unconcernedly browsing." The ground surface became regular, "very grand in vastness and simplicity" and followed "Hogarth's line of beauty," with "a grade of mathematical exactness."[6]

Throughout his writings Olmsted reveals his agrarian/scientific farming background, with many references to Southern farming techniques, methods of cultivation, and lack of agricultural management. In the "Highlands" of Virginia, he notes the good natural conditions of the terrain, and the fact that all the level ground he had seen in three weeks was fenced and was either under tillage or producing grass for hay. With some dismay, however, he reports that the

agricultural management is nearly as bad as possible. Corn, planted without manure, even by farmers who have large stocks of cattle, is cultivated for a long series of years on the same ground; the usual crop being from twenty to thirty bushels to the acre. Where it fails very materially, it is thought to be a good plan to shift to rye. Rye is sown in July, broadcast, among the growing corn, and incidentally covered with a plow and hoes at the "lay by" cultivation of the corn. It is reaped early in July the following year with cradles, an acre yielding from five to fifteen bushels. The following crop of corn is said to be much better for the interpolation. Oats in the eastern parts, buckwheat, are sowed in fallow land, and the crops appeared to be excellent, but I could learn of never a measurement. Herds-grass (*agrostis vulgaris*), is sown on the valley lands, (rarely on the steep slopes of the mountain,) with oats, and the crop, without any further labor, pays for mowing and making into hay for from four to eight years afterward. Where it becomes mossy, weedy, and thin, it is often improved by harrowing or scarifying with a small "bull-tongue," or counter plow, and meadows thus made . . . are considered "permanent." The hay from them soon becomes in large part, however, coarse, weedy and bushy.[7]

Traveling through the rice-producing states of the South, Olmsted is quite absorbed in the cultivation of that grain and expresses "little doubt that . . . many [northern] swamps . . . could be converted into fields of irrigation . . . with great profit."[8] For this reason, he gives an extensive account of the techniques of rice cultivation.[9] A similarly detailed discussion is given for sugar cane[10] but not for cotton; apparently, he assumed the reader was familiar with the simplicity of this crop's culture. In these accounts, Olmsted discusses the characteristics of the plant and growing conditions, explains the methods of cultivation, describes the necessary tools, and analyzes the systems of production.

Olmsted's frequent references to the landscape indicate how closely he observes native scenery and specific plant materials as well as the man-made elements. The frequent swamps of South Carolina have cypress, sycamores, gray beech, black-jack oak, red cedar, and holly. Vines and creepers grow to the tops of the trees, and tylandria (Spanish moss) dangle from the branches, clothing the trunks and lower limbs.[11] In eastern Mississippi, the scenery is "monotonous and somber" with the predominant trees being black oak, black-jack oak, and pine, with "profuse and bright colored vegetation."[12] Around St. Francisville, Louisiana, Olmsted notes that the soil is a friable, sandy loam, "generally rich, though much washed off higher ground."[13] The landscape around this region, known as the Feliciana, has

an open, suburban character, with residences indicative of rapidly accumulating wealth, and advancement in luxury among the proprietors. For twenty miles to the north of the town, there is on both sides a succession of large sugar and cotton plantations. Much land still remains uncultivated, however. The roadside fences are generally hedges of roses—Cherokee and sweet brier. These are planted first by the side of a common rail fence, which, while they are young, supports them in the manner of a trellis; as they grow older they fall each way, and mat together, finally forming a confused, sprawling, slovenly thicket, often ten feet in breadth and four to six feet high. Trumpet creepers, grapevines, greenbriers, and in very rich soil, cane, grow up through the mat of roses, and add to its strength. It is not as pretty as a trimmer hedge, yet very agreeable, and the road being sometime narrow, deep and lane like, delightful memories of England were often brought to mind.

There were frequent groves of magnolia grandiflora, large trees, and every one in the glory of full blossom. The magnolia does not, however, show well in masses, and those groves, not unfrequently met, were much finer, where the beech, elm, and liquid amber formed the body, and the magnolias stood singly out, magnificent chandeliers of fragrance. The large-leafed magnolia, extremely beautiful at this season of the year, was more rarely seen.[14]

Olmsted's recorded observation of native plant materials and the effects they produced extended to several references of extensive gardens that often adorned the wealthy planter's mansion in this area. One such reference occurs in the previously mentioned Feliciana region of Louisiana, when Olmsted talked to a fellow traveler:

"Do you remember a place you passed (describing the locality)?"
"Yes" said I [Olmsted]; "a nice house, with a large garden, and a lawn with some statues or vases in it."
"I think it likely; got a foreign gardener, I expect; that's all the fashion with them; a nigger isn't good enough for them. Well, that belongs to a Mr. A. J. Clayborn. (?) He's got to be a very rich man; I suppose he's got as many as five hundred people on all his places. He went out to Europe a few years ago, and sometime after he came back, he came up to Natchez. . . . [M]y wife . . . and Mrs. Clayborn . . . used to know each other when they were girls . . . and she [went] . . . to see her. Mrs. Clayborn could not talk about any thing but the great people they had seen . . . of some great nobleman's castle they went to, and the splendid park there was to it, and how grandly they lived.[15]

Another Olmsted reference to landscape gardening occurs in the Natchez area. Approaching the suburbs of this important river town, Olmsted finds the country "beautiful," the soil "very rich," most of the land enclosed in plantations, and the roadside boundaries made of rose hedges. The road, with high banks on either side, is "well constructed," with trees bending over the traveler, resembling "Herefordshire lanes." The frequent oak woods have a "park-like character" and, when enclosed and slightly thinned out, form "noble grounds around the residences of the planters," which were "cottages or very simple and unostentatious mansions." Within three miles of Natchez

the country is entirely occupied by houses and grounds of a villa character, the grounds usually exhibiting a paltry taste, with miniature terraces, and trees and shrubs planted and trimmed with no regard to architectural and landscape considerations. There is, however, an abundance of good trees, much beautiful shrubbery, and the best hedges and screens of evergreen shrubs that I have seen in America. The houses are not remarkable.[16]

At first reading, it might seem curious that Olmsted dismissed the grounds of the plantations as "paltry" and the many imposing mansions around Natchez as "not remarkable," for the population of that city at this time was one of the wealthiest per capita in America. His seemingly inconsistent judgment that the grounds were planted "with no regard to architectural and landscape considerations" resulted perhaps from Olmsted's predeliction to base his judgments on the writings of Andrew Jackson Downing and the architecture of Alexander Jackson Davis. In Natchez, there were few examples corresponding to the ideals of either, inasmuch as its mansions featured the Greek Revival styles rather than the newer "Italianate" or "Gothic Revival" period fashions popularized by the philosophy of Downing and the examples of Davis.

Other contemporary accounts of Natchez contrast with Olmsted's. *DeBow's Review* in 1861 cited Natchez for its "classic antiquity,"[17] a reference no doubt to its Greek Revival architecture. James Silk Buckingham, the English observer who preceded Olmsted by a decade in this area, had found Natchez quite impressive, with regularly laid streets, "well furnished" and "substantial" stores, "built after the New York fashion," and "no less than twelve hotels." He found the "private dwellings are well built, and constructed with verandahs, and furnished with gardens, so as to adapt them to the climate."[18] Another contemporary account of Natchez mentions that the "houses are very neat in their appearance, and many of them have pretty porticos in front and neat gardens around them."[19]

Leaving Natchez, Olmsted came upon a large plantation where he spent the night with the overseer and toured the plantation the next day.

This particular one, described as being "first-rate," was managed entirely by the overseer; as was often the case, the owner lived somewhere else. Although there was a "large and handsome mansion" there, it had not been occupied for several years. Olmsted compared the "conditions of the fences, of the mules and tools, and tillage" with the "best farming districts in New York," and noted that overall, it is quite admirably managed.[20]

Olmsted found the roads south of Natchez, around Woodville, "well engineered"[21] but in north Mississippi, quite poor. Farming only small crops of maize, grain, and cotton that their families could work, these planters formed the majority of the white population of the South and had few, if any, slaves. A typical house in the area, Olmsted observed, was a "neat building of logs, boarded over and painted on the outside." Smaller cabins in the square yard surrounding the house included the smoke house, several Negro cabins ("small, dilapidated, and dingy"), and the kitchen/dining room adjoining the main house.[22]

Although most of Olmsted's observations concern impressions of rural conditions, his itinerary included many of the largest Southern cities (New Orleans, Louisville, Charleston, Richmond, Mobile, Savannah, Norfolk, Lexington, and Nashville, which, according to the 1850 census, ranged in population from 116,000 to 10,000, respectively) and several of the smaller, albeit important, ones (Natchez, Vicksburg, Selma, and Montgomery). The impressions of natural elements and open spaces in the cities he visited strongly confirmed Olmsted's earlier conviction that for many reasons open space in urban areas was necessary. He recorded his delight in reaching the Place d'Armes (now Jackson Square) in New Orleans:

. . . now a public garden, bright with the orange and lemon trees, and roses, and myrtles, and laurels, and jessamines of the south of France. Fronting upon it is the ancient Hotel de Ville, still the city court-house, a quaint old French structure, with scaly and vermiculated surface, and deep-worn door-sills, and smooth-rubbed corners; the most picturesque and historic-looking public building, except the highly preserved, little old court-house at Newport, that I can now think of in the United States.[23]

Another significant discussion concerning an urban open space occurs in Natchez. The public park overlooking the Mississippi River apparently made an indelible impression:

But the grand feature of Natchez is the bluff, terminating in an abrupt precipice over the river, with the public garden upon it. Of this I never had heard, and . . . I strolled off to see the town, I came upon it by surprise. I entered a gate and walked up a slope, supposing that I was approaching the ridge or summit of a hill, and expecting to see beyond it a corresponding slope and the town again, continuing in terraced streets to the river. I found myself, almost at the moment I discovered that it was not so, on the very edge of a stupendous cliff, and before me an indescribably vast expanse of forest, extending on every hand to a hazy horizon, in which, directly in front of me, swung the round, red, setting sun.

Through the otherwise unbroken forest, the Mississippi had opened a passage for itself, forming a perfect arc, the hither shore of the middle of the curve being hidden under the crest of the cliff, and the two ends lost in the vast obscurity of the Great West. Overlooked from such an eminence, the size of the Mississippi can be realized—a thing difficult under ordinary circumstances; but though the fret of a swelling torrent is not wanting, it is perceptible only as the most delicate chasing upon the broad, gleaming expanse of polished steel, which at once shamed all my previous conceptions of the appearance of the greatest of rivers. Coming closer to the edge and looking downward, you see the lower town, its roofs with water flowing all around them, and its pigmy people wading, and laboring to carry upward their goods and furniture, in danger from a rising movement of the great water. Poor people, emigrants and niggers only.

I laid down, and would have reposed my mind in the infinite vision westward, but was presently disturbed by a hog which came grunting near me, rooting in the poor turf of this wonderful garden. I rose and walked its length. Little more has been done than to inclose a space along the edge, which would have been dangerous to build upon, to cut out some curving alleys now recaptured by the grass and weeds, and to plant a few succulent trees. A road to the lower town, cutting through it, is crossed by slight wooden foot-bridges, and there are some rough plank benches, adorned with stenciled "medical" advertisements. Some shrubs are planted on the crumbling face of the cliff, so near the top that the swine can obtain access to them. A man, bearded and smoking, and a woman with him, sitting at the extreme end, were the only visitors except myself and the swine.[24]

This description, as the previous ones in Kentucky and Texas, reveals Olmsted's tendency to observe significant landscape elements: the scale of the river, the view from the bluff to the west, the condition of the town below the park, the plant materials in the park, the use of unbuildable ground for open space, and the other people in the park. It also demonstrates his recognition of the importance of providing a public facility to accompany an existing natural feature, a propensity which occurred throughout Olmsted's later career in practically all his many plans for public parks and reservations.

Among the other urban areas he visited, Olmsted found Montgomery a "prosperous town, with pleasant suburbs." Sailing down the Alabama River for Mobile, he noted that Selma was a "pleasant village" with "a number of pretty gardens."[25] Olmsted found Mobile

in its central, business part, . . . very compactly built, dirty, and noisy, with little elegance, or evidence of taste or public spirit, in its people. A small, central, open square—the only public ground that I saw—was used as a horse and hog pasture, and clothes-drying yard. Out of the busier quarter, there is a good deal of the appearance of a thriving New England village—almost all the dwelling-houses having plots of ground enclosed around them, planted with trees and shrubs. The finest trees are the magnolia and live oak; and the most valuable shrub is the Cherokee rose, which is much used for hedges and screens. It is evergreen, and its leaves are glossy and beautiful at all seasons, and in March it blooms profusely. There is an abundance, also, of the Cape jessamine. It is as beautiful as the camelia; and, when in blossom, scents the whole air with a most delicate and delicious fragrance. At a market-garden, near the town which I visited, I found most of the best Northern and Belgian pears fruiting well, and apparently healthy, and well suited in climate, on quince-stocks. Figs are abundant, and bananas and oranges are said to be grown with some care, and slight winter protection.[26]

Again, Olmsted's observations foretell his future handling of open space. At Mobile, he noted the location of the park, the conditions of the town, the current use of the space, and the use of indigenous plant material. His reference to the "best Northern and Belgian pears" resulted perhaps from his attempts at scientifically raising pears on his Staten Island farm in 1848.[27]

Olmsted's earlier travels in England had sparked his interest in the landscape and the public park as a means of making the cities more humane for the poorer classes.[28] The convergence of these ideas through his environmental observations is the key to the theoretical evolution from landscape gardening, in the tradition of Andrew Jackson Downing, into landscape architecture, represented by Olmsted's career. The significance of his Southern experience was derived from the observation of diverse elements that were later synthesized into a rationale for his designs. Olmsted's Southern journals are more than a comprehensive and fascinating record of Southern life and culture in the decade before the war. These works assume added importance by revealing the sturdy foundation for a multifaceted career and for the beginning of landscape architecture, a new profession based on social conscience and on dedication to design of the total environment.[29]

NOTES

1. Frederick Law Olmsted, *A Journey in the Back Country in the Winter of 1853–54* (London, 1860), p. vi.

2. Broadus Mitchell, *Frederick Law Olmsted: A Critic of the Old South* (Baltimore, 1924), pp. 43–44.

3. Laura Wood Roper, *FLO: A Biography of Frederick Law Olmsted* (Baltimore, 1973), p. 44.

4. Andrew Jackson Downing, *Treatise on the Theory and Practice of Landscape*

Gardening Adapted to North America, 6th ed. (New York, 1859), p. 49.

5. Frederick Law Olmsted, *Journey Through Texas; or a Saddle Trip on the Southwestern Frontier* (New York, 1957), pp. 10–11.

6. Ibid., pp. 97–99. The Hogarth referred to here is William Hogarth, the German painter, who introduced the romantic concepts of "line of beauty" and "line of grace."

7. *Back Country*, pp. 222–23.

8. Frederick Law Olmsted, *A Journey in the Seaboard Slave States, with Remarks on Their Economy* (New York, 1856), p. 465.

9. Ibid., pp. 466–78.

10. Ibid., pp. 663–73.

11. Ibid., pp. 382–84.

12. *Back Country*, p. 162.

13. Ibid., p. 14.

14. Ibid., pp. 13–14.

15. Ibid., pp. 32–33. Rosedown, one of the more elaborate plantations in this area, fits this description rather closely. After construction began in 1835, Daniel Turnbull and his new wife left for an extended buying expedition in Europe to furnish their home. A French landscape gardener was sent home to manage the thirty-one acre gardens of native, European, and oriental plant material. The garden had seven levels, divided by paths and walkways which constantly revealed garden features or structures. Between each oak in the allee leading to the house was a Carrara marble statue from classical mythology. For a more extensive discussion of this and other Louisiana plantations, see Harnett Kane, *Plantation Parade: The Grand Manner in Louisiana* (New York, 1945), pp. 295–305.

16. *Back Country*, pp. 34–35.

17. *DeBow's Review* 31 (August 1861): 189.

18. James Silk Buckingham, *The Slave States of America* (London, 1842), 1: 118–19.

19. Bishop Whipple, *Southern Diary, 1843–1844*, edited, with an Introduction by Lester B. Shepp (Minneapolis, 1839), pp. 126–27.

20. *Back Country*, p. 53.

21. Ibid., p. 17.

22. Ibid., p. 140.

23. Frederick Law Olmsted, *The Cotton Kingdom: A Traveller's Observations on Cotton and Slavery in the American Slave States*, edited, with an Introduction by Arthur M. Schlesinger (New York, 1953 and 1969), pp. 227–28.

24. *Back Country*, pp. 37–38.

25. *Cotton Kingdom*, p. 214.

26. Ibid., pp. 219–20.

27. Roper, *FLO*, p. 60.

28. Ibid., p. 71.

29. For a detailed analysis of landscape architecture as a "profession based on total environmental planning," see Albert Fein, "Frederick Law Olmsted: His Development as a Theorist and Designer of the American City," Ph.D. dissertation, Columbia University, 1969. This essay, it should be noted, began as a paper in Professor Fein's seminar at Harvard.

Howard L. Preston and Dana F. White

KNICKERBOCKER ILLUSTRATOR
OF THE OLD SOUTH:
John William Orr

At the same time that Frederick Law Olmsted was beginning his career as a professional man of letters, the American public was being introduced to a new dimension in popular literature—the engraved illustration. Prior to the 1850s, publishers of books and periodicals used illustrations sparingly, and the publications in which readers found the most space devoted to them were mainly art journals, such as *The New-York Mirror* and the *Bulletin of the American Art-Union*. One year before Olmsted published his *Walks and Talks of an American Farmer in England* (1852), however, the first two illustrated weeklies, *Gleason's Pictorial Drawing-Room Companion* and the *Illustrated American News*, appeared, and by 1852, *Harper's New Monthly Magazine* was making unprecedented use of woodcut illustrations.[1] Over the next five years, woodcut illustrations became so common in the pages of popular magazines and books that one contemporary literary authority observed that an " 'illustration mania' " had overcome American publishers.[2]

The illustrators themselves comprised a small band of artists and engravers who, in the decades preceding the 1850s, had found little market for their work. One of these men was John William Orr, an Irish-born immigrant, whose family settled in Buffalo, New York. Orr spent his childhood and adolescence in upstate New York, and in 1836, at the age of twenty-one, he studied under the nationally recognized engraver, William Redfield. A year later, Orr established his own business in Buffalo, but he soon moved to Albany to accept a position with the state, illustrating geological reports. In 1844, he again relocated—this time to New York City—and entered into partnership with his brother, Nathaniel, under the name, J. W. & N. Orr. Within two years, the brothers' working relationship was dissolved and, once again, John continued in business on his own. Thereafter, he sought the best staff available and launched an extensive advertising campaign which, by 1850, when publishers and journalists had begun to seek qualified engravers to furnish illustrations for their publications, helped earn him recognition as a first-rate engraver.[3]

Orr's first major opportunity came in 1850 when he was retained by Andrew Jackson Downing to engrave a series of woodcuts for the famous landscape gardener's book, *The Architecture of Country Houses*[4] (Figure 1). A year later, fellow engraver and founder of the *Illustrated American News* T. W. Strong hired Orr to assist him in the publication of that news weekly.[5] These opportunities, together with his desire to establish himself professionally, undoubtedly put Orr in contact with members of the Knickerbocker literary set at the same time that Olmsted was attempting to cultivate his own personal relationships with men such as George Palmer Putnam, Parke Godwin, and William Cullen Bryant. It is not known how close the ties were between Olmsted and Orr; still, between 1851 and 1852, both men were certainly moving in that same small circle of New York writers and publishers that Olmsted knew as the "Literary Republic." This circumstance, together with Orr's growing reputation, helps to explain why Olmsted selected him to engrave the dozen illustrations—originally sketched by Olmsted himself, then redrawn by Marryat Field—which were to appear in *Walks and Talks*[6] (Figures 2 and 3).

Following the period of his first association with Olmsted, Orr found his talents much in demand. Between 1852 and 1855, an increasing number of authors retained him to illustrate material for such nationally circulated periodicals as *Graham's Monthly, Leslie's Weekly,* and *Harper's New Monthly Magazine.* What is more, Orr's work also appeared in *Putnam's Monthly,* the same journal that Olmsted began editing in April 1855. Orr's engravings were also solicited for a variety of book illustrations: for Daniel Curry's *New York: A Historical Sketch* (1853); for several of the best-selling "Harper Story Books" of the mid-1850s, from the hyperactive pen of Jacob Abbott, creator of the famed "Rollo Books"; and for the New York Ladies of the Mission tract, *The Old Brewery and the New Mission at the Five Points* (1854).[7] This last assignment, it should be noted, suggests still another possible connection between Orr and Olmsted, for it was at the Five Points Mission that Charles Loring Brace, Olmsted's fellow Connecticut Yankee and life-long friend, began his career as a "professional altruist" with the publication in the *New-York Daily Times* of his series "Walks Among the New York Poor" (Fall 1852). Brace, who had accompanied the Olmsted brothers on their tour abroad in 1850 and who was later to attain national fame as founder of the Children's Aid Society—"with," Albert Fein has noted, "Olmsted's assistance"—also introduced FLO to Henry J. Raymond, co-founder and editor of the *New-York Daily Times,* and recommended Olmsted for a projected series

1. *JWO engraving of an Elizabethan-style antique apartment, which appeared in Andrew Jackson Downing's* Architecture of Country Houses *(1850).*

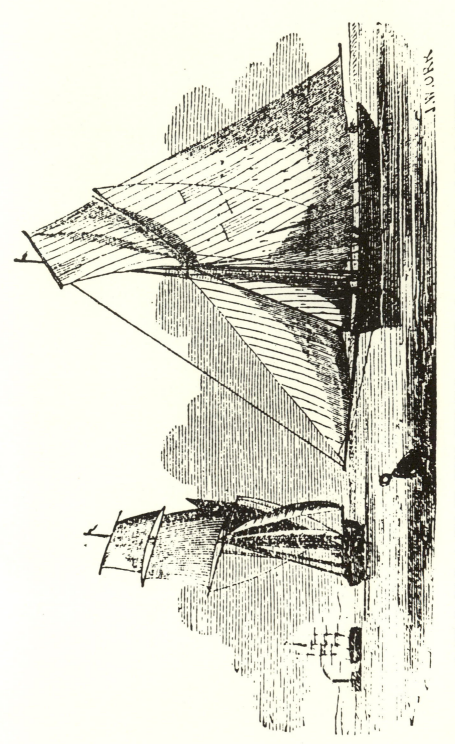

J.W.ORR

2. "The English Coaster (Calm)" by JWO for FLO's Walks and Talks of an American Farmer in England (1852).

3. "The Timber House (old farmhouse)" by JWO for FLO's Walks and Talks of an American Farmer in England (1852).

of articles on the South that was to develop, eventually, into "Our Slave States."[8]

Still another author who engaged Orr to illustrate his work was Calvert Vaux, the English-born protégé of Andrew Jackson Downing and later partner of Frederick Law Olmsted. Vaux's "Hints for Country House Builders," which appeared in the November 1855 number of *Harper's Monthly*, drew upon Orr's skills to represent the various types of houses then popular among American builders. With the publication of his *Villas and Cottages* in 1857, again with the assistance of Orr, Vaux expanded considerably on this same theme[9] (Figure 4).

Concurrent with Olmsted's travels in the South and the publication of his *Journey in the Seaboard Slave States* (1856), Orr was busy engraving woodcuts for a number of articles about the South, including those of David Hunter Strother, better known as "Porte Crayon," and T. B. Thorpe for *Harper's New Monthly* between 1853 and 1855[10] (Figures 5 and 6). The wide variety of Orr's work suggests, however, that he never allowed himself to become stereotyped as an engraver on any particular topic or subject matter. There is also nothing to indicate that he ever developed any long-term interest in any one author, school of writing, or region of the country—including the antebellum South.

Like other woodcut illustrators in New York City during the 1850s, Orr worked from sketches of characters and scenes presented to him by writers and/or artists who required engraving for their works. The most common practice was for an artist to sketch the desired picture in reverse on a smooth-sided block of wood. The engraver carved away the light area, leaving the lines and shaded portions slightly raised. An ordinary lettering press could then be used to reproduce the illustration on a printed page. In addition to this process, by the mid-1850s woodcut illustrators were also able to obtain an image on a block of wood by means of photography. At the same time that woodcut illustrations were becoming popular, Americans were beginning to experiment with early forms of photography, and in 1857, the August issue of the *Scientific American* described the process of capturing a photograph on a block of wood, attesting that "we have seen some wood blocks bearing very fine pictures produced by this means. . . ."[11]

New York City was a center for the developing American fascination with photography, and by the mid-1850s some one hundred daguerreotype studios and galleries were located there.[12] The two illustration disciplines—photography and engraving—then, both had as their headquarters the city of New York, but how much overlap there was between the two trades remains to be determined. Restricted in their subject matter by lengthy exposure times, most early professional photographers, like Matthew Brady, specialized only in portraits. It was not until

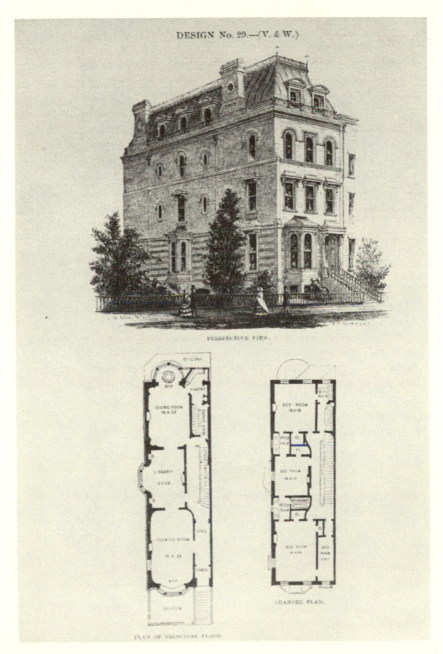

DESIGN No. 29.—(V. & W.)

PERSPECTIVE VIEW.

PLAN OF PRINCIPAL FLOOR.

CHAMBER PLAN.

4. *"A Town House"* designed by Calvert Vaux *"for Mr. John A. C. Gray, . . . to be executed for him in Fifth Avenue, New York, on a valuable lot, 25 feet wide, adjoining the grounds occupied by the Church of the Ascension"; and "to be built by day's work, and will cost about $20,000 when properly finished." Engraving by JWO,* Villas and Cottages *(1857), pp. 301–303.*

VOL. XI.—No. 63.—U   NATURAL BRIDGE.

5. *The Natural Bridge in Virginia, engraved for "Porte Crayon's" third article in his series on Virginia,* Harper's New Monthly Magazine, *August 1855.*

COTTON AND ITS CULTIVATION.

6. *Engraving for* T. B. Thorpe's *"Cotton and Its Cultivation,"* Harper's New Monthly Magazine, *March 1854.*

the 1870s that a recognized "landscape school" of photography developed. However, this did not mean that the early "artists of the sun," as photographers were sometimes called, limited themselves only to portraiture.[13]

As early as 1838, the federal government had sent a group of daguerreotypists to northwestern Maine to help settle the boundary dispute there between Great Britain and the United States. A series of highlands were the center of the controversy, and the daguerreotypes that the expedition submitted to the joint United States-Great Britain commission charged with settling the dispute are said to have figured significantly in the resolution of the dispute.[14] Amateur photography also abounded in the late 1850s, and photographers all across the country tramped over hill and dale for weeks at a time in search of "views."[15] It is therefore conceivable that some of Orr's engravings of the South could have been produced from photographic sources. But what is more important, whether they worked from an artist's sketch or a photograph, engravers seldom had any personal contact with the subjects of their work, which lends further credence to the supposition that Orr, and others of his profession, were interested more in their craft and their business than in any particular facet of American landscape or culture.

By the late 1850s, Orr succeeded in establishing his firm as the leading house in the field, with his business, from that point on, nationwide[16] (Figure 7). In 1862, he became editor and publisher of the *American Odd Fellow*, the periodical of the Odd Fellows Society, an organization to which he had belonged for over a quarter of a century. Orr ran this journal until 1871, when he renewed his business association with both Olmsted and Vaux, now engaged in the development and management of New York City's Central Park. The partners selected Orr as an illustrator for several annual *Central Park Reports*.[17]

In 1883, Orr agreed to edit a new Odd Fellows' monthly magazine. Designed to appeal to an urbane audience, *The Manhattan* published in its twenty-one consecutive issues the work of such noted nineteenth-century literati as Matthew Arnold, Thomas Hardy, Sidney Lanier, and James Whitcomb Riley. Still, it failed to survive; it ceased publication in 1884.[18]

Three years after the demise of *The Manhattan*, the seventy-two-year-old Orr died. For the last thirty-five years of his life, he had played a leading role in helping to promote the use of illustrations by American publishers. Prior to the days when a procedure for reproducing photographs cheaply had been introduced, Orr and his contemporaries had made it possible for the reading public to visualize events and places which previously could only be described in words. Theirs was a magic that Jacob Abbott—himself the author of over two hundred books, many

7. JWO engraving of the original Kimball House, *which was opened in 1870 and destroyed by fire in 1883.*

of them illustrated (some by Orr)—likened to that of "a *poet* whose hand has been trained to express his mental conceptions by drawing." "Designing," Abbott reflected," . . . is purely an intellectual process, and it requires intellectual qualities of the highest order to perform it successfully." And the next step, the actual engraving, was perhaps the most important. "This process of engraving," Cecil D. Eby, Jr., pointed out a century later, "was by far the most tedious, and no matter how excellent an artist's sketch was, it was at the mercy of the engraver."[19]

Without question, the artistic magic of the Knickerbocker illustrators had transformed the conventions of narration, but while their engravings intrigued and delighted readers, they also placed a stylistic burden on whatever their subject happened to be. This was certainly true for the antebellum South.

Like many other Knickerbocker engravers who illustrated writings concerned with the Old South, Orr and his associates depicted the region without ever having studied it first-hand, as Olmsted had. The objective of the Orr firm and other New York-based engravers was obviously less reportorial than it was aesthetic. Their inclination was to produce high-quality illustrations that would complement accompanying articles and simultaneously stimulate public interest. The result was a series of illustrations in the tradition of the picturesque, which portrayed the day-to-day South with the same degree of accuracy that one might expect to find in present-day picture postcard "art" (Figures 8 and 9).

The Knickerbocker engravings may well be compared, in kind, to those stereotyped views of the familiar which Grady Clay illustrates and analyzes in his recent *Close-Up: How To Read the American City.* Clay calls them "fixes."[20] Each represents a *gestalt* that has been stylized, standardized and, finally, been made acceptable as *the* correct manner for framing a scene—i.e., achieving the *proper* perspective on it. "Of all the fixatives still permeating the modern vision," Clay observes, "the perspectivist tradition is one of the most rigidifying."[21] Similarly, the romantic perspective of the Knickerbocker engravers—their own special "fix"[22]—inclined these absentee observers of the Old South toward a portrayal of the region and its inhabitants that was often sentimentalized, oversimplified, and not necessarily in agreement with the more extensive and, frequently, more accurate verbal descriptions of Southern culture presented by Olmsted and other travelers south.

Without question, an Olmsted was a more reliable witness than an Orr or one of his artist-engravers. Still it must be asked: whose "picture" of the South was the more widely disseminated and accepted—the verbal description of the perceptive traveler *or* the engraved image of the absentee observer? What was the impact of the "illustration mania" upon a public opinion which, before the 1850s, had been more exposed to a print medium than to a pictorial one? What relationships, finally, may we infer here between the medium and the message? Some answers immediately suggest themselves; others seem all but self-evident. Nevertheless, before any one answer (or set of answers) can be advanced confidently, extensive and comparative research into the histories of engraved illustration, photography, popular culture, and public opinion must be undertaken.[23] Then, and only then, might the formation of the image of the antebellum South in the mind of the North be fully comprehended.

MOONLIGHT IN THE SALUDA GAP, S C

8. *A bucolic vision of "Moonlight in the Saluda Gap," South Carolina, engraved by T. Addison Richards for "The Landscape of the South,"* Harper's New Monthly Magazine, *May 1853.*

LOUISIANA CANE FIELD.

9. A "Louisiana Cane Field," as engraved by JWO for "Sugar and the Sugar Region of Louisiana," Harper's New Monthly Magazine, November 1853.

NOTES

1. "John William Orr," *Appleton's Cyclopaedia of American Biography*, 1888, 4: 593; James T. Callow, *Kindred Spirits: Knickerbocker Writers and American Artists, 1807–1855* (Chapel Hill, N.C., 1967), pp. 94–102; Frank Luther Mott, *A History of American Magazines, 1850–1865*, (Cambridge, 1957), 2: 43, 193, 384ff.; William Charvat, "The People's Patronage," pp. 513–25 in Robert E. Spiller, Willard Thorp et al., *Literary History of the United States*, rev. ed. (New York, 1959).

2. *Cosmopolitan Art Journal* 1, No. 3 (January 1857); quoted in Mott, *History of American Magazines*, 2: 192.

3. James F. Carr, ed., *Mantle Fielding's Dictionary of American Painters, Sculptors, and Engravers* (New York, 1965), p. 265; "John William Orr," *Appleton's Cyclopaedia*, 1888, 4: 593; George C. Groce and David H. Wallace, *The New York Historical Society's Dictionary of Artists in America, 1564–1860* (New Haven, Conn., 1957), p. 479.

4. Andrew Jackson Downing, *The Architecture of Country Houses* (New York, 1850).

5. Mott, *History of American Magazines*, 2:, 43.

6. Laura Wood Roper, *FLO: A Biography of Frederick Law Olmsted* (Baltimore, 1973), Chap. 7. The price agreed upon by Orr and Olmsted was $150. Frederick Law Olmsted to John Olmsted, January 17, 1852, Olmsted Papers, Library of Congress. (Nine of FLO's sketches would later appear in *Journey in the Seaboard Slave States;* one in the *Journey Through Texas.)*

7. See, for example, "New York Daguerreotyped," *Putnam's Monthly Magazine* 1 (April 1853): 353–68; Henry William Herbert, "Etna and Its Eruption," *Graham's Magazine* 42 (January 1853): 15–32; John A. Kouwenhoven, *The Columbia Historical Portrait of New York* (New York, 1953), pp. 199, 246–47, 261, 280. Jacob Abbott was the older brother—and sometime co-author—of John S.C. Abbott, the polemicist and partisan critic of the Old South, whose work was examined above in "Olmsted as Observer."

8. Thomas Harry Bender, "Discovery of the City in America: The Development of Urbanism in 19th-Century Social Thought," Ph.D. dissertation, University of California, Davis, 1971, pp. 185–87, 191–93; Roper, *FLO*, p. 84; and Albert Fein, "Frederick Law Olmsted: His Development as a Theorist and Designer of the American City," Ph.D. dissertation, Columbia University, 1969, pp. 254–55.

9. Calvert Vaux, "Hints for Country House Builders," *Harper's New Monthly Magazine* 11 (November 1855): 763–78 and *Villas and Cottages* (New York, 1857). Vaux and Radford (the successor firm to Olmsted, Vaux & Company) was later to design the lodging houses for Charles Loring Brace's Children's Aid Society (Henry Hope Reed Introduction to Vaux's *Villas and Cottages* [New York, 1968], p. xii).

10. David Hunter Strother (Porte Crayon), "Virginia Illustrated" (Third Paper), *Harper's New Monthly Magazine* 11 (August 1855): 289–311; and T. B. Thorpe, "Cotton and Its Cultivation," ibid., 8 (March 1854): 447–63.

11. "Photographing on Wood," *Scientific American* 12 (August 15, 1857): 390; "Photographs for Wood Engraving," ibid., 13 (December 19, 1857): 117; Robert Taft, *Photography and the American Scene* (New York, 1938; paperback reprint

edition, Dover, 1964, pp. 420–23). According to Taft, "In the early illustrated magazines (those of the fifties and early sixties) an occasional illustration . . . [would] be marked 'after a photograph on wood' " (p. 512, n. 448).

12. By the mid-1850s, a photographic image could be produced by a number of different processes. Similar methods produced Plumbeotypes, Crystallotypes, Ferrotypes (Tintypes), Ambrotypes, Talbotypes, and others (Taft, *Photography and the American Scene*, pp. 46–137).

13. Ibid., p. 311.

14. Ibid., p. 52.

15. Ibid., Chaps. XII and XIV.

16. In his Introduction to *The Old South Illustrated by Porte Crayon* (Chapel Hill, N.C., 1959), Cecil D. Eby, Jr., suggests that "the Orr firm was the center of illustration in New York for over forty years" (p. xiii).

17. Many of his engravings for this account are reproduced in Albert Fein, *Frederick Law Olmsted and the American Environmental Tradition* (New York, 1972), Figures 100–01 and p. 180; and *Frederick Law Olmsted's New York*, text by Elizabeth Barlow and illustrative portfolio by William Alex (New York, 1972), passim.

18. Mott, *History of American Magazines*, 3: 37, 191; Dana F. White, "The Self-Conscious City: A Survey and Bibliographical Summary of Periodical Literature on American Urban Themes, 1865–1900," Ph.D. dissertation, George Washington University, 1969, pp. 595–96.

19. Jacob Abbott, *The Harper Establishment; or, How the Story Books Are Made* (New York, 1855), p. 110. Eby, *The Old South Illustrated*, p. xiii.

20. Grady Clay, *Close-Up: How to Read the American City* (New York, 1973), pp. 23–37.

21. Ibid., p. 23.

22. Their special fix was, as indicated above, to be found in the tradition of the "picturesque." The word itself, as Leonard J. Simutis has noted in his "Frederick Law Olmsted's Later Years: Landscape Architecture and the Spirit of Place," Ph.D. dissertation, University of Minnesota, 1971, "is derived from the Italian *pittoresco*, 'after the manner of painters' " (p. 27). Simutis later quotes William Gilpin's (*The Essay on Prints*, 1768) description of the picturesque as being " 'a term expressive of that peculiar kind of beauty, which is agreeable in a picture' " (p. 31). This definition might almost have served as motto and advertisement for the Knickerbocker engravers.

23. One recent venture into comparative research, a series of essays in H. J. Dyos and Michael Wolff, eds., *The Victorian City: Images and Realities*, 2 vols. (London, 1973), relates revealingly, albeit indirectly, to the "illustration mania" in Victorian America. Nicholas Taylor's "The Awful Sublimity of the Victorian City: Its Aesthetic and Architectural Origins" (2: 431–47) adds significantly to our understanding of the evolving tradition of the picturesque (especially pp. 432–34), as it was confronted with both a changing landscape/cityscape and new technologies for visual representation. E.D.H. Johnson's "Victorian Artists and the Urban Milieu" (2: 449–74) uncovers the conflicts inherent between established "hierarchies of artistic expression" and "the harsher actualities of the world about them [*viz.*, artists]" which resulted in such compromises as "the vogue for

incorporating realistic detail in romantic scenes": a level of compromise suggestive of that employed by Knickerbocker illustrators of the "Peculiar Institution." G. H. Martin and David Francis's "The Camera's Eye" (1: 227–46) is especially valuable for its analysis of changing photographic technologies, the early (1850s) reliance upon photographs "as a basis for engraved illustrations," and "the connection between photography and other recording arts"—including the written record. Michael Wolff and Celina Fox's "Pictures from the Magazines" (2: 559–82) is perhaps the most applicable to the American scene. Its attention to technique—especially to the "history of news illustration," including engraving—and, even more importantly, to the cultural significance of "pictorial conventions"—the social implications, for example, of "the progressive simianization of the Irish" in English periodicals—suggests many parallels, both direct and indirect, with the American experience. Their conclusion, that "The way of seeing of both artist and audience was governed by the techniques available and by the artistic traditions which were conventional to that particular framework," fits neatly with our own concerning Knickerbocker illustrators of the Old South.

Victor A. Kramer

HARRIET BEECHER STOWE'S IMAGINATION AND FREDERICK LAW OLMSTED'S TRAVELS:
The Literary Presentation of Fact

Generalizations about the conditions of slavery and abuse of slaves were relatively easy to make in the 1850s as newspaper reports, slave narratives, and information from abolitionist societies became available. Yet, many facts were not easily authenticated, and fiction sometimes embellished truth. It was within this milieu that Harriet Beecher Stowe, perhaps the most famous and controversial of antislavery writers, produced her work. It was also this atmosphere which compelled the young Frederick Law Olmsted to travel throughout the South in search of the facts of a slave-bound economy. Olmsted's emphasis upon documentation sharply contrasts with the sentimentalized fiction of his contemporary, Mrs. Stowe.

Stowe herself recognized the value of Olmsted's travel writing. When his first book about the South appeared, she wrote to compliment him and to inquire if he could read her manuscript of *Dred,* then in progress, so that he might give her first-hand information about North Carolina. Although Olmsted was well acquainted with the Stowes and the Beechers, it is not known if he conferred with her about this manuscript. Her interest demonstrates the value of Olmsted's accomplishment and also reveals her concern about the accuracy of romance.[1] *Uncle Tom's Cabin,* one of the most debated documents of the period, added heat to arguments about slavery. Olmsted himself reports that Stowe's novel was often read in the South, although it was sometimes sold surreptitiously, under the counter. Mrs. Stowe herself probably had conceived of her role more as historian than as novelist. More than likely, when readers felt *Uncle Tom's Cabin*—or the later romance *Dred*—significant, the apparent accuracy of these works was the heart of their appeal. Southerners had objected to Stowe's fictionalization as misrepresentation even while the novel was being serialized. The fact that objections were so strong finally suggests that she must have presented, in many ways, an accurate picture. Inaccuracies must also have been present, however, because her fictional world was essentially determined by what she imagined as correct, and her primary concern was the conviction that slavery was immoral.

Originally announced in 1851 and subtitled "The Man That Was A Thing" in its advertisement of forthcoming publication, *Uncle Tom's Cabin* actually began appearing in June 1851 with a changed subtitle: "Life Among the Lowly."[2] That change suggests the direction in which Stowe's contribution to fiction about slavery developed, for she attempted two things as she wrote both *Uncle Tom's Cabin* and the later romance *Dred*. First, she emphasized her moral outrage about the status of slaves, who were often considered things by owners; that outrage is only slightly veiled by plots she contrived to represent a slave society. In *Uncle Tom's Cabin*, she implies that men of changed heart might voluntarily emancipate slaves. She hoped for a gradual change in the way individuals think about society, for with such change society itself might change. (Related to this view, however, is the implication that individual change would be difficult given the sinful institution of slavery.) In addition to a moral responsibility to report what she assumed was wrong with slavery, the second thing Stowe attempted was to provide believable settings for her fiction. One of the successes of *Uncle Tom's Cabin* is its believably imagined characters. Early in the novel, several realistic scenes quickly follow each other to establish the credibility of what follows. The book is episodic (it was originally written in installments), but the episodes seem real, and from the episodic structure develops a moral force from objections that a man could be a "thing." That moral force establishes a rhythm which emphasizes her belief that society failed in its responsibility.

Stowe's fiction stands as an indictment against an immoral society, and her writing had an immense influence on other antislavery novels. It is significant that when later appraisals of antislavery writing were made, some commentators felt that Olmsted's writing stood as an equally important indictment.[3]

When Olmsted writes of the same society—but as witnessed, not imagined—he minimizes moral questions and simply reports. His vision is of a society inefficient because it does not properly utilize resources. He provides example after example of the debilitating effect of a slave economy while the option of free labor remained. Olmsted set out to document slavery, but since he did so as an agricultural economist, he saw his job as that of reporting how resources were used, and not as passing judgment on the morality of actions accompanying slavery. The practical Olmsted seemed to sense that man's pocketbook was as important a factor in the continuance of slavery as religious or moral beliefs. Thus, a basic difference of assumption separates Stowe and Olmsted. A fundamental point made in this essay is that his objectivity, in essence, provided a new method for looking at the culture of the South at precisely the time when fanciful pictures of romance were becoming less trustworthy and less capable of mirroring reality.

Mrs. Stowe hoped that the power of God might change the hearts of sinful men. After all, she argued, it was God who wrote *Uncle Tom's Cabin* and she was simply His medium. Her 1856 novel, *Dred,* apparently was more consciously her choice as a novelist, for she emphasizes her decision to choose a subject "once more . . . from the scenes and incidents of the slaveholding states" as twofold. Stowe noted, from "a merely artistic point of view, there is no ground, ancient or modern, whose vivid lights, gloomy shadows and grotesque groupings, afford . . . so wide a scope as did the South." She insisted that these mines of "inexhaustible stores have but begun to be developed."[4] But artistic aims, she insisted, were not her highest motivation. She wanted primarily to give an accurate picture of the South. In a manner suggestive of her praise of Olmsted's *A Journey in the Seaboard Slave States,* which she had reviewed earlier that year, she commented on her aims.[5]

Moral bearings have had the chief influence [in the decision to write *Dred*]. The issues presented . . . between liberty and slavery do not grow less important, their interest increases with every step in the development of the national career. Never has there been a crisis in the history of this nation so momentous. . . . Under such circumstances the writer felt that no apology was needed for once more endeavoring to do something toward revealing . . . the true character of [slavery].

No doubt, Stowe's writings were read by a wide audience, and her moral suasion was of significance. But her procedure of depicting the conditions of slavery in a romance did cause problems in documentation of the reality theoretically reported. This seems especially true with *Dred, A Tale of the Great Dismal Swamp,* where the attempt to document fact finally was overwhelmed by the complexity of a situation where family, region, and economic circumstances combined to produce fiction with few clear-cut answers. Since the form of *Dred* was the popular romance, more closely associated with entertainment than with information, Stowe's desire to reflect truth was further complicated by the limitations of this genre.

Earlier in the same year that *Dred* appeared, Olmsted's first volume on his Southern travels, *A Journey in the Seaboard Slave States,* was published. Given the facts of his biography, his enjoyment of investigation, his success with experimental agriculture, and his successful *Walks and Talks of an American Farmer in England* (1852), along with his desire to become a literary personage, it is predictable that Olmsted would attempt a book which might serve as a balance against weighted evidence, so often the standard fare of his times. During this period, for example, slave narratives were sometimes the product of intermediaries who assisted in editing. That there were doubts about the authenticity of materials about slavery is indicated by the common practice in the mid-1850s of publishing as verification letters, affidavits, and other documents which attested to truthfulness. As it was, Mrs. Stowe's own *Uncle Tom's Cabin* was followed by a full volume of documentation, *The Key to Uncle Tom's Cabin*. Olmsted's desire, then, as he wrote to a friend, was to produce "a valuable book of observations on Southern agriculture and general economy as affected by slavery [which would be] matter of fact . . . after the deluge of spoony fancy pictures now at its height shall be spent."[6]

When one begins to read *Dred*, the initial impression is that it is far removed from the pressures which generated its predecessor. The book's romantic setting is North Carolina, and the descriptions of the plantations upon which much of the action transpires are lavish with detail. As Mrs. Stowe emphasized however, in the preface, *Dred* was intended primarily as an exploration of moral problems. Such exploration remains bounded by an elaborately imagined setting.

Edward and Anne Clayton have established reforms on their plantation, Magnolia Grove, which suggest that Utopia might be possible in North Carolina. With their concern for education and the trust of their slaves, backward servants are painfully being made over in their benevolent masters' image. Parts of *Dred* are so fanciful, however, that even Anne Clayton, despite her good intentions, blushes as she witnesses some actions. One event involves a group of happy slaves singing improvised folk melodies for the welcoming home of their master. Anne remarks that young Lettice "who has a natural turn for versifying, quite extraordinary [if encouraged] might turn out a second Phillis Wheatley." Such fanciful claims do not even hold Stowe's attention, and it is revealing that she begins the chapter following with a comment: "Would the limits of our story admit of it, we should gladly linger many days in the shady precincts of Magnolia Grove . . . where the hours flew by on flowery feet; but the inevitable time and tide, which wait for no man, wait not for the narrator." The narrator's comment stands as a revelation of the problems involved in writing romance which purports to be a revelation of the truth. Fanciful Magnolia Grove provides an entertaining setting, but it is like an idyll. Surely Olmsted saw nothing like it in the Carolinas.

Opposed to the benevolence of the younger Claytons is their father,

Judge Clayton, who argues that the law, like it or not, calls for slavery. In the ensuing family controversy, which is quickly extended to other parts of the novel, Stowe reveals her awareness of the complex problems related to slavery. But as Alice Crozier remarks, "the high-minded reforms of the Claytons' model plantation are not severely urged upon the reader; it is all too good to be true."[7] On the other hand, by the time the novel is completed the horrors of abuse and brutality recorded in *Uncle Tom's Cabin* have been far surpassed.

An abrupt change in the mood of this novel takes place when Dred, a fugitive slave, is introduced midway. Contemporary events, such as the Fugitive Slave Act and the beating of Charles Sumner by Preston Brooks of South Carolina in the Senate, seem to have added urgency to Stowe's message, as she wrote episodes, chapter by chapter, to meet her deadlines. The result is that a book which begins as a romance, and with a large element of reformism at its base, suddenly changes. The wild character Dred is an unlikely combination of prophet and barbarian. From the time he first appears, he functions as central character by upstaging the action. Yet, none of the other characters has any firm relationship to him. Dred has long speeches which echo the prophets of the Old Testament. While perhaps the rhetoric of Dred, and the rhetorical language of many other characters of the book, ultimately ruin the novel as a work of art, Dred does remain an interesting character. He is close to mad with hatred of the injustice which has driven him into seclusion. And as he listens to the mounting evidence of white oppression, he has still more reason to call for destruction of the slaveholders. The most interesting aspect of Dred's characterization, and as a revelation of Stowe's mind, is that he makes none of the assumptions which young Edward Clayton does about the possibility of reform. Dred sees little hope for society as it is structured, and like Nat Turner, upon whom his characterization is partially based, he believes terrorism, as inspired by God, may be necessary.

The difference between *Uncle Tom's Cabin* and *Dred* is well summarized by Crozier when she argues that in both the dilemma of slavery will be resolved only through Christian love. In *Dred,* however, Mrs. Stowe's presentation of the effectiveness of Christian love is not so forcefully argued as is the case with the characterization of Little Eva or Uncle Tom. Two things occurred in the second novel: Dred, as a near-crazy religious mystic, "had become a plausible, even fascinating and certainly frightening figure, [and secondly,] Harry Gordon's situation had occurred as symbolical of one of the real dilemmas of a slavery society." Gordon is perhaps the most interesting character in the novel because he is truly caught between his status as slave and his desire for freedom. Harry Gordon, the black-white brother of Nina, the heroine, is an illegitimate son and thus unfree. His brother, Tom Gordon, functions as evil symbol for the continuance of the status quo. Harry remains torn between rebellion wherein he could assert his dignity, and loyalty to his sister, Nina. Finally, Harry does not know what to do. Crozier says the result is an inconclusive novel: "The disintegration of this novel at the end, and its failure to impose even a spurious fictional pattern on the arguments over slavery, suggest the disintegration of the nation during the next five years and anticipates the chaotic failure of all argument and all bonds that finally led to the Civil War."[8] The complexity of a slave economy seems thus to have been too much for fiction heavily reliant on a romantic mode.

Parallels might be drawn between the monomania of Dred and the ferocity of action of Ahab in *Moby Dick*. This is not to suggest literary influence, but the fact is that both Melville and Mrs. Stowe saw the dangers implicit in an American course which seemed hell-bent. In fact, the failure of *Dred* as a work of art derives from Mrs. Stowe's attempt to articulate the complexities of her subject. *Dred* is an honest attempt to document reality, and just as was the case with slave narratives edited by abolitionists and many earlier works of fiction about slavery, Stowe bases her fictive world on fact. All of the horrible stories related by slaves to Dred are based on true accounts. Judge Clayton's decision to reverse a lower court's decision of his own son's defense of a slave woman is given by Stowe in the actual words of a case decided in North Carolina. Thirty pages of appendices follow the text of *Dred*. It is not a matter of whether much (or even most) of what Stowe fictionalizes has a basis in truth. The question becomes, is her procedure an effective means of documentation? More importantly, is a feel for the culture as a whole suggested, or are particular facts exaggerated?

What seems to have occurred was that the facts of slavery had outdistanced the power of Stowe's fictive imagination to corroborate them within a conventional romance. Other and different methods were becoming necessary to document the facts. Effective objective correlatives were demanded; or at the very least, an objectivity which would report unblemished facts. Olmsted seems to have sensed this need.

It is significant that in the spring of 1855, Olmsted had assumed editorship of *Putnam's Magazine*, the first important national magazine to take a stand against slavery. In addition, in the spring of 1855 Herman Melville submitted the manuscript of "Benito Cereno" to *Putnam's*. (In the last three numbers for 1855, Olmsted, as a free-soil journalist, and his colleagues of the magazine included not only Melville's tale, but also articles on the threat of slavery in Kansas and a review of Frederick Douglass's *Autobiography*, which was recognized for its probity and directness.) Melville's tale of insurrection at the turn of the nineteenth century centers on American, Spaniard, and African, but the readers of *Putnam's Magazine* would more than likely have recognized these figures as Yankee, Slaveholder, and Negro. Melville's tale can be read as allegory about the facts of American slaveholding society. Jean Yellin argues that "in 'Benito Cereno' Melville used the standard literary version of slavery and the black man, displayed [its] falseness, and destroyed [stereotypes.] Melville's tale, like the slave narratives, reveals the stereotyped faces worn by black characters in our fiction to be masks."[9] Stowe and Olmsted did not attempt to use symbolism such as that employed by Melville, but their contributions were significant attempts to reveal truth. Stowe's fiction is, however, sometimes "spoony"; Olmsted's deliberately prosaic documentation provides balance.

Olmsted and Stowe each consciously attempted to shed light on the complexity of the institution of American slavery. On first appearance, it might even be assumed that Mrs. Stowe's sometimes melodramatic plots and pious moral arguments are distinct from Olmsted's objective approach to a slave economy. In fact, the two approaches—romance and objectivity—are related, and both Stowe, in the structure of *Uncle Tom's Cabin* and *Dred*, and Olmsted, by the examples he provides, make this clear. The two writers were convinced that slavery meant degradation for both owner and owned. Stowe's method, however, often seemed to rely on stereotypes. Olmsted usually attempted to let facts speak and to allow the reader to draw inferences. The result was that, like Melville, he was able to get below the mask.

When, for instance, he reports his travels through Louisiana, his rendition of a conversation between a buyer and seller of slaves is telling because of the context of its being observed. Within a section where Olmsted systematically reports facts about the district near Washington and Opelousas, he provides information about knife fights, a Creole ball he attended, and free Negroes. Then he quietly reports an after-dinner conversation overheard on the gallery of his hotel. A Negro trader opened the conversation by saying, " 'I hear you were unlucky with that girl you bought of me, last year?' " Some exchanges follow, and finally, the slave owner admits: " 'Yes, I was foolish, I suppose, to risk so much on the life of a single woman; but I've got a good start again now, for all that. I've got two right likely girls; one of them's got a fine boy, four months old, and the other's with child—and old Pine Knot's as hearty as ever.' "[10] Just as is often the case in Olmsted's books, indication of moral judgment, or outrage, is minimized. He does not comment on what he observes, yet the reader surely draws appropriate conclusions. It seems fantastic that apparently civilized men could talk as these did. Had Olmsted imagined a land such as Swift's Gulliver had visited, more damning conversation would have been hard to contrive.

In Olmsted's works, many little incidents factually observed cumulatively have force: "As I was walking in the outskirts of the town this morning, I saw squads of negro and white boys together, pitching pennies and firing crackers in complete fraternization. The white boys manifested no superiority, or assumption of it, over the dark ones."[11] But just as matter-of-factly, Olmsted also reports how he witnessed "chained negroes walking down the streets."[12]

The nuance of what he reports can be contrasted with the way Stowe imagines what Harry, or Milly, or other slaves feel: In a slave dealer's establishment, Olmsted reports seeing "neatly clad negroes, who appeared perfectly cheerful; each grinning obsequiously, but with a manifest interest, or anxiety, when I fixed my eye on them for a moment."[13] Similarly, his announcement in *Journey in the Seaboard Slave States* that he has seen but one example of whipping of slaves is all the more startling for its restraint: "The only whipping of slaves that I have seen in Virginia, has been of . . . wild, lazy children as they are being broke in to work. It is at this moment going on in the yard beneath my window. They cannot be depended upon a minute out of sight."[14]

Both Olmsted and Stowe set out to verify many of the same parts of the South. Stowe's *Uncle Tom's Cabin* comes up in conversations reported by Olmsted; and once he engages a defender of harsh authority in an exchange which corroborates the truthfulness of the Red River episode of that novel. And just as Stowe, in *Dred*, imagined a plantation which had instituted humane practices toward slaves, Olmsted reports actually meeting a former slaveholder who had liberated his slaves.[15]

It is in the particulars upon which Stowe and Olmsted focus that both the similarities of subject and their differences of method are most readily seen. In *Dred*, the fictional setting is the region of the Great Dismal Swamp of North Carolina, a region where Olmsted had traveled. The swamp as depicted by Stowe is a wonderfully mysterious place appropriate for the hiding place of the near-mad mystic, Dred, in flight from his pursuers. Olmsted's account of the Dismal Swamp area is strictly factual. Yet, his facts support the basic arguments he develops in the course of his several accounts. Slave labor is inefficient. Olmsted, therefore, was especially interested in the way slaves, who worked without overseers, did work as lumberers in the Swamp. Those somewhat independent slaves, he reported, seemed fairly happy. Olmsted does verify that the Swamps were still "noted places of refuge for runaway negroes," and he even speculates about the lonely life for those born and bred there; but he notes that there could be "few . . . of those 'natives' left."[16] His interview with Joseph Church verifies that runaways to the Swamp in North Carolina are still hunted with dogs. Such data make clear that Stowe's setting was in many ways accurate, but Olmsted also provides many less romantic facts about the geographical area unused (unknown?) by Stowe. In contrast,

Stowe's fictionalized Swamp seems much less real than Olmsted's reported one.

Olmsted's observations about religion among slaves might have given Mrs. Stowe pause to wonder. For while the character Dred is imagined as a fanatic who finally preaches rebellion, another character, the patient Milly, remains the embodiment of Christian submission. Both seem stereotypes. Milly's counsel in the novel is to wait patiently. Olmsted's admittedly cursory survey of religious practices among slaves shows that few of them had absorbed sufficient Christian teaching to make such waiting possible. He reports that in one parish near Richmond fewer than one-fifth of the black population living within convenient distance of the church were even in the habit of going there. Of those who did come, many arrived late, and "many more slept through the greater part of the service."[17] Olmsted's qualification reveals some of his own bias. He notes that many blacks profess religion,

but it is evident, of the greater part even of these that their idea of religion, and the standard of morality which they deem consistent with a "profession" of it, is very degraded. That they are subject to intense excitements, often really maniacal, which they consider to be religious, is true; but as these are described, I cannot see that they indicate anything but a miserable system of superstition, the more painful that it employs some forms and words ordinarily connected with true Christianity.[18]

He does insist that house servants are in a different situation. Still other details add to the complexity of what he observed, as, for instance, his report of witnessing a church service by whites, while the blacks remained quietly seated. Although he did not actually witness the subsequent service, he infers that the services blacks enjoy most "are rather hard upon the lungs, whatever their effect may be upon the soul."[19] A related passage in *Journey in the Back Country* supports the believability of Stowe's characterization of Dred, but it in no way makes readers feel comfortable about religious zeal. Speculating about the dangers of religious enthusiasm, Olmsted stated that he felt many blacks are "grossly ignorant and degraded in mind, with a crude, undefined, and incomplete system of theology and ethics, credulous and excitable, intensely superstitious and fanatical, what better field could a cunning monomaniac or sagacious zealot desire in which to set on foot an appalling crusade."[20] That Olmsted would draw such conclusions only after witnessing many slaves in many situations makes his data more trustworthy than Stowe's somewhat contrived, imagined situations.

An even more important area of difference between these two writers who sought to provide documentation involves the benevolence of master to slave. Stowe implies through the fictional setting of Magnolia Grove that good Christians like the Claytons might choose to educate and fit slaves for freedom. It is just such a suggestion, however, that casts doubt on the validity of Stowe's setting. Thus, young Clayton, early in the novel, says he regards his "plantation as a sphere for raising men and women, and demonstrating the capabilities of a race."[21] But Olmsted's systematic observations cast doubt upon such possibilities ever becoming reality. He expresses reservations about how slaves accept paternalism and about paternalism even working successfully: "The patriarchial condition is a transitional one. If long maintained it must be by an abuse of intelligence and at the expense of comfort and morality."[22] Clayton's fictionalized schemes about freeing slaves sound good in theory, but Olmsted's observations suggest that throughout the South there was a general indisposition to emancipate slaves, and this was connected with the economy of the entire system. (For Milly, the model slave in *Dred*, whose many children have been sold from her to meet the pressing financial needs of the Gordon family, finally all that is left her is comfort through Christianity.) In Olmsted's account about Louisiana, he observed that the slaves nearer the frontier were in better circumstances because they enjoyed privileges unavailable to those on large plantations. He noted that he was even "inclined to think that the greatest kindness that can be done a slave, is to neglect him and so encourage, if not force him to exercise some care over himself."[23]

Perhaps the most important single difference in how Olmsted and Stowe focus on the facts of slavery is revealed in the way Olmsted attempts not to "overlook the working classes." Olmsted noted that men of "literary or clerical habits" often forget the masses who have a real influence on the "fortune and fate" of nations.[24] Through the careful observation of detail surrounding everyday life, Olmsted is able inductively to arrive at conclusions. Because of what he observed, Olmsted suggests that many Southerners are, in a sense, in a state of involuntary servitude. Carelessness, heedlessness, and inconstancy of purpose, which had become a way of life for those who unconsciously assumed that more slaves and more land would always be available, affected the entire culture. Whether Olmsted's observations are presented in terms of how slaves are abused, land consumed, or through his minute recollection of how his umbrella was not repaired in Norfolk, he martials evidence to show that those who "must have dealings or be in competition with slaves . . . have their standard of excellence made low . . . until they are content with slight, false, unsound, workmanship."[25]

Olmsted's observations are essentially about the proper use of capital and labor, but human life was the most valuable of resources. Writing of the wealth accumulated in Louisiana, Olmsted states flatly, "I question if greater wealth would not have been obtained by the same expenditure of human labor, and happiness, and life, in other directions."[26] That it would become increasingly more difficult to squeeze wealth from the enforced labor of slaves is implied throughout the detailed reports of Olmsted's observations.

The problems of management and discipline were quickly multiplying. Surely these are, as Stowe insists, moral problems as well as economic. But Olmsted's restrained and unembellished manner of presenting such facts allows readers to see the culture clearly. This is different from the exaggeration of romance within *Dred* or *Uncle Tom's Cabin*. Through the cumulative effect of details recorded, Olmsted gives a feel for the inter-relations of an entire culture. It is that overview, more than anything else, which had become impossible to achieve in a romance like *Dred*. Olmsted's books finally provide an introduction to the culture, something impossible when bounded by the limitations of romance.

NOTES

1. Charles Eliot Beveridge, "Frederick Law Olmsted, The Formative Years 1822–1865," Ph.D dissertation, University of Wisconsin, 1966, pp. 226–27; Laura Wood Roper, *FLO: A Biography of Frederick Law Olmsted* (Baltimore, 1973), pp. 40, 79.

2. John William Ward. "Afterword," *Uncle Tom's Cabin* (New York, 1966), p. 478.

3. Lorenzo Dow Turner, *Anti-Slavery Sentiment in American Literature Prior to 1865* (Port Washington, N.Y., 1966). See p. 86 where Turner cites Jesse Macy's *The Anti-Slavery Crusade* (New Haven, Ct., 1921).

4. Harriet Beecher Stowe, "Author's Preface," *Dred, A Tale of the Great Dismal Swamp* (New York, 1967), p. xiii.

5. When Stowe reviewed Olmsted's initial volume, she praised him for "the most thorough exposé of the economical view of this subject which has ever appeared." Indeed, she may have relied upon Olmsted for some of her own factual data. Cited by Arthur M. Schlesinger in his edition of *The Cotton Kingdom: A Traveller's Observations on Cotton and Slavery in the American Slave States* (New York, 1953), p. xxvi. Original source: *Household Words* 14 (August 23, 1856): 138, and the *Independent* 7 (February 21, 1856): 57.

6. Frederick Law Olmsted, quoted in Edmund Wilson, *Patriotic Gore: Studies in the Literature of the Civil War* (New York, (1962), p. 108.

7. Alice C. Crozier, *The Novels of Harriet Beecher Stowe* (New York, 1969), p. 39. My reading of *Dred* has been aided by the perceptive insights of this study.

8. Ibid., p. 54.

9. Jean Fagan Yellin, *The Intricate Knot: Black Figures in American Literature, 1776–1863* (New York, 1972), p. 224.

10. *A Journey in the Seaboard Slave States, with Remarks on Their Economy* (New York, 1904), 2: 302.

11. Ibid., pp. 125, 32.

12. Ibid., p. 32.

13. Ibid., p. 34.

14. Ibid., p. 163.

15. Ibid., pp. 105–107.

16. Ibid., pp. 177–79.

17. Ibid., p. 126.

18. Ibid., pp. 126–27. But note also that Olmsted will at times qualify h: remarks with statements such as the following: "Opinions as to the gener; standard of morality among the slaves are strongly contradictory" (p. 138).

19. Ibid., 2: 93.

20. *A Journey in the Back Country in the Winter of 1853–54* (New York, 1970), ɪ 105.

21. *Dred*, p. 23.

22. *Back Country*, p. 289. In this volume, which is sometimes more speculati\ than the other two, Olmsted uses fairly strong language to suggest his positio Compare the indirection of *Seaboard Slave States*, 1: 321–22.

23. *Seaboard Slave States*, 2: 273.

24. Ibid., 1: 240.

25. Ibid., pp. 163–64. See also p. 102.

26. Ibid., 2: 322–23.

Victor A. Kramer and Phillip R.
Rutherford, with Dana F. White

FREE-SOIL ADVOCACY AND
THE NEW ENGLAND EMIGRANT
AID SOCIETY:
Five 1857 Letters by Olmsted

Twelve years ago, Mr. James Harmon, a firearms and military accoutre-
ments collector from Bridgton, Maine, purchased an accumulation of old
letters and documents from a vendor at a flea market in southern New
Hampshire. Harmon was especially interested in two invoices of the
Sharps Rifle Company. In examining the approximately one hundred
and twenty-five items in the collection, Harmon found about forty related
to guns, and set them aside. The remainder concerned various aspects of
Kansas politics from 1855 to 1858 and held no interest for him. Subsequently, all the letters about guns were offered for sale to local collectors.
No one was interested until 1975, when the collection of documents and
letters was shown to Phillip R. Rutherford who was at first intrigued with
the possibility that one of the Sharps invoices, which contained the serial
numbers of one hundred carbines, might refer to the guns used by John
Brown in the raid on Harpers Ferry. With cursory research, it was evident
that the numbers were not those of the John Brown Sharps, but those of
another shipment which also had an exciting history, as they were stolen
from the river steamer *Arabia* by the Missouri "border ruffians" in March
1856.

   In examining the first group of documents, it was easily determined
that they all had to do with arms purchases made by the New England
Emigrant Aid Company of Boston, Massachusetts. This organization was
established to help free-state settlers migrate to Kansas so that when the
referendum was held about whether Kansas would enter the Union as a
slave or free state, the free-state forces would triumph.

   As Rutherford studied these materials, Harmon told him that he had about another one hundred which were not nearly so interesting, but he would show them to him. Upon inspecting this larger group, Rutherford was shocked to see such signatures as Charles Robinson, free-state governor of Kansas in 1856; Sarah Robinson, the governor's wife; Eli Thayer, founder of the Aid Company; Amos Lawrence, Massachusetts industrialist and namesake of Lawrence, Kansas; Edward Everett Hale, clergyman and noted author; Thomas Wentworth Higginson, later commander of black troops in the Civil War and Emily Dickinson's mentor; Adolf Douai, pioneer San Antonio, Texas, editor; and Frederick Law Olmsted. Fearful of letting such a treasure escape him and become separated without adequate study, Rutherford bought the entire collection.

After several months of research, the relationship of all the documents to the Aid Company, their separation from the mass of the company records now located at the Kansas State Historical Society at Topeka, and the correspondence from such a variety of historic personages became apparent. Almost all of the letters in the collection were addressed to Samuel Cabot, prominent Boston medical doctor and member of the executive committee of the Aid Company. The letters could be divided into roughly three groups: one concerned arms purchases; another, the raising of clothing and money for indigent Kansas settlers; and a third, the proposal of settling western Texas with free-state emigrants.

As to the first group of letters, the Aid Company had been inveterately attacked by the South for not only aiding free-state emigrants to Kansas, but also supplying them arms. (There had even been an important congressional debate concerning the charges.) Having expected trouble on this score, the members of the company had set up a clandestine, semi-separate Rifle Committee early in its history and justified the act to itself by saying that the Aid Company would never deal in arms, but what its members did as private individuals through the Rifle Committee was their own business. That this was "a distinction without a difference" they ignored. Dr. Cabot was elected chairman of this committee, and to preserve the illusion that he and its members, who were all important men in the company, were acting as private citizens, it was imperative that he kept his records separate from those of the company. Then, as they did during the congressional debate, they could piously state that "This Company has never invested a dollar in cannon or rifles, in powder or lead, or in any of the implements of war."[1]

In reference to the second group of documents, Dr. Cabot also was evidently head of the committee which raised material aid for the Kansas settlers through solicitation of charitable donations throughout the Northeast. Naturally, many of the freight bills, receipts, and communications with various shipping companies would have been in his private possession. He probably deemed them too insignificant to place with the company records.

The separation of the group of letters dealing with the proposed free-soil settling of western Texas, which include the Olmsted letters, can be essentially accounted for in the same way as above. In 1857, after it was evident that Kansas had been saved for freedom, the Aid Company looked afield to duplicate its triumphs. At the suggestion of Colonel Daniel Ruggles of the United States Army, it decided on sparsely settled southwest Texas. To investigate the possibilities of success, the Texas committee was formed and Dr. Cabot was again made chairman. No doubt Cabot got in touch with Olmsted because of Olmsted's close relationship with Edward Everett Hale—a member of the company; because it had already dealt with Olmsted on the shipping of his howitzer to Texas; because it had given money to free-soil editor Douai at his request; and because of his being hailed as the northern "Texas expert" for his *A Journey Through Texas*. The five recently discovered letters ensued. Again, possibly through oversight, Cabot did not place the Texas committee's correspondence with the company records.

When Cabot's papers were donated to the Massachusetts Historical Society in Boston, the records of the Aid Company committee that he headed were not with them. Miraculously, they stayed intact and will now be preserved.

These autograph letters are valuable as additional documentation of Frederick Law Olmsted's sustained involvement with free-soil activities, specifically with the New England Emigrant Aid Company during those months which coincide with his gradual movement from aspiring man of letters toward the incipient landscape architect of late 1857. Olmsted's thinking on the free-soil movement is illuminated by this correspondence, most especially in relation to his hopes for the settlement of the Neosho Territory (Oklahoma), which in his mind, was apparently the logical place for further extension of free-soil activities. With the discovery of these letters, Olmsted's relationship with the New England Emigrant Aid Company can be further clarified. It has long been recognized that Olmsted was actively engaged in free-soil activities, but until these letters were discovered the extent of that involvement and the fact that he was seriously entertaining the possibility of serving as Texas agent for the New England Emigrant Aid Company remained unknown.[2] These materials, which constitute the first new published information on this subject since 1917,[3] are perhaps of most importance because they indicate Olmsted's enthusiasm about the future possible settlement of the Red River Valley.

Olmsted's enthusiasm about both arms provision and the possibility of emigration to free-soil territories by Germans and other Europeans is known, and some of those facts provide the necessary background for understanding interests reflected in these letters. Many passages in Olmsted's *Texas* volume document his distinct pleasure with the German settlements of southcentral Texas in comparison with other parts of the South supported by slave labor. He was convinced that free labor, such as he observed north and west of San Antonio, would finally be the most effective way to defeat the advance of slavery. He and his brother were so enthralled with the German emigrant communities, such as Neu Braunfels, which they observed in Texas that they seriously considered settling in Texas themselves. While in Texas Olmsted had befriended Dr. Adolf Douai, editor of the *San Antonio Zeitung*, a semi-covert free-soil German language newspaper. In 1854, when Douai's apparently radical views concerning free-soil possibilities in Texas alarmed financial backers, he was given a chance to purchase outstanding shares of the paper. Douai wrote the Olmsted brothers to inquire if they might provide him with the necessary $350. The Olmsteds contacted friends, including Charles Loring Brace and Henry Ward Beecher, and while the Olmsteds had little money of their own, they were soon able to raise the needed funds.[4] Olmsted and Douai remained active in Texas free-soil activities throughout 1855; Olmsted wrote an article for the *Zeitung* on Know-Nothingism, and he may have been instrumental in founding a colony headed by a French Fourierist near San Antonio. Roper suggests that Olmsted may also have pursued the possibility of sending the unemployed from New York to areas such as Texas.[5]

It was during this period that Olmsted first contacted the New England Emigrant Aid Company to investigate the possibilities of cooperation between Kansas and Texas free soilers.[6] (The New England Emigrant Aid Company was then sending groups of settlers to the Kansas-Nebraska Territory in the hope it would soon become a free state.) Olmsted was concerned that the Aid Company must minimize emphasis on the free-soil aspect of immigration which it sought to stimulate, although clearly he favored this activity.

During this time, Douai continued to seek assistance for free-soil efforts in Texas. It is clear that Olmsted continued to assist Douai's cause. Because of such interests, and also through the reputation that he was gaining by his travel books, he was fast becoming considered a Yankee expert on Texas. Such a reputation was reinforced by his sustained efforts to raise money for free-soil activity in Texas and Kansas.[7]

Olmsted's second definite contact with members of the New England Emigrant Aid Company concerned just Kansas, not Texas. In early September 1855, he had met a free-soil agent, Major James B. Abbott, who was raising funds for arms to defend Kansas. Olmsted quickly got involved with what was privately known as the Rifle Committee of the Aid Company, and Abbott delegated Olmsted to raise money for guns. Olmsted initially sought funds for one hundred carbines. To provide so many arms would have taken approximately $3,000, and upon the advice of an anonymous military friend Olmsted purchased a cannon. Another newly discovered letter from Abbott to Samuel Cabot, dated November 3, 1855 (found with these edited Olmsted letters), states that Abbott was eagerly awaiting the mountain howitzer. The facts about the subsequent use of the cannon have been subject to debate.[8]

Additional correspondence also shows that Olmsted maintained a regular correspondence about Texas with Edward Everett Hale, who also was a member of the Aid Company. This fact is supported by company records now in Kansas. Much of the Hale correspondence concerns Olmsted's contact with Texas, specifically with Olmsted and Hale's friend, Douai. The interests of Douai, Olmsted, and various other members of the New England Aid Company were apparently drawing closer throughout 1855. On December 21, 1855, Olmsted wrote to Hale to explain that he was planning to have his correspondence to Douai translated into German because it was arriving in Texas with broken seals, and he did not want information about the "Abbott Howitzer" (and it might be assumed other information as well) to get into the wrong hands.[9] In another letter, of January 23, 1856, Olmsted suggested that he and Hale might send sections of his *Texas* book to New England editors in the hope of luring additional emigrants to Texas.[10] Thus, considerable evidence demonstrates that Olmsted pushed hard for emigration to Texas throughout 1855. Unfortunately, by the spring of 1856, his friend Douai had given up his efforts as an editor and had departed from Texas.[11]

It is somewhat ironic then that, while Douai had been forced out of his editorship, Olmsted was being thought of more frequently as a Texas expert. He was considered to be extremely knowledgeable about Texas, and that expertise was valued. There was a sense of urgency about such matters because when Texas was annexed in 1845, it was with the provision that it could be divided into five states. It was not commonly thought that Texas would remain one state very long. What was called western Texas was an extremely likely candidate for a new soil-free state. Furthermore, by 1857, Kansas had been won by the free soilers, and the New England Aid Company even considered closing down. However, Colonel Daniel Ruggles met with the executive committee on May 15, 1857, and began to interest them in Texas as a site for their operations.[12] Such interest apparently grew rapidly, and this is why Olmsted's letters to Samuel Cabot are of special importance. The company formed a Texas Commission with Dr. Cabot as its chairman; he soon contacted Olmsted. Earlier, during 1857, Olmsted himself had already contacted the Cotton

Supply Association of England in hopes of interesting emigrants to Texas. During 1857, Olmsted became increasingly interested in Neosho and northern Texas as promising places for colonization. Such convictions apparently had been strengthened by the problems he had already experienced concerning Texas. Given different circumstances, he might well have become still more involved with free-soil activities in the Southwest. The New England Emigrant Aid Company was undoubtedly interested in Olmsted as its representative.

Still other letters, which were in the private possession of Cabot, shed additional light on Olmsted's relationship with the company. On July 8, 1857, Charles J. Higginson, a company member, wrote Cabot to say that he wanted to show the enthusiastic parts of Olmsted's letter of July 4 to the local Boston-Kansas Club so as to interest them in Texas colonization. Apparently, the Boston-Kansas Club had $1,000 which they wanted to invest. Because the New England Emigrant Aid Company was without funds (as a result of the financial Panic of 1857), it was thought that the Boston-Kansas funds might be used to start a Texas venture.[13] Clearly, members of the New England Emigrant Aid Company respected Olmsted's opinions concerning Texas, and that is why he was among the first contacts made by their Texas Commission. Such facts were the stimulus for the exchange of letters with Cabot who must have sought information about whom they should contact and how ready Texas might be for exploitation.

In retrospect, that Olmsted would be so enthusiastic about the possibilities of Oklahoma as a place for settlement is surprising. Apparently, he had not traveled there, and it is questionable if Douai or Ruggles would have agreed with such a move. However, Olmsted seems to have anticipated problems with advocating additional emigration to what was called western Texas, problems which would not be easily surmounted. His appraisal of the situation is outlined at length in the July 4 letter. The fact is, however, that Olmsted misjudged the probable role that the Red River Valley would play in the years before the war, and decades passed before Neosho actually opened for settlement.

A significant point clarified by these letters is that Olmsted was evidently thinking seriously about accepting a position as Texas agent for the company.[14] It sometimes seems that his choice to go into landscape work was almost a matter of circumstance. While this is not the case, at this point in his life Olmsted did entertain many options and was quite flexible. The financial Panic of 1857 was apparently the major contributing factor in his decision to remain in New York.

This correspondence also demonstrates that Olmsted remained concerned about the Neosho-Texas project for several months. His October 2 letter, with its mention of the Weston book, emphasizes that sustained interest.[15]

It is fascinating to speculate how Olmsted's career may have taken a different turn if it had not been for the Panic of 1857 and the fall of his publishing house. He could well have gone to Texas, not been offered the Central Park position, and thus had a different life. Yet, as the details of his July 4 letter suggest, Olmsted was capable of thought on a grand scale. He might well have ended as the architect of new cities in Neosho or Texas, for his talent as a planner on a regional scale is foreshadowed by the enthusiasm of these letters. Within them are indications of the powerful imagination that would create a park from the slagheaps of central Manhattan, reorganize a mining empire in the mountains of California, and conceive of plans for forest reservations in the West, Northeast, and South.

NOTES

1. From New England Emigrant Aid Company broadside entitled "To the Senate and House of Representatives, in Congress Assembled" included in the Rutherford collection.

2. That FLO was offered a position as Texas agent is confirmed by the minutes of the executive committee of the New England Emigrant Aid Company: "Minutes, July 19, 1857," from "Records of meetings of the board of trustees, July 24, 1854 to April 20, 1868." New England Emigrant Aid Company Papers, Kansas State Historical Society, Topeka, Kansas, Roll Seven.

3. Earlier letters by Olmsted were edited by Percy W. Bidwell in the *American Historical Review* (October 1917); they include a July 6, 1857, letter to the secretary of the Cotton Supply Association of England and a July 26, 1857, letter to Dr. Samuel Cabot, pp. 114–19.

4. Laura Wood Roper, *FLO: A Biography of Frederick Law Olmsted* (Baltimore, 1973), p. 102.

5. Ibid., p. 104.

6. Ibid.

7. Ibid., p. 105.

8. JBA to SC, November 3, 1855, Rutherford Collection. According to Samuel A. Johnson, the cannon was used in Kansas, surrendered by the Free-Soilers at the Sack of Lawrence on May 21, 1856, then held by "Missouri Border Ruffians" until mid-August when it was traded back to the Free-Soilers in exchange for prisoners. Samuel A. Johnson, *The Battle Cry of Freedom: The New England Emigrant Aid Company in the Kansas Crusade* (Lawrence, 1954), p. 159, + p. 202. Beveridge and Roper say the cannon was never used.

9. FLO to EEH, December 21, 1855, Hale Collection, New England Emigrant Aid Company Papers, Kansas State Historical Society, Topeka, Kansas, Roll Two.

10. FLO to EEH, January 23, 1856, ibid.

11. Roper, *FLO*, p. 105.

12. Minutes, Board of Trustees, New England Emigrant Aid Company Papers, Kansas State Historical Society, Topeka, Kansas, Roll Seven.

13. CJH to SC, July 8, 1857, Rutherford Collection.

14. See August 15; August 18; and September 14 letters.

15. Olmsted refers to *The Progress of Slavery* by George M. Weston (Washington, D.C., 1857), a systematic study of the advantages of free emigration in the southwestern United States.

APPENDIX

92 Grand St.
July 4th, 1857

My Dear Doctor

I have just received your favor of July 2d.

"A good plan of action in a matured form" implies fuller knowledge and consideration than is yet possible. I have written in various directions for information and in about a month's time, I shall be glad, if you will allow me, to propose a plan for provisional movements at least.

Mr. Desel,[1] one of the few determined, avowed and laboring free-soilers of Western Texas has been here this week and I have had much conversation with him. Two successive bad crops—entire failures—a recurrence of Indian troubles, robberies and murders, an increased and more general ruffianism and barbarism on the part of the Americans, the total cessation of immigration of Germans, the increasing demoralization of those resident and the entire abandonment of hope of a free state, are exceedingly discouraging circumstances. On the other hand however it is to be considered that the crop-failures have damaged the slave-holders as much as the Germans, that there has been very little American immigration, and that the landowners have been greatly dissapointed [sic] and are now in a condition of mind to resort to expedients they would have scorned a few years ago, or to sell at low prices. And that there seems to have been some reaction among thinking men from that fanaticism which effected the expulsion of Douai.

I think we should now find the large majority of Germans against us in any movement which was suspected to have a free state as one of its objects, because they consider the last movement in that interest to have been ill-judged and harmful to them, they have made up their minds to slavery, consider a free state utopian, & desire to make the best of what is inevitable;—I mean that we should, if such a purpose was suspected at the outset, have their opposition to it. Secretly and at heart it may be understood that all Germans are opposed to slavery. It is more their natural character, than of any other people in the world—not by any means excepting the English.

These things I am inclined to consider essential to forming a free-state in Western Texas. An organization for land-speculation and the collection and assistance (by means of agents in Europe) of emigrants or colonists, with a cash capital at the outset of not less than $100,000. 2nd that this organization has not the aim to make a free state, but merely a community of freemen, 3rd the co-operation cordially, fully, and extensively, of certain large land-owners in Texas who are probably *at present*, pro-slavery partisans.

If the charter under which the organization operated could be granted by the Texas or the Louisiana legislature and the head quarters of the Company appear to be, not at New York as you suggest, but at New Orleans or San Antonio, I should consider its power for good certain to be three times as great as would otherwise be the case.[2]

These questions, however, are for the future. The Red River project is one which requires to be defined to a certain extent, more immediately.

Assuming that the pro-slavery party expect ever to make a slave-state West of Arkansas and between Kansas & Red River, it may be reckoned upon with confidence that they will take the earliest possible opportunity to throw that country open to settlement—For the following reasons: an extensive movement of slaveholders & slaves is certain to take place from Missouri during the next two years. This movement will most naturally and cheaply take a Southwesterly course; i.e. into Neosho, if that territory is open to it. If the organization of that territory is delayed two years; this emigration will not only have passed by & be lost, but Missouri will have become much more practicable for emigrants, to cross from the free-states—both on account of the retreat or the defection of the resident ruffians and by the progress of rail-roads and free-state settlers on routes leading across Missouri towards Neosho. Secondly, because every month's delay increases the free-soil force on the Northern border of Neosho—Kansas—and sets free the men and the capital which have together conquered Kansas to freedom.

For these reasons, and because also of the very clear intentions of Governor Walker[3] & because I see in various quarters indirect efforts to prepare the public mind for it, I think it may be considered to have been determined on the part of the administration to throw open Neosho as soon as practicable to slave-holding settlement. (It must be our congressional policy to postpone it as long as possible and to insist on Squatter Sovereignty & that as well guarded as possible when it must come. It must be fought off till next spring at any rate that the Southerners do not have the advantage of the open Red River entrance, when the Missouri and Ohio are closed to us).

If Neosho is to open settlement as preemption [*sic*] next summer, is it possible to secure it for freedom? Is it worth while to undertake to do so by organized emigration?

These questions I do not feel able to answer with confidence at present, but there are two points upon which I have made up my mind—1st. If it is to be done, the bulk of emigration to be relied upon must be composed of Germans and not of New Englanders [.]

New England and all the east has been pretty severely dragged for emigrants lately. A reaction to the emigration furor is probable. Stimulating emigration from New England is going to be unpopular with our conservative rich and patriotic old gentlemen and old women—ministers doctors & lawyers especially. Better keep these on our side.

German settlers for Neosho must be composed in about equal measure of those who have had some experience in the country and of newcomers. One Yankee to five Germans will be sufficient to give the latter courage and unity to oppose slavery actively, with arms, should arms become necessary.

2ndly. If at any time in the next ten years, Neosho should become a free-state, it will very soon be the most profitable field of free-labor in the union. I should like what I say to be remembered—though anyone who looks at the map, seeing its waters, its relations to the East, West and South, and considers the advantages of its climate, the variety of its productions, which is to be immensely greater than that either of Kansas or Texas, the variety, extent and accesibility [sic] of the mineral resources which the most superficial observations have already disclosed, anyone must at once perceive that no free state or territory has half the attractiveness which it would possess. It has every advantage of Kansas with the addition of much more navigable and mill-power water, better soils*, more wood* & more mineral wealth, more valuable forage, and a climate, which while equally healthy, permits the growth of cotton and figs and almonds and pecan nuts & olives, is acceptible [sic] to camels, cashmere goats, alpacas + Llamas (as our own & the Kansas climate is not), and (in the South), allows sheep, horses & neat-stock to be reared with no more than three weeks' winter foddering or shelter, being required for their perfect health and improvement.

If Neosho should become a free state there will be some large towns in it: probably one or two of the largest interior towns on the continent. These will be the market towns not only of Neosho but of the great continental pastoral region lying west of the 100° of longitude. One of these towns will be on the Arkansas [.] Another or others on the Red R. or its tributaries, probably. If Neosho becomes a free state Northern, and especially North Western Texas will not be a regular slave-holding community. That part of Northern Texas lying to the west of the counties at present occupied by Slave-holders is not likely in the event of Neosho's becoming a free state, to be settled upon by them: it is likely to be attractive to free-laborers and to capital.** Land can not be bought at present in Neosho, but land can be bought in that part of Texas referred to, and at very low prices, as low perhaps as 30 cts an acre. It is not possible to settle free soilers in Neosho at present but it is possible to settle them in that part of Texas on the opposite side of the river. If Neosho becomes a free state it is certain to have intimate & important commercial relations with Western Texas—an important town in that vicinity is likely to be established—and even if Texas adjoining remains a Slave State, as likely to grow on her side the river as the other (vide Louisville & St. Louis & their rivals New Albany & _____).⁴ Consequently here is a good place to speculate.

Also, if we are to fight for Neosho, it will be of great service to have a quiet unobserved post in that Southwestern quarter. It may also be of great value to have established an entrance for emigration by Red River before that object is suspected.

Suppose that land can be bought here at 50 cts. an acre, that 20,000 acres should be bought; 2000 reserved for town lots, alternate lots to be given away to trades-

*See Marcy's Exploration, p. 111.
**See Marcy's Explor. p. 113 & 114. Debow Vol. III pp. 338 & 340.

men, mechanics etc. for a while—9000 acres to be offered to colonists in Germany in farms of say 100 acres each, at $1.00 an acre payable in five years after occupation, with interest at _____ per ct, payable annually after the first year, with mortgage security on the farms and improvements; 1000 acres to be given to old, free soil, experienced, German, Texan frontiersmen & frontier farmers; 1000 to Yankee farmers (from Kansas) $5000 to $10,0000 be expended in mills, cotton-gins, school-houses etc. & in payment of agents, advertising in Germany etc. Within a year I think there would be established a colony of 500 souls, the foundation of a town made and the speculators would have some 1900 acres of "town lots;" 7000 acres of agricultural land still to dispose of to new-comers, and notes safe for $9000.—mills school-houses etc. Capital invested so far $20,000.

It is the opinion of Mr. Desel that land in the part of Texas towards which we are looking has not yet been taken up; if it has not it may be bought at 25 cts an acre (and certain fees) that being the value of Texas land-warrants of which the Rail Roads will have plenty to be disposed next winter.

Of the value of the town lots & farm-lots you are better able from your Kansas observation, to judge than I am. 500 Germans however never fail to draw 500 after them & no frontier farmer was ever long satisfied to own no more than 100 acres around his "improvements."

This suggestively with reference to the Land Trust Company.

The fact you state with reference to the navigable condition of upper Red R. was mentioned by me to Dr. Webb.[5] I have written to a cotton merchant at N. Orleans and to the postmaster at Preston to ascertain what may be depended upon.

I have written to the Cotton Supply Associations of Liverpool and Manchester and engaged Mr. W. Neill, who sails next Wednesday to urge the subject on their attention. Mr. N. is a Cotton Merchant. I have also written fully to Lord Goderiche [sic] requesting his influence with these associations to be used to favor our scheme. I should be glad to see Mr. Paddleford [sic] and could probably supply him with some important facts and arguments.[6]

Yours Very Truly

Fred. Law Olmsted.

New Haven. Aug. 15th
57

My Dear Sir

The failure of Miller & Curtis, which occurred last week, deprives me of all my property & involves me almost hopelessly in debt. This of course interrupts & dissaranges [sic] all my plans & I must ask your Society not to depend on me for any services which I have heretofore given you reason to expect of me.

Any information of value which I may receive regarding the Texas project, I will of course lay before you.

Yours Respectfully

Fred. Law Olmsted.

Dr. Cabot.

New Haven. Aug. 18th
57

My Dear Sir

After dispatching a letter to you yesterday I recd yours of 12th.

I wrote to you saying that you could not depend on me, for the purpose of freeing myself from any thing like an engagment [sic] to you—or rather that you might not be dissappointed [sic] hereafter if I should not be able to meet your expectations of me. I have not determined not to go on your business, my heart is in it, but I am under the necessity now, much more than I have been, of making a permanently lucrative disposition of myself. I shall be closely engaged for a month or more to come. My eyes have failed lately & I have lost a fortnight in writing in consequence. So I shall not immediately form determined plans. Probably I shall come to Boston as you wish, to see you early in September.

I at present incline to think that Texas should be considered as a secondary & entirely subordinate field and that all possible capital, study, forecasting and statesmanship, should be given immediately to Neosho. I believe a coup de main will be attempted there and it is better that New England be depopulated than it succeed. Anything & everything can be suspended if not sacrificed to gain that position. I am disposed to think therefore that whatever is done in Texas should be done chiefly with reference to Neosho. The *chief* object of large (general) operations in Texas, at this time should be, to gain the land-interest & revive the German Anti-Slavery party.

The Kansas Zeitung,[7] has been well noticed in the Tribune; I dont know about the German press of N. York—will enquire; you can send some copies to Mr Kapp[8] & I will call on him, & see that is noticed and recorded in the Post & Times.

I hope to hear of your successes with the Land & T Comp. soon.

Yours very Truly

Fred. Law Olmsted.

New York, Sept. 14th
1857

Dr. S. Cabot.
    N.E.E. Aid Soc.
My Dear Sir,

From the tenor of your last communication I infer that it is not probable that your Society would wish me to make the journey in Neosho and Texas at this time, as was proposed in June.

I have to-day received notification of my appointment to the office of Superintendent of the Central Park of New York, with a request that I would enter upon the duties of the office immediately. I have determined to do so to-morrow and therefore relinquish the intention I have hither too [sic] had to visit you this week.

It is unnecessary to assure you of the very deep interest I have in the scheme of free colonization, Southward from Kansas. My duties at the park will occupy my time & mind very closely for some time to come, but I wish as far as possible to be allowed to actively co-operate with you in your great work.

Since I saw you I have taken a good deal of pains to obtain information regarding Neosho, and the result is the highest possible estimate of its attractiveness to Northern settlers. I earnestly advise you to send a judicious person to carefully survey the ground, especially the Southeastern part, from the Arkansas to the Red River, adjoining Arkansas. It is my impression, from a great variety of indications, that no part of the United States, ever offered greater natural attractions (as respects productiveness & salubrity), than this part of Neosho. I would urge the importance of early steps in this direction. An expenditure of a great treasure of money and life would be justified to establish firmly a respectable colony of brave and careful New Englanders, South of the Arkansas river near the State line. It is my conviction, however, that if Neosho is thrown open, and it is undertaken to prevent its becoming a slave state, during the next two years, success can only be secured by the aid of a transatlantic organization for directing German emigrants directly thither. I mean the organization of an extensive system of agencies and canvassing—with inducements similar to those offered by the Illinois Central R.R., and carefully systematized, cheap & comfortable facilities of transit.

I have been dissapointed [sic] in the receipt of information from Texas. I believe Dr. Douai has been more fortunate and he will translate for you a letter from Mr. Riotte,[9] of which I can only say the author is deserving of the highest confidence and the warmest sympathy for his personal sacrifices for the principles of free men.

I enclose a letter giving some important information with regard to Red River. The information with regard to the wheat producing qualities of the soil of Northern Texas, is not to be disregarded. I have received numerous confirmations of it & I am inclined to believe that Southern Neosho & Northern Texas may become the most productive wheat districts *in the world*. There are tolerably authentic statements of 50 bushels of wheat of the heaviest description having been produced here to the acre, with the rudest frontier cultivation.[10] At the same time North *Eastern* Texas & South eastern Neosho have apparently *unequalled* cotton-growing advantages.

I have received a reply to my communication to the Manchester Cotton Association, which I enclose. I also send you a letter from Lord Goderiche [sic] which I have this day received. I beg for various reasons that your Society will give very early attention to this subject and that you will soon return this letter with some advice about a reply. The matter should not be allowed to drop. A well defined scheme should be presented to our English friend, as soon as practicable, but in the mean time they must not be allowed to loose [sic] sight of the importance of the subject both materially & philanthropically. Col. James Hamilton[11] wrote me last week that he contemplated making a trip to Europe soon (in a few weeks, I judge,), "should I do so," he says, "I will certainly employ all the time I may be on the other side to impress influential persons with my views of the advantages of your project. It is a glorious one & if successful would be of infinite service to both countries." Col. H's facilities of reaching influential persons both political &

mercantile in England are of the best, & the opportunity should not be lost. If you are ready to do anything or to propose anything definitely, & will write me soon, I will take a day to visit Col H. at his residence, to consult with him & give him all the information likely to assist his purpose, which I can obtain.

The Kansas Zeitung has been well noticed in the German papers here, & several copies are taken in New York. From what I have, I infer that it is conducted with remarkable good judgment, and is likely to be very useful.

Be kind enough to show this letter & its enclosures to Dr. Douai, with warm regards.

I shall always esteem it an honor and a favor to be entrusted with any duty for your Society in New York.

Faithfully Yours

Fred. Law Olmsted.

92 Grand St. Oct. 22, 1857.

My Dear Doctor Cabot,

I have begun writing an article which I intend for the "Atlantic Monthly" based on Weston's "Progress of Slavery" which I consider the most respectable book which has been published in my time in the United States. As he had publickly refferred [sic] to the chances of occupying Neosho by free men, I mean to treat that point frankly, and confidently, and especially advertise the advantages which milder climates offer to emigrants.

Please write me if Dr. Webb has returned & if he brings any further information regarding the country [.]

Write me also if your Society "still lives" & how you feel & what you expect in Boston-Kansas-ward and politically, if you have time.

I have further letters from England intimating great interest in the Neosho project, but I take it any movement is at present out of the question.

Everything is black & blacker in New York. Slavery has nothing to gain however by the present condition of things.

Yours most cordially

Fred. Law Olmsted.

Editorial Notes:

These letters are transcribed exactly as Olmsted wrote them. All editorial annotations are indicated with brackets. Olmsted's spelling is retained, and marginal notes are included in the transcriptions. All of these letters (preserved in original envelopes) are written on eight by five inch paper (folded from 8" x 10") and are in excellent physical condition. Brown ink was used consistently.

1. Possibly one of the Desel Brothers (Julius?), active in the German Immigra-

tion Company. Cf. Max Freund, ed., *Gustav Dresel's Houston Journal: Adventures in North America and Texas, 1837–1841* (Austin, 1954).

2. Proposed land company to be operated under the direction of the New England Emigrant Aid Company.

3. Samuel Walker, governor of Kansas Territory.

4. Olmsted's omission.

5. Thomas H. Webb, secretary of the NEEAC.

6. William Neill, of Neill Brothers and Co., Cotton Merchants; Lord Goderich, courtesy title, M. P. from West Riding, George Frederick Robinson; Seth Padelford, of Providence, Rhode Island, member of the NEEAC.

7. Newspaper supported by the NEEAC and edited by Charles F. Kob. (The Rutherford collection contains a number of Kob's letters to the NEEAC.)

8. Friedrich Kapp, FLO's history of Neu Braunfels in *Journey Through Texas* is based on a published lecture by Kapp.

9. Charles N. Riotte, German lawyer whom FLO met in San Antonio.

10. This sentence is a postscript; it was written in the left margin.

11. Colonel James A. Hamilton, son of Alexander Hamilton; interestingly, Colonel Hamilton drew up a petition signed by Peter Cooper, Washington Irving, and others in support of FLO's Central Park post (Roper, *FLO*, p. 128).

Timothy J. Crimmins

FREDERICK LAW OLMSTED AND JONATHAN BAXTER HARRISON:
Two Generations of Social Critics of the American South

"I find in my 'deep-laden notebooks'—to borrow a phrase from a recent work of the most competent observer who has ever studied the South *in extenso*—many sketches and incidents which illustrate no theories . . . but which simply reveal the life of the people as I saw it."[1] Thus did Jonathan Baxter Harrison—a former abolitionist and Union soldier who returned to describe the South fifteen years after the end of the Civil War—pay tribute to Frederick Law Olmsted whose writings about his Southern journeys in the 1850s depicted the American slave states with a detailed accuracy which had seldom been accomplished prior to his visit. When Harrison went south in the fall of 1880 and began to publish his travel accounts the following February as an anonymous special correspondent for the *New-York Daily Tribune,* he declared his intention to describe the "New South" with detachment, a quality which had also characterized Olmsted's studies twenty-five years earlier.[2] These two men were excellent reporters, but they went beyond the mere recording of observations: by drawing deductions about the nature of the society which they analyzed, they were among the forefathers of modern social science.

Jonathan Baxter Harrison met and became a collaborator of Frederick Law Olmsted in the early 1880s under the influence of a common acquaintance, Charles Eliot Norton, the Boston Brahmin whose advice was instrumental in launching or guiding the careers of such nineteenth-century New England writers as Henry Wadsworth Longfellow, James Russell Lowell, and William Dean Howells.[3] The Olmsted-Norton friendship began in the Civil War years, with their initial exchange of letters in 1862 and their first meeting in 1863.[4] In that same year, Norton took notice of essays Harrison had written in *The Students' Repository,* a quarterly published by a Quaker-staffed school for blacks, the Union

Literary Institute. Harrison was then assisting the black editor of the *Repository*, a journal whose stated goal was "to cultivate the moral, intellectual, and religious character of the colored people, and to afford the scope for their rapidly rising talents and aspirations."[5] Norton, who was then editor of *Broadsides*—a compendium of the Loyal Publication Society (an organization strongly endorsed by Olmsted)—and of the *North American Review*, was attracted by the straightforwardness and sincerity of Harrison's writings. Norton published a favorable review of Harrison's periodical in the *North American Review*, solicited Harrison's contributions for *Broadsides*, and entered into a remarkable correspondence of forty-one years, during which time his advice helped shape and reshape Harrison's career.[6]

In their earliest exchange of letters, Harrison provided biographical details by way of introduction which later enabled Norton to describe him as having traits similar to those of Lincoln.[7] Of his young adulthood Harrison said:

My father has always been very poor and I have gone to school very little since I was ten years old. From twelve to twenty I worked, at clearing land, raising corn, and hiring out by the month much of the time. We lived in the backwoods. When at home I studied some at night by firelight. My parents were not able to use candles. I thus learned something of the common English branches, but there was no one to whom I could recite.[8]

Harrison's account—particularly his implied plea for someone to whom he could recite—must have struck a sympathetic chord in the Harvard professor, for Norton undertook the responsibility for further educating his rough-hewn pupil. As his mentor, Norton guided Harrison's complete adult educational development. Harrison, who had been ordained a Methodist minister in 1860, occupied a pulpit in Kendallville, Indiana, during the first year of his correspondence with Norton. But as a result of a dialogue in which his "unorthodox" beliefs were nurtured, Harrison soon withdrew from the church of his birth and converted to the Unitarianism espoused by Norton.[9]

As he grew more "liberal" in his religious beliefs, Harrison continued to enlarge his world view with readings suggested by Norton. His appreciation for Norton's guidance was apparent in the earliest years of their correspondence: "I acknowledge that my hunger for books with substance in them increases and I cannot well conceal it. . . . The books you have sent to me are of such help to me that I think it would be impossible to go on in my work without them."[10] With Norton's encouragement, Harrison traveled east in 1866 to meet the great writers of nineteenth-century America. He visited with Emerson, Bronson Alcott,

Longfellow, and Lowell before capping off his journey with a trip to "Ashfield," the country home of Norton.[11] From this point, it is clear that Norton became the most influential person in Harrison's life. After their first meeting, Harrison wrote: "I shall always remember my visit to Ashfield as a time of deep, pure happiness; and I know I shall always be better equipped for my work for having met you."[12] Not long after, Harrison pleaded for continued tutelage:

And finally, and most important of all, please tell me how, in your judgement, I *may improve myself.* I desire above all things to have an ideal life. . . . Now be truly my friend, as you have begun to be. I have nobody else to help me in this way. I have almost infinite *willingness* and will improve. Give me a little heroic treatment, and I shall in no way embarrass our future intercourse.[13]

Harrison's intellectual development was accompanied by a series of moves eastward in search of positions which would provide the financial security that seemed always to elude him. He worked as an editor of *The Liberal Christian,* a New York-based Unitarian weekly, while preaching at a small Unitarian church near his home in Montclair, New Jersey, from 1870 until 1875.[14] Thereafter, he held a Unitarian pulpit in Vineland, New Jersey (near Philadelphia), where he eked out a living as a writer and lecturer until 1879, when he accepted a position as Unitarian minister in Franklin Falls, New Hampshire, the base of his operations until his death in 1907.[15]

Harrison's continued intellectual maturation under Norton's watchful eye brought remarkable results in late 1878 with the publication of the first in a number of essays for the *Atlantic Monthly.* Norton had submitted a paper, which he had encouraged his pupil to write, on developments in American life and thought to William Dean Howells, editor of the *Atlantic.* Howells, in turn, was so impressed that he not only published the piece but also encouraged Harrison to contribute additional essays. Three of these articles, which appeared between 1878 and 1880, were later published under the title (suggested by Norton) *Certain Dangerous Tendencies in American Life, and Other Papers.*[16]

Encouraged by his initial success as a contributor to the *Atlantic,* Harrison wrote to Howells in 1878 suggesting that the magazine subsidize a trip to the South where he might observe and record current conditions. When Howells approved the project, Harrison wrote to Norton for advice. This step ultimately brought him into contact with that most famous of all Southern travel writers, Frederick Law Olmsted.[17]

The Harrison-Olmsted working relationship was initially suggested by Albert Fein in *Frederick Law Olmsted and the American Environmental Tradition,*[18] the study that provided the direct stimulus for this essay. This relationship can now be established and documented. While Harrison and Olmsted had not corresponded during the writing of the Southern travel narratives, which were first published in the *Tribune* and later serialized in the *Atlantic Monthly,* they did exchange ideas through their mutual friend, Norton.

It was actually the project to conserve Niagara Falls which began a decade of direct cooperation among Harrison, Olmsted, and Norton. In early 1882, Norton recruited Harrison to write a series of newspaper articles on the preservation movement; to facilitate this work, he brought Harrison and Olmsted into personal contact that summer. By fall, the two were in direct correspondence. Although their letters dealt primarily with the Niagara Falls case, Harrison was eager to solicit Olmsted's guidance on other matters, prompting Olmsted to assume the same role of adviser already undertaken by Norton.[19] Harrison became the subject of the Norton-Olmsted correspondence. For example, they conferred about the title for Harrison's 1882 pamphlet, *The Conditions of Niagara Falls and the Measures Needed to Preserve Them.* They again consulted concerning the difficulties their pupil was having in getting his Southern narratives into book form.[20] Once more, in 1885, the trio worked together in the movement to conserve the Adirondack region, with Harrison acting as field agent—writing newspaper articles and ultimately gathering them together in the booklet *The Adirondack Forest and the Problem of the Great Natural Waterways of the State of New York.* No sooner were their preservation efforts guaranteed than Norton was writing to Olmsted about Harrison: "I should like to get him on the Indian Committee."[21] He did, and Harrison became an agent for the Indian Rights Association. In 1887, he undertook an extensive investigation of the plight of the American Indian, publishing a number of articles and a book on the subject.[22]

Harrison received the counsel of both mentors in the writing of *Notes on Industrial Conditions,* a follow-up examination of the shortcomings of post-Civil War American culture that was to reintroduce a number of the ideas first expressed in *Certain Dangerous Tendencies.*[23] Harrison's period of close collaboration with Olmsted finally came to a close in 1889 with their co-authoring of "Observations on the Treatment of Public Plantations, More Especially relating to the Use of the Ax." This report (which grew out of Harrison's work on the New Hampshire Forestry Commission) justified the thinning out of unsightly trees from Central Park.[24]

Harrison and Olmsted were able to enter into such a fruitful working relationship because, with Norton, the two shared a common view of nineteenth-century society, a perspective which is apparent in both of their travel narratives and which could be described as that of the early social scientist. A common feature of their approach was seeming detachment, a quality which James Russell Lowell noted when he reviewed

Olmsted's *Journey in the Back Country*. Lowell was so impressed with the keenness of Olmsted's observations that he noted: "We cannot help wishing that he would make a journey through New England and make us as thoroughly acquainted with its internal condition as we ought to be."[25]

Lowell's call for disinterested observers who would discern and record the internal workings of society was part of a wider movement in the mid-nineteenth century which led to the establishment of the American Social Science Association. This organization, which Olmsted helped to found, mirrored his interest in fact-finding as a prelude to social control.[26] When Olmsted read Harrison's narratives, he was impressed with their insights into what he thought was the real condition of Southern society. In this regard, Olmsted wrote to Norton that Harrison's narratives were "much more valuable than any other book on the subject" because of the detachment which Olmsted thought they exhibited.[27]

Harrison's training in the detached approach of social science came from instruction provided by his original mentor. In 1866, while he was in Kendallville, Indiana, Harrison wrote to Norton: "I am interested in all that I can learn about Social Science movements. What should I read to learn more about it?"[28] The books and articles discussed in subsequent letters helped to answer Harrison's questions. Fourteen years later, when he was seeking Norton's advice for a title of his first book of essays, Harrison suggested that "Social Studies" might be appropriate.[29]

Harrison's initial proposal to Howells that he travel south for the *Atlantic* reflected Harrison's scientific perspectives. He suggested that the journey would test his hypothesis "that the Southern States will perhaps be *conservative* and so be of help to the nation against the wild and revolutionary tendencies of the time."[30] While it might seem that Harrison was predisposed to find evidence to buttress his thesis (one with which Howells and Norton were in sympathy), he nonetheless sought to put it to the test of observation: "I wish to see if the facts of life and thought in the states support this hope of mine."[31] With Howells' encouragement, Harrison wrote to Norton seeking advice on the methods which he might use to observe the true conditions of the Southern states. Norton, in turn, asked his most appropriate contact—Olmsted—for his opinions. The result was a remarkably succinct statement of Olmsted's method of acquiring data for his own ambitious survey:

There are two ways by which a traveller can get information of the opinions inclinations and tendencies of a population the particular characteristic of which is feebleness of community. One is by taking the judgment of well-informed and leading men, of which there are in the South two classes to be sought. The first by letters of introduction; the second, as Mr. Harrison proposes, by such chance acquaintance as one may hit upon at inns and in public conveyances. Of the latter class my best finds were coarse men with whom I could take a glass of toddy in the bar room. . . . To proceed in this way in the South one should be prepared to stay not only at the inns which are the resort of the farmers drovers and small country traders . . . in the larger towns, . . . but should do a good deal in the smaller places. . . .

The other process is to get below second hand information by personal acquaintance with the people in their homes. For this a man must go on horseback and take his chances.[32]

Olmsted's advice (relayed through Norton) provided Harrison with excellent guidance for undertaking his journey.[33] However, because of a delay resulting from a lack of financing, Harrison did not begin until late 1880. Since part of the money for this trip came from the *New-York Daily Tribune*, Harrison's observations were first published (anonymously) in February 1881 and continued on a relatively regular basis through August of that year. The original plan was to follow his reports with detailed studies—which would be published serially in the *Atlantic* and reissued in book form. This plan ran awry when Whitelaw Reid, the editor of the *Tribune*, put out a special edition of his newspaper which collected all of Harrison's special reports. This edition, "Glimpses of a New Dixie: Unsectional Views of Sectional Questions, A Series of Letters from an Unprejudiced Observer," scooped the publications planned by the publishers of the *Atlantic*.[34]

The naive Harrison, caught between the conflicting interests of two publishers, also suffered because William Dean Howells, his sympathetic editor, had recently resigned from the *Atlantic*.[35] Henry O. Houghton, a principal in the company which published the *Atlantic* as well as book-length manuscripts, had agreed to have Harrison write a Southern series for his magazine. Because of the competition problem created by the *Tribune* extra, however, he refused to publish the narrative in book form. At this point, Olmsted urged Norton to help Harrison find another publisher. Norton tried, without success, to pressure Houghton (to whom he referred as an "ugly old dog in the manger") into releasing the Southern studies. As a result, the only records of Harrison's trip remain in the *Tribune* and the *Atlantic Monthly*.[36]

Olmsted, who had been alerted by Norton to follow Harrison's *Tribune* series and had been asked for comments, wrote to Norton suggesting questions which Harrison might consider for his *Atlantic* series. These questions again reflected the concern of the social scientist:

The interesting question of the South is to what social conditions is it heading? . . . Are white and black to grow into more or less distinct communities? . . . Is there any tendency among the lower orders to live more in harmony—to unite in churches, schools &c.? Is that coming, or the reverse? . . .

. . . Is it too soon to see the beginning of what is to come? . . . Anything that Mr. Harrison can write even negatively upon it will be valuable.[37]

Olmsted's influence on Harrison's Southern narratives can be seen in his early suggestions on how best to go about the gathering of information on the true condition of the region and in his probing questions about the patterns of social life which were emerging. While Harrison's *Tribune* series report the conditions of the South, his *Atlantic Monthly* essays go further in their attempt to analyze social patterns and to predict trends of community development. Here again, Harrison was demonstrating a concern with the social order which had characterized Olmsted's studies a quarter of a century earlier.

Harrison's travel reports were first given prominence in the *Tribune* special edition, "Glimpses of a New Dixie," published on August 17, 1881. The editorial which accompanied the series commented that "the writer visited all the Southern States except Arkansas and Florida, talked with all sorts of people, and observed all phases of industrial enterprise and social life."[38] Indeed, Harrison's journeys took him to such places as the clandestine hideaway of a community of mountain moonshiners, where he transcribed conversations with his hosts which revealed their feelings about the federal laws threatening them with imprisonment, and to a city, where he described what he thought to be the idyllic conditions of docile industrial workers. The *Tribune* editorial proclaimed that the section described by Harrison was "a new South, fermenting with new thoughts, beginning to feel itself an important part of the great American Republic . . . anxious for capital, immigration, and better educational facilities and earnestly at work developing industrial resources." A close reading of Harrison's narratives also reveals that the region still had such very real problems as agricultural and industrial inefficiency, and the open deprivation of the civil rights of blacks.[39]

Harrison's correspondence in the *Tribune* included such datelines as Salisbury, North Carolina; Chattanooga, Tennessee; Huntsville, Alabama; Corinth, Mississippi; New Orleans, Louisiana; San Antonio, Texas; and Columbus, Georgia. But his narrative summaries in the *Atlantic Monthly* eliminated many of these specifics in favor of a more generalized description. Like Olmsted before him, Harrison made a point of claiming anonymity for himself and his subjects: "Very few men in the South learned that I was a writer or a correspondent for the press. It may be that some persons would have been less frank if they had known what use would be made of the information which they so freely and courteously aided me to obtain . . .; but, of course, I do not use names, nor in any way designate individuals."[40] Harrison's invisibility as an observer helped him to capture life in the post-Reconstruction South. Following Olmsted's formula, his approach was personal. He entered into frank dialogue with politicians who described the peaceful means which they used to disfranchise black voters, spoke to management and workers in textile mills in small towns, and discoursed with Southerners on how Northerners viewed the proper relationship between blacks and whites. In all of these conversations, Harrison revealed that he possessed independent judgment, as well as some of the prejudices of his Northern environment. He believed that any restriction of voters—even the literacy requirement used in New England—threatened the entire democratic order, that the Southern factory operatives were more placid and content than their restless Northern cousins, and that Yankees never intended blacks to be regarded as their companions and friends. Harrison was also not an infallible prophet of the future course of events in the South. In reaction to the Olmsted-inspired question—is there any tendency for the lower orders to unite in schools—Harrison noted: "After attentively studying the subject everywhere, I am convinced that there will soon be mixed schools for white and colored children, in many parts of the South."[41]

On the whole, however, the quality of the observations and judgments which Harrison offered in his narratives is somewhat above that of his contemporaries. Paul H. Buck notes that Harrison effectively presented "through the columns of a great Northern newspaper and a staunch Yankee periodical, a popular narrative which portrayed a reconciled South, indifferent to partisan controversy, and devoting its strength to work, education, and the improvement of race relations."[42] Yet, Buck is critical of the contemporary claim that Harrison's account was the best since Olmsted's. In Buck's judgment, little that was new could be said in a Southern narrative which had not already been written by Edward King in *The Great South* (1875) or by Charles Nordhoff in *The Cotton States in the Spring and Summer of 1875* (1876). Since Buck's theme of reconciliation is buttressed by the conclusions of both of these books, that the time had come to end federal reconstruction, he seemingly preferred their partisan approach to the more detached descriptions of Harrison.

More recently, in his comments on such 1880s travel narratives as Carl Schurz's *The New South* (New York, 1885), Thomas D. Clark notes that such works made little mention of the crime of lynching, the plight of blacks, and the woes of farming.[43] Since Harrison was doing something other than painting a picture of a reconciled South, his narratives do include descriptions of each of these topics. Harrison's "Studies in the South" are thus more inclusive than other contemporary studies because his purpose, like Olmsted's before him, was to record the internal workings of Southern society.

Although Harrison's travel narratives have never reached an audience comparable to Olmsted's, they still provide a remarkably similar approach to describing conditions in the South. Harrison and Olmsted reflected the universal interests of the early social scientists; in their writings, they spoke as sociologists, planners, statisticians, nutritionists, advocates of scientific agriculture, and historians. Their all-encompassing vision typified the approach of the American Social Science Association (ASSA) which viewed social science as an undifferentiated discipline embracing all aspects of social life. Only in the 1880s and 1890s, when the specialized disciplines began to define their own scope and methodologies, did the universal interest of ASSA begin to diminish.[44] Harrison and Olmsted, then, represent the consciousness of the early, nonspecialized social scientists who were free to roam the fields which have since been so carefully fenced off by historians, political scientists, economists, sociologists, and statisticians.

The quality which distinguished the work of Harrison and Olmsted from most travel accounts of their day was the appearance of impartiality, the absence of polemic. When Olmsted undertook his journeys, the rhetoric of antislavery abolitionists and proslavery Southerners had reached a fever pitch. As a Northern observer in the South, he set out to describe the "real condition" of the slave states; throughout his narratives, Olmsted emphasized that he recorded what he saw, not what he believed as a result of preconceptions.[45] When Harrison went south a generation later, he wanted to dispel the political fog which had been spread by Republican and Democratic partisans. He told one such advocate that he "had come to the South to see as much as possible, and to report accurately and impartially all that [he] could learn of the facts of the time."[46] While Olmsted's writings have been described by others as photographic presentations, Harrison himself actually used that metaphor to depict what he was attempting: "It is knowledge which is needed, wide observation of facts, accurate, photographic reporting."[47] Yet, these two authors wanted to go beyond impartial accounting in their writings; they wanted their revelations to change people's lives. Harrison continued his argument by saying that what was needed after knowledge was "such comparison and discussion of the results, of the facts of the situation, as the thoughtful people of our country are abundantly capable of conducting when they are possessed of sufficient information."[48] Olmsted, too, believed that knowledge based on an accurate presentation of facts could free people from their prejudices and lead to improved social conditions. He wrote that only after the delusions in the South about slavery were dispelled would "any general policy for remedying the evils . . . be initiated."[49]

Harrison and Olmsted were more than reporters; they were social critics who devised plans to remedy the disorders which they observed. Olmsted argued that the inefficiencies of slavery could be eliminated by engineering a program which would condition blacks to become more productive workers. In his view, slavery was to be extinguished by "educating the negro for taking care of himself in freedom."[50] This plan of education was designed to create a "self-respecting laboring people" by crediting each slave for a day's work until a sufficient amount of money had been accumulated to pay for his freedom. Olmsted predicted that the transformation of all slaves into productive workers would be a long process, but that the undertaking was vital to the regeneration of a territory which he observed to be an economic and cultural wasteland.[51]

Harrison, on the other hand, visited the South after the Emancipation Proclamation. Still, he reported that blacks had not yet overcome the unproductive habits inherited from slavery. He noted that "the feeling and conviction, of the white people of the South, that the elevation of the negro race is indispensible [sic] to the safety of society, and that their present condition of ignorance and debasement is full of danger for both races, is a most wholesome sentiment."[52] Harrison's method of uplifting was one of political amalgamation of the two races. He believed this course of action would provide the social control which Olmsted envisioned in his plan of emancipation. "Nothing should be done," he wrote, "to release these white people from their proper duties and responsibilities connected with the education of negroes, and their guidance and control."[53]

Both Harrison and Olmsted, like other members of the American Social Science Association, were interested first in fact-finding and second in developing procedures to direct human actions. These two planners envisioned a system of social conditioning which also epitomized the thinking of many late nineteenth-century theorists who equated education with social engineering.[54]

Far from considering themselves outsiders who had no business telling citizens from another section of the country how to govern their own affairs, Harrison and Olmsted felt that as detached observers they could discern the real condition of the society better than those who participated in its day-to-day operations. Like many present-day social scientists and "experts," these two authors were convinced of the objectivity of their position, a conviction that they bolstered through the use of statistics and case studies. Olmsted, who had more time to analyze the supporting materials for the transformation of his narratives into book form, made much more extensive use of statistical analysis. He frequently quoted material from the Census of 1850 to substantiate his generalizations, but his real understanding of the value of statistics came in his refutations of the misuse of numbers in the proslavery *DeBow's Review*.[55] Since Harrison never had the opportunity to publish his accounts as a book, in his necessarily brief summaries in the *Atlantic Monthly* he relied much more on the use of case studies. He described such "Southern types" as the optimist, the poor white, the moonshiner, the black planter, and the common black fieldhand.[56] But Harrison was aware of the need for statistics: he lamented a lack of accurate figures for Ku Klux Klan violence which prevented the construction of a true picture of that organization's influence on the reconstructed South.[57]

Both Harrison and Olmsted were critical of the agricultural practices they observed in the South. Olmsted bemoaned the influence of slavery which made it more economical for individual planters to exhaust the soil—by neglecting to replenish it through draining, manuring, and fallowing—and then to move on to new cheap land. He noted that the baneful influence of this practice had not only ruined good farmland for future generations, but had also contributed to the paucity of expenditures in the South for sturdy housing, good schools and churches, and adequate roads and bridges. Olmsted also observed that stock raising was at the same pitiful level of economy. In the highlands of Tennessee, Georgia, and North Carolina, he found no attempt to feed and shelter cattle in the winter, no understanding of the techniques of fattening through mixed grain feedings, and little effort to exterminate the beasts of prey which further thinned the already sparse ranks of emaciated livestock.[58] Harrison's travels indicated that little had changed in the intervening years: "I saw nothing in my journey through the South which appeared to me more imperatively to require . . . immediate and earnest attention . . . than this evil of the rapid denudation of large areas of fertile country of the entire body of their soil."[59] Harrison remarked that the dependence of Southern planters on cotton cost them hundreds of thousands of dollars a year because they had to import staples such as corn and pork which they could produce themselves. He also recorded that there still appeared to be insufficient feeding and a lack of winter shelter for livestock.[60]

In urging scientific agricultural practices on farmers in the South, Harrison and Olmsted were also suggesting that steps be taken to improve the diet of Southerners. Both men complained of their daily fare while on the road. Olmsted summarized the situation: "Wholesome water and wholesome fresh fruits are not to be obtained by the traveller, in the largest part of the United States. Bacon, fat and salt, is the stock article of diet. He must satisfy his appetite with this, or with coarse or most indigestible forms of bread. In either case he will have an unnatural thirst, the only means . . . for satisfying this will be an exceedingly dirty and unpalatable decoction of coffee . . . or alcoholic liquors."[61] Although he was not as carping as Olmsted, Harrison did note that there was still the demand for the "old stand-bys"—bread and bacon.[62] The solution which both proposed was a deemphasis on cash-crop production of cotton, tobacco, sugar, or rice and the development of New England gardening practices which would produce a far greater variety in table foods.[63]

One final concern of these two social scientists was with the writing of history. Olmsted devoted long sections in his *Journey in the Seaboard Slave States* to an unraveling of the history of the states which he visited. However, he revealed his real historical concern in a remarkable passage which called for the re-creation of the past of all men, not just influential men.

Men of literary taste . . . are always apt to overlook the working classes, and to confine the records they make of their own times . . . to the habits and fortunes of their own associates, or to those people of superior rank to themselves. . . . The dumb masses have often been so lost in this shadow of egotism, that, in later days, it has been impossible to discern the very real influence their character and condition has had on the fortune and fate of nations.[64]

This insight into the need to expand the scope of historical inquiry motivated Olmsted to provide extensive detail on the conditions of the slaves and ordinary workers. However, this interest in the "dumb masses" is one which only recently has begun to capture the imagination of the historian. Unfortunately, since in the intervening century care has not been taken to record the living conditions and influences of common men, current historians still face the paucity of sources which Olmsted decried.

Harrison's narratives reveal the same concern for recording the life-style of the "inarticulate classes." In fact, long before it had become fashionable, Harrison encouraged the practice of writing oral history: "A vast amount of rich material for history . . . will soon perish and be lost forever, unless somebody has the patience to live and talk with the common people of the South, and transcribe their accounts of what they have seen and known."[65] Echoing Olmsted's conviction, Harrison went on to argue that without this input, "our national history for that time can never be truthfully or adequately written."[66]

In the travel accounts of Harrison and Olmsted, we see two generations of social scientists recording what they saw as the true conditions of the South. Olmsted's two short letters to Norton with suggestions for Harrison provided excellent guidance. However, the many similarities in their studies were more probably the direct result of Olmsted and Harrison being cut by the same die of nineteenth-century social criticism. The press of duties kept Olmsted engaged in the practice of landscape architecture in the 1880s. Nonetheless, his recognition of the value of Harrison's observations indicated a continued interest in an "objective" description of American society and the formulation of strategies for a more workable social order. In Jonathan Baxter Harrison's "Studies in the South," then, we have a remarkable followup to the work of the "most competent observer who ever studied the South *in extenso*."[67]

NOTES

1. "Studies in the South," *Atlantic Monthly* 50 (October 1882): 476.

2. "Life in the South," *New-York Daily Tribune* (February 21, 1881): 2.

3. Martin Green, *The Problem of Boston: Some Readings in Cultural History* (London, 1966), p. 137. Kermit Vanderbilt, *Charles Eliot Norton: Apostle of Culture in a Democracy* (Cambridge, Mass., 1959), pp. 88, 152.

4. In *Frederick Law Olmsted: A Critic of the Old South* (Baltimore, 1924), Broadus Mitchell suggested that Norton was Olmsted's mentor (pp. 52–53), a misconception recently corrected by Laura Wood Roper in *FLO: A Biography of Frederick Law Olmsted* (Baltimore, 1973).

5. "What Shall Be Done with the Negro," *The Students' Repository* 1 (July 1863): 1.

6. Jonathan Baxter Harrison to Charles Eliot Norton, October 15, 1863, Norton Papers, Harvard University. Charles Eliot Norton to J. B. Ward in Sara Norton and M. A. DeWolfe Howe, eds., *Letters of Charles Eliot Norton, with Biographical Comment* (Boston, 1913), 2: 292–93. Charles Eliot Norton and Jonathan Baxter Harrison hereafter will be abbreviated CEN and JBH, respectively. *North American Review* 47 (October 1863): 557–59. Vanderbilt, *Charles Eliot Norton*, p. 86.

7. CEN to J. B. Ward in Norton and Howe, eds., *Letters of Charles Eliot Norton*, pp. 292–93.

8. JBH to CEN, October 15, 1863, Norton Papers, Harvard University.

9. JBH to CEN, November 16, 1865; December 9, 1864; August 4, 1866, Norton Papers, Harvard University.

10. JBH to CEN, January 31, 1866, Norton Papers, Harvard University.

11. JBH to CEN, September 14, 1866, Norton Papers, Harvard University.

12. JBH to CEN, October 8, 1866, Norton Papers, Harvard University.

13. JBH to CEN, February 8, 1867, Norton Papers, Harvard University.

14. JBH to CEN, February 18, 1871, Norton Papers, Harvard University.

15. JBH to CEN, December 18, 1879, Norton Papers, Harvard University.

16. JBH to CEN, June 17, 1878; August 11, 1878; January 16, 1880. "Certain Dangerous Tendencies in American Life," *Atlantic Monthly* 42 (October 1878): 385–402. "Sincere Demagogy," *Atlantic Monthly* 43 (October 1879): 488–500. "People of a Factory Village," *Atlantic Monthly* 44 (October 1880): 460–64.

17. JBH to CEN, September 8, 1878, Norton Papers, Harvard University.

18. (New York, 1972), pp. 44–45.

19. JBH to CEN, March 9, 1882; Frederick Law Olmsted to CEN, July 17, 1882, Norton Papers, Harvard University. (Frederick Law Olmsted will hereafter be abbreviated FLO.) JBH to FLO, October 24, 1882, Olmsted Papers, Library of Congress. Roper, *FLO*, pp. 397–98. Vanderbilt, *Charles Eliot Norton*, pp. 189–93. Alfred Runte, "Beyond the Spectacular: The Niagara Falls Preservation Campaign," *New-York Historical Society Quarterly* 57 (January 1973); 33–34, in which JBH appears, erroneously, as "James B. Harrison."

20. CEN to FLO, October 1882; FLO to CEN, March 14, 1883, Olmsted Papers, Library of Congress.

21. CEN to FLO, May 3, 1885, Olmsted Papers, Library of Congress.

22. Jonathan Baxter Harrison, *The Latest Studies on Indian Reservations* (Philadelphia, 1887). J. B. Harrison, "Education for Indians," *Critic* 11 (December 24, 1887): 321–22. J. B. Harrison, "A Typical Indian Removal," *Boston Evening Transcript* (December 17, 1887).

23. Jonathan Baxter Harrison, *Notes on Industrial Conditions* (Franklin Falls, N.H., 1886). Fein, *Olmsted and the American Environmental Tradition*, p. 51.

24. Reprinted in Frederick Law Olmsted, Jr., and Theodora Kimball, eds., *Frederick Law Olmsted: Landscape Architect, 1822–1903* (New York, 1928), pp. 362–75.

25. *Atlantic Monthly* 6 (November 1860): 636.

26. L. L. Bernard and Jessie Bernard, *Origins of American Sociology: The Social Science Movement in the United States* (New York, 1965), p. 544. Albert Fein, *Landscape into Cityscape: Frederick Law Olmsted's Plan for a Greater New York City* (Ithaca, N.Y., 1968), p. 169.

27. FLO to CEN, March 14, 1883, Olmsted Papers, Library of Congress.

28. JBH to CEN, January 31, 1866, Norton Papers, Harvard University.

29. JBH to CEN, January 16, 1880, Norton Papers, Harvard University.

30. JBH to CEN, August 11, 1878, Norton Papers, Harvard University.

31. Ibid.

32. FLO to CEN, September 19, 1878, Norton Papers, Harvard University.

33. JBH to CEN, September 25, 1878, Norton Papers, Harvard University.

34. *New-York Daily Tribune* (August 17, 1881). JBH to CEN, November 11, 1881, Norton Papers, Harvard University.

35. In a letter to Howells expressing sorrow that he was leaving the *Atlantic*, Harrison wrote: "If it had not been for you, I had not been—as a 'man of letters'! Mr. Norton begot in me the purpose to write and you smiled on the birth that followed." JBH to William Dean Howells, Howells Papers, Harvard University.

36. FLO to CEN, March 14, 1883, JBH to FLO, March 10, 1883; CEN to FLO, March 15, 1883, Olmsted Papers, Library of Congress.

37. FLO to CEN, November 11, 1881, Norton Papers, Harvard University.

38. "Glimpses of a New Dixie," *New-York Daily Tribune* (August 17, 1881): 4.

39. Ibid.

40. "Studies in the South," *Atlantic Monthly* 69 (July 1882): 100.

41. Ibid. (September 1882): 359; (June 1882): 747–50; (August 1882): 197–98; (December 1882): 754. FLO to CEN, November 11, 1881, Norton Papers, Harvard University.

42. Paul H. Buck, *The Road to Reunion, 1865–1900* (Boston, 1937), pp. 130–33.

43. Thomas D. Clark, "The New South, 1880–1900," in Thomas D. Clark, ed., *Travels in the New South: A Bibliography* (Norman, Okla., 1962), 1: 135.

44. Bernard and Bernard, *Origins of American Sociology*, pp. 605–606.

45. *A Journey Through Texas* (New York, 1860), p. xii. *A Journey in the Seaboard Slave States, with Remarks on Their Economy* (New York, 1904), 1: 96. *A Journey in the Back Country in the Winter of 1853–54* (New York, 1863), p. v.

46. "Studies in the South," *Atlantic Monthly* 69 (February 1882): 195.

47. Mitchell, *Olmsted: Critic of the Old South*, p. 91. "Studies in the South," *Atlantic Monthly* 50 (August 1882): 198.

48. Ibid.

49. *Back Country*, p. ix.

50. *Seaboard Slave States*, 2: 76.

51. Ibid., 1: 331. *Back Country*, p. ix.

52. "Studies in the South," *Atlantic Monthly* 50 (September 1882): 352.

53. Ibid.

54. Bernard and Bernard, *Origins of American Sociology*, p. 544. Dana F. White, "The Self-Conscious City: A Survey and Bibliographical Summary of Periodical Literature on American Urban Themes, 1865–1900," Ph.D. dissertation, George Washington University, 1969, p. 430.

55. *Seaboard Slave States*, 2: 175–76. *Back Country*, 99–103.

56. "Studies in the South," *Atlantic Monthly* 49 (January 1882): 79–82. Ibid. (February 1882): 182–85.

57. Ibid. (July 1882): 106.

58. *Back Country*, pp. 223–25, 374–75.

59. "Studies in the South," *Atlantic Monthly* 49 (June 1882): 744.

60. Ibid., p. 742. Ibid. (May 1882): 680.

61. *Seaboard Slave States*, 2: 279.

62. "Studies in the South," *Atlantic Monthly* 49 (May 1882): 675.

63. Ibid., p. 674. *Back Country*, p. 394.

64. *Seaboard Slave States*, 1: 240.

65. "Studies in the South," *Atlantic Monthly* 50 (November 1882): 633.

66. Ibid.

67. Ibid. (October 1882): 476.

PART TWO

New South

Dana F. White

". . . THE OLD SOUTH UNDER NEW CONDITIONS"

During the 1880s, more than thirty years after his first travels through the Cotton Kingdom, Frederick Law Olmsted once again turned south. In that long interval, professional commissions had taken him only to the borders of the Upper South: to Washington, D.C., in 1866 to lay out the campus for Gallaudet College, in 1874 to relandscape the grounds of the United States Capitol and, at different times throughout the 1880s and early 1890s, to undertake various federal commissions; and to Baltimore, Maryland, during the mid-1870s for the landscaping of the Johns Hopkins University campus. Earlier still, in the opening years of the Civil War (1861–1863), Olmsted, as secretary general of the United States Sanitary Commission, had maintained offices in the Union capital. From this post, in 1862, he had joined McClellan's Army of the Potomac in the field, to serve aboard the hospital ship *Daniel Webster* throughout those months of carnage officially designated the "Peninsular Campaign." Still, despite the historical significance of many of his Southern activities between the late 1850s and the mid-1880s, 1888 should be marked as the year of Olmsted's return south.

The Biltmore Estate—the more than 100,000-acre Vanderbilt barony near Asheville, North Carolina—became the focus for Olmsted's professional activities in the South from 1888 until his forced retirement in 1895. From Biltmore, he undertook commissions across the Upper South: in Baltimore, once again in 1889, to lay out the subdivision of Sudbrook Park in that city's northwestern suburbs; in Louisville, Kentucky, at various times between 1891 and 1893, to organize the park system and to landscape Boone Square, Logan Place, and Kenton Place; and in Kansas City, Missouri, in 1893, to consult on that city's proposed park-boulevard system. He also ventured farther south into the old Confederacy: to Montgomery, Alabama, in 1889, to outline the concept of a plan for relandscaping the State Capital grounds (Figure 10); to Hot Springs, Arkansas, in the early 1890s, to consult on the establishment of a United States military reservation there; and to Atlanta, Georgia, between 1890

STATE CAPITOL OF ALABAMA.

10. *View of the state capitol at Montgomery, Alabama, in 1858. FLO first visited this "fine and promising town" in August 1853 (Journey in the Seaboard Slave States, p. 574); more than thirty-five years later, he was to prepare the concept of a plan for the relandscaping of the Capitol grounds in 1889. It was never enacted by the state.*

and 1894, as a consultant to the Kirkwood Land Company and, for a time, to the Exposition Company, charged with the planning of the Cotton States and International Exposition of 1895.[1] Once again, then, Olmsted was to travel the American South, but this time with a difference. This time, although he maintained the firm's main office in Brookline and added another in Chicago during the planning stages for the World's Columbian Exposition, he was to work out of the South—no sometime traveler through it—with Biltmore as home base.

Olmsted's work at Biltmore was the focus of his postwar activities in the South. It promised to be a professional and aesthetic triumph, equal to—if not actually surpassing—his other major projects of the period: the design of the Stanford University campus (1886–1889) and the site plan for the World's Columbian Exposition at Chicago (1890–1893). Biltmore was also an experiment in resource management. Although, as Olmsted's biographer has cautioned, it might be judged "in the form it eventually took, . . . a callous anomaly; it was a regal estate, with French Renaissance chateau, gardens, amd dependencies, set down in a mountainous region of rural America, and of poor rural America at that. . . . Yet it was more than a stately pleasure dome." The estate was "a product of Olmsted's double-edged genius, [for] it justified itself artistically as a superb piece of landscape design and socially as the first large experiment in America in practical forestry."[2] "It was unique in America as a large-scale demonstration of economical forest management; he [FLO] intended to start the first national school of forestry on it; [and] the arboretum, for which more thousands of species and varieties had been collected than were shown even at Kew, was to be an experiment station and dendrological museum of large practical and scientific interest."[3] In sum, it was envisioned as becoming the embodiment of many of the concepts set forth in *Observations on the Treatment of Public Plantations* by Jonathan Baxter Harrison and Olmsted, published during the early (1889) part of Olmsted's tenure at the Estate. But even more than a demonstration of forest management, Biltmore represented an essay in regional planning. It seemed to offer an opportunity to reorder, almost recreate, an environment: to develop and harvest its natural resources; to lay out its transportation lines; to plan its towns and villages; and to establish mechanisms for promoting social betterment and control.[4] The Estate, then, would introduce "Civilization" into a "frontier condition" and mark, thereby, another step forward in the progress of "History."[5] Last and certainly not least significant, Biltmore was Olmsted's final great enthusiasm. His consummate work, it monopolized his time, inspired his love, and even determined what other projects he might undertake. Fortunately for the city of Atlanta, its proximity to Asheville persuaded the founder of landscape architecture in America to venture even farther south and to inspire still another *Olmsted city.*

During the early 1890s, Atlanta was becoming for its region what Chicago was becoming for the nation and what, fifty years before, Manchester had become for the industrializing world—a "shock city."[6] That is, each for its own time and culture seemed to embody both a promise *and* a threat: in England's first industrial city, a breakthrough into a new economic age *and* the potential for open class warfare; in the giant metropolis of the Midwest, a new "melting-pot" urbanity *and* a "foreign city" set down in the nation's "heartland"; in the Gate City to the South, the modernization of an anachronistic, semifeudal economy *and* the legitimation of a rigidly ordered racial distance. And in the Atlanta for which Olmsted was to plan, both promise and threat were articulated in a "New South creed."[7]

"The recognized apostle of the new faith," Henry W. Grady, promoted region and city as one.[8] His Atlanta—a " 'giant young metropolis,' " " 'a town of giants,' " " 'a creation of the day before yesterday' "[9] this "city from the ashes" with its motto of "Atlanta *Resurgens*"—seemed the very embodiment of a New South (Figures 11 & 12). It was perhaps never more so than on the evening of December 21, 1886, when, in his famous speech before the New England Society of New York, Grady won the title of " 'pacificator' " between North and South.[10] Turning then to the guest of honor, Grady assured General William Tecumseh Sherman that he was "considered an able man in our parts, though some people think he is a kind of careless man about fire" and that, more seriously, "from the ashes he left us in 1864 we have raised a brave and beautiful city; that somehow or other we have caught the sunshine in the bricks and mortar of our homes, and have builded therein not one ignoble prejudice or memory."[11] "I shall often use Atlanta as an example," Grady explained on another occasion to his Northern audiences, "for it is a typical Southern city. None is generally thought to be so largely the result of Northern capital and enterprise, . . . [and] this is the city that is oftenest cited as a 'Northern city in the South.' " Nonetheless, both Atlanta and the New South that it seemed to epitomize had been rebuilt, Grady proclaimed, "by Southern brains and energy."[12]

The people of Atlanta in 1864 crept out of the diagonal holes cut, like swallows' nests, in the hillsides, in which they had abided the siege, to find their city in ruins. Old citizens could scarcely thread the course of familiar streets through ashes and debris. . . . Strenuous as life had been in the South for four years, its most desperate struggle had but begun. . . . From defeat and utter poverty were to be wrought victory and plenty. There was no faltering—no repining—but Atlanta worked as she had fought, for all that was in her. . . . In 1866, there were but four men in Atlanta worth $10,000. In 1889, there are six millionaires whose wealth aggregates $10,000,000; nine others assessed at more than $750,000 each; fourteen others worth over $500,000 each; and twenty-one worth from $250,000 to $500,000 each. These fifty citizens, now worth over $30,000,000 were not worth $250,000 in 1865. Back of them is a prosperous city filled with well-to-do people and capital of a prosperous state.[13]

Unquestionably, such Atlantans merited the highest accolade that a New South spokesman could suggest to New Yorkers gathered together in the New England Society: that of "Georgia Yankees."[14]

11. Atlanta's central business district, c. 1895. The view is of Marietta Street looking west from Five Points—the major node of twentieth-century Atlanta—toward the Henry W. Grady statue, which can be seen in the background (left-center).

12. Bird's-eye view of Atlanta to the west, looking away from the central business district, c. 1895. Buildings on the campus of Atlanta University—occupied since the 1930s by Morris Brown College—can be seen on the horizon (center).

As Paul H. Buck has confirmed, Henry Grady's Atlanta was clearly the "most energetic and alert of the new cities" in the postwar South. "Favorably situated and admirably served by a network of railways, the Georgia capital forged ahead as the chief distributing center of the Southeast." To most contemporary observers, Buck tells us, "there seemed little of the Old South about it. Many described it as a Southern Chicago. But the model city which all Atlantans hoped to pattern after was New York." The ever-present boosterish "spirit of Atlanta," incarnate in her all-time champion tub-thumper Henry Woodfin Grady, could be satisfied with nothing less. Yet, as Buck has also cautioned, "If Atlanta epitomized the spirit of the New South, it was still, in spite of its proud pretense at being a metropolis, like Chattanooga and Birmingham, little more than an overgrown town." That is, it was an overgrown town at a stage of development approximating that of Boston or New York a half century earlier; an urban organism that was beginning to grow and spread and reach out into the countryside around it; a municipality without pattern or plan.[15] Atlanta was at that stage in her development when Olmsted's influence might prove most beneficial. As Grady boasted, "The time will come when there will be an amendment to the shibboleth 'Westward the star of empire hold its sway.'"[16] For the Olmsted firm, that time had come: with the southeastern United States *the* new planning frontier and Atlanta, the capital of the New South, its focal point.

The essays in Part Two document what Olmsted was able to accomplish *and* what he failed to achieve in the Gate City through his own efforts, those of his firm, and the weight of an established tradition of landscape architecture, to which he himself had contributed immeasurably. They detail the record—archival and material—of Olmsted's, his firm's and his profession's influence upon the development of Atlanta's suburbs, parks, and parkways from the 1880s into the 1910s, with some glimpses into the very recent past. These studies offer the first full documentation of the second reshaping of Atlanta: the first, after Sherman, of the old inner city; this next, with the Olmsteds, of its outlying suburbs. Here, then, is the story of the suburbanizing of Henry Grady's "Georgia Yankees," the shaping of their "overgrown town" into a new metropolis, and their search for environment.

Here, also, are intimations of the second major doctrine propounded in the New South Creed. This tenet, it must be stressed, is equal in importance to the initial call for the modernization of the Southern economy: namely, the establishment and legitimation of a fixed and rigidly ordered color line. As the Prophet of the New South interpreted this proposition, it demanded "that the whites and blacks must walk in separate paths in the South. As near as may be, these paths should be made equal—but separate they must be now and always."[17] Although there were "fanatics and doctrinaires" who held that such separation constituted discrimination and "that discrimination is offensive," Grady denied that this was the case.[18] This policy of "equal—but separate" had been initiated, Grady argued, by "resolute, clear-headed, broad-minded men of the South—. . . whose energy has made bricks without straw and spread splendor amid the ashes of their war-wasted homes"; "men of common sense and common honesty—wisely modifying an environment they cannot wholly disregard—guiding and controlling as best they can the vicious and irresponsible of either race. . . . and conscious all the time that wrong means ruin."[19] And "ruin" meant any threat to the "clear and unmistakable domination of the white race." As Grady and his contemporaries would have it, "the supremacy of the white race of the South must be maintained forever, and the domination of the negro race resisted at all points and at all hazards—because the white race is the superior race. This is the declaration of no new truth. It has abided forever in the marrow of our bones, and shall run forever with the blood that feeds Anglo-Saxon hearts." Indeed, it was "no new truth," for Frederick Law Olmsted had heard it propounded thirty years before, during his travels in the Cotton Kingdom. What is more, he was equally familiar with biblical injunctions on this issue. "The races and tribes of earth," ran Henry W. Grady's version of the same, "are of Divine origin. . . . What God hath separated let no man join together."[20]

Olmsted's return south was prompted largely by his "desire to get a footing at the South" and to "make the firm favorably known at the South and 'extend its connections' as the merchants say."[21] Despite the urgings of his friends and associates—as has been demonstrated in the first half of the present study—he never did "review" or "re-create" his early travel writings to produce some sort of "Cotton Kingdom Revisited." Still, he did find the time to answer one prominent Southerner's question as to "how I look upon the after troubles of slavery."[22] Parts of Olmsted's answer to Thomas H. Clark's query would certainly have pleased New South boosters. "The negroes have been doing a great deal better as freedmen than I had ever imagined it possible that they would," Olmsted confessed. "The whites have accepted the situation about as well as it was in human nature that they should, and we have been advancing toward prosperity and in prosperity under the new state of things at the South amazingly more than I had thought would be possible in so short a time after so great a catastrophe."[23] At the same time, he was firm in his conviction that it was "now as one of the fixed conditions of the country, as surely fixed, for all practical purposes, as its geological conditions, that our people of African blood are to stand on the same political footing as citizens of any other blood."[24] His tone throughout this letter to Clark was conciliatory but firm.

I would not have you think that there is not yet a good deal of jealousy and anxiety and a sense of antagonism among people here growing out of the conviction that the whites of the South are not "playing fair" about the negroes at elections, but I am inclined to believe that while most of us deplore the state of things in this respect, we think that it was, for a time, in a large degree, inevitable. We are only anxious to have the more intelligent people of the South show a disposition and purpose to struggle out of it as fast as possible.[25]

Whether it was as clear to Olmsted then as it is to us today that the New South propagandists were moving in the opposite direction cannot be determined. And one can only guess as to whether, eventually, the elderly and increasingly infirm landscape architect of the 1890s might have become as "radicalized" as did the youthful "Yeoman" of the 1850s. But if Frederick Law Olmsted had experienced the sharpening of the "color line" at the close of the century, and if he had heard Booker T. Washington pronounce his "Atlanta Compromise" at the Cotton States and International Exposition of 1895, he might well have agreed with Henry Grady that "The new South is simply the old South under new conditions."[26]

NOTES

1. This listing is based upon currently available sources. Within the next few years, as the Olmsted Papers at the Library of Congress and, hopefully, the firm's records at Brookline are processed and released, it is likely that this list will be expanded.

2. Laura Wood Roper, *FLO: A Biography of Frederick Law Olmsted* (Baltimore, 1973), pp. 414–15.

3. Ibid., p. 455.

4. The immense gap between Olmsted's initial expectations for the estate and his actual achievement there is the subject of the concluding chapter of this book, Frederick Gutheim's "Olmsted at Biltmore."

5. An excellent statement of Olmsted's *Weltanschauung* is found in his *Public Parks and the Enlargement of Towns* (Read before the American Social Science Association, Boston: February 25, 1870; Cambridge, Mass., 1870). For a thoughtful and concise explication of the same, see Victoria Post Ranney, *Olmsted in Chicago* (Chicago, 1972), pp. 9–11.

6. Asa Briggs, who coined the term, also includes Los Angeles as the shock city for the first stage of the automotive age in *Victorian Cities* (London, 1963), p. 108. For the 1970s, Houston, undoubtedly, would earn the title.

7. Paul M. Gaston, *The New South Creed: A Study in Southern Mythmaking* (New York, 1970); C. Vann Woodward, *Origins of the New South, 1877–1913* (Baton Rouge, La., 1951).

8. Paul H. Buck, *The Road to Reunion, 1865–1900* (Boston, 1937), p. 194.

9. Quoted in Mills Lane, "Introduction: The New South in Georgia," *The New South: Writings and Speeches of Henry Grady* (Savannah, 1971), pp. ix–x.

10. Gaston, *The New South Creed*, p. 90.

11. *The New South*, pp. 7–8.

12. Ibid., pp. 119–20.

13. Ibid., pp. 114–15. Grady's statistics ought to be judged in the same light as his claims and predictions for city and region—i.e., not so much as statements of fact, but as advertising claims.

14. Ibid., p. 8.

15. Buck, *The Road To Reunion*, pp. 185–86. The fifty-year lag between the development of Northern and Southern cities was spelled out first in T. Lynn Smith's classic essay, "The Emergence of Cities," pp. 24–37, in Rupert B. Vance and Nicholas J. Demerath, eds., *The Urban South* (Chapel Hill, N.C., 1954). Its application here to Atlanta is intended to be more figurative than literal. For this author's perspective on Atlanta's historical development, see Dana F. White and Timothy J. Crimmins, "Urban Structure, Atlanta," *Journal of Urban History* 2 (February 1976): 231–52.

16. *Atlanta Constitution*, August 20, 1884; quoted in Gaston, *The New South Creed*, p. 43.

17. The development of these "separate paths" in Henry Grady's own Atlanta is examined in Dan Durett and Dana F. White, *An-Other Atlanta: The Black Heritage* (Atlanta, 1975), especially pp. 3–5.

18. *The New South*, p. 141.

19. Ibid., pp. 92–93.

20. Ibid., pp. 19–21.

21. Frederick Law Olmsted to John C. Olmsted, March 13, 1894.

22. Thomas H. Clark, "Frederick Law Olmsted on the South, 1889," *South Atlantic Quarterly* 3 (January 1904): p. 13.

23. Ibid., p. 15.

24. Ibid., p. 14.

25. Ibid., p. 15.

26. *The New South*, p. 107.

Elizabeth A. Lyon

FREDERICK LAW OLMSTED AND JOEL HURT:
Planning for Atlanta

I want the firm to have an established "good will" at the South. Then, as we would all be called abolitionists at the South, I think a demonstration that the time has passed in which hatred of abolitionists is an element of consequence in matters of professional business is of some value. . . . With reference to your future business it is very desireable to make the firm favorably known at the South and "extend its connections" as the merchants say.[1]

It was on the eve of one of several visits to Atlanta in the early 1890s that Frederick Law Olmsted expressed this concern for the future business of his landscape architecture firm. Believing that all Northern cities would soon be provided with parks, he was looking for new design opportunities when he arrived in Atlanta in March 1894. He came to meet with the directors of the Cotton States and International Exposition to convince them that Olmsted, Olmsted, and Eliot should design the grounds for their fair. During this visit, he was successful in selling his services to the directors, but ultimately, because of their delay in honoring a preliminary agreement, he found it necessary to give up this project. Although his initial offer was withdrawn, the advice he offered during his visit may have influenced some elements of the Exposition plans. In another Atlanta project, however, the influence of this extraordinary man, who had designed so many parks and residential areas for other American cities, was more direct. He prepared a preliminary plan in 1893 for the suburban area northeast of the city which later became Druid Hills, and he made several trips to the city in the early 1890s for consultation on this residential development. In both park and suburb, his landscape concepts, which have given the two areas their distinct shape, were realized through the work of his sons, the Olmsted Brothers. In 1905, these men drew the final plans for a major portion of the Druid Hills subdivision. They also provided a plan of improvement in 1910 for the Cotton States

Exposition grounds, which had been purchased in 1904 by the city for what was to become the present Piedmont Park.

The senior Olmsted's interest in Atlanta, stimulated in part by his concern for his sons' future business, was encouraged and promoted by a local entrepreneur, Joel Hurt, the original developer of Druid Hills. Hurt shared some of the landscape architect's ideas about the urban environment. He was familiar with Olmsted's work in other cities, sought his help with the early plans for Druid Hills, and urged his participation in planning the Cotton States Exposition. By 1890, when Hurt first invited Olmsted to Atlanta, he already enjoyed an established reputation as a successful businessman and developer. He had lived in the city for fifteen years, having come there in 1875 with a degree in civil engineering from Franklin College (now the University of Georgia) and four years of experience as a railroad surveyor. From an initial and brief partnership with another civil engineer, he had organized a series of successful businesses that were predominantly involved with the physical development of the rapidly growing city. In 1887, with the founding of the East Atlanta Land Company, he began implementation of a coordinated development scheme.[2] With this company he developed Atlanta's first planned residential suburb, engineered and built the city's first electric street railway, and constructed at the town end of his railway line the South's first skyscraper, the Equitable Building. (Plans for this building were prepared by Georgia-born John Wellborn Root of the Chicago firm, Burnham and Root.[3]) These interrelated projects were well under way when Hurt first began negotiations with the senior Olmsted on Druid Hills. During this period he also bought, consolidated, and converted to electric power almost all of the street railroads in the city, organized the Trust Company of Georgia, managed the Georgia Iron and Coal Company, and served a term as president of the American Street Railway Association.[4]

Clearly, Joel Hurt was not only a successful businessman, but also an important developer who brought to Atlanta some of the most advanced technological innovations and urban land-use ideas of the time. While exact details on most of Hurt's forays outside of Atlanta in search of information, skills, and financial support are not available, it is known that he frequently traveled to other sections of the country. Several visits to Boston are recorded in the Olmsted files and another visit is reported in a local newspaper.[5] That he went to Chicago to consult with Burnham and Root on the construction of the Equitable Building is also recorded. Hurt may have met Frederick Law Olmsted in Chicago, since the landscape architect was often there during this period, working on the grounds for the World's Columbian Exposition, for which Daniel H. Burnham was chief of construction. Whether or not it was Burnham who first suggested that Hurt employ Olmsted is not certain, but it is recorded that he advised Hurt to hire the landscape architect's firm on an annual basis to guide the development of Druid Hills.[6]

Hurt's career resembles Olmsted's in many ways. Hurt pursued a similarly varied list of vocational interests, informed himself in a pragmatic manner on diverse topics, and shared an abiding interest in late nineteenth-century technology. His scrapbook reveals the diversity of his interests: articles appear on such subjects as electric generators, streetcar building methods, health and disease problems, and sewerage systems.[7] His library included such volumes as the *Cyclopedia of American Horticulture*, voluminous nurseryman's catalogues, numerous encyclopedia sets, art and travel books, and histories of Georgia.[8] Unlike Olmsted, Hurt was a college graduate, but both men were civil engineers who developed an enthusiasm for landscape design and a concern for a healthful environment. During all the long years of planning for the Druid Hills subdivision, Hurt studied botany and kept a nursery of plants and trees on the company property. Many specimens were gathered on his travels: creeping cedars from North Georgia, white holly seeds picked up in the Okefenokee swamp, and barberry seeds gathered on the Boston Common.[9] In one of his earliest letters to Olmsted, Hurt described in detail two sample branches taken from Georgia trees which he had sent to the landscape architect for identification.[10] When he later sold the Druid Hills property, Hurt required that he be allowed to select samples of each variety of shrub and tree and remove them from the nursery.[11]

Hurt's intense curiosity was supported by energy and bold vision. His enterprising nature was the subject of numerous newspaper articles which described his office habits, powers of organization, spartan living habits, and long working hours. Writers commented on his methodical manner of thinking, meticulous way of working, and careful supervision of all of his projects. Even at an advanced age, when his second skyscraper, the Hurt Building, was under construction, he was seen climbing the steel skeleton, checking the plumb lines to be sure they were true.[12] Observers ascribed his direct approach in problem-solving to his engineering background, but his directness often created enemies.[13] For example, it was asserted that he was successful in consolidating Atlanta's street railroads and saving them from receivership in 1893–1894 because of "the Napoleonic manner in which he surmounted opposition from numerous sources and the unusual number of overpowering obstacles."[14] He was roundly criticized for pulling up company streetcar tracks where he would have been compelled by a new ordinance to pave the streets.[15] His determination is further evident in instances such as his refusal to divert the straight-line route of Edgewood Avenue and his rejection of an offer to finance an office building only half as large as the one he planned. In the first instance, he persuaded the city council to condemn property along the route which property owners had refused to sell, and in the second, he insisted on a conference with the president of the Equitable Company and convinced him to finance his complete plans.[16] He was an extremely self-confident man who investigated his projects until he was convinced he was right and then went ahead, whatever the opposition. He encountered opposition not only because of his determined tactics but also because—like Olmsted—he was able to see the trends of future changes and developments. Further, he believed he had a key role to play in those developments. He seems to have thrived on the challenge of new and, to the general public, impossible projects. He initiated a variety of businesses and projects, but then often tried to resign from them once they were launched. Apparently, the excitement lay in the challenge of a seemingly insurmountable task, not in the daily routine. "He has a passion for developing great enterprises," a local newspaper reported, "and will never be content to jog along with one after it is fairly established and running smoothly."[17] This attitude would affect his work in Druid Hills. Hurt ultimately gave up the development of this property, but throughout the early 1890s his enthusiasm for building the "ideal residential suburb" remained strong.

Hurt's hopes for Druid Hills and his other projects were supported by the remarkable growth of the city itself. Atlanta's rapid recovery from the ravages of the Civil War and its emerging importance as a railroad center were factors which had attracted him there in 1875. The first postwar federal census of 1870 had shown a population of 21,789. By 1880, it had increased to 37,409, and in 1890, stood at 65,533. Although Atlanta was not large when compared with older cities in the North, its rate of growth had far outstripped that of older established cities in the South and compared favorably with similar, newer Southern cities (Table 1).

The business atmosphere was vigorous and had been stimulated by the activities of several "New South" promoters. Among these was Henry Grady, flamboyant editor of the *Atlanta Constitution*, who promoted Atlanta as the hub of a New South. Through a series of expositions in the 1880s and 1890s, Grady and other Atlanta boosters sought to increase the city's economic activity. The Cotton States and International Exposition of 1895, the largest and most ambitious of these fairs, emphasized the trade and transportation potential of Atlanta and presented the city as the ideal distribution center for the southeastern region.[18]

By 1890, when Frederick Law Olmsted arrived in Atlanta for his first visit, signs of expansive activity would have been evident everywhere (Figures 11 and 12). The Union Depot, where his train arrived, stood astride a wide swath of railroad tracks in the center of the city. Between this iron shed and his hotel, the Kimball House, was Wall Street with the noise and confusion of hacks and carriages clattering over its granite block

Table 1
POPULATION OF SELECTED SOUTHERN CITIES

New Cities:

Year	ATLANTA Population	% Growth	BIRMINGHAM Population	% Growth	CHATTANOOGA Population	% Growth	MEMPHIS Population	% Growth
1880	37,409	—	3,086	—	12,892	—	33,592	—
1890	65,533	75.2	26,178	748.3	29,100	125.7	64,495	92.0
1900	89,872	37.1	38,415	46.7	30,154	3.6	102,320	58.6
1910	154,839	72.3	132,685	245.4	44,604	47.9	131,105	28.1
1920	200,616	29.6	178,806	34.8	57,895	29.8	162,351	23.8

Established Cities:

Year	NEW ORLEANS Population	% Growth	SAVANNAH Population	% Growth	CHARLESTON Population	% Growth
1880	216,090	—	30,709	—	49,984	—
1890	242,039	12.0	43,189	40.6	54,955	9.9
1900	287,104	18.6	54,244	25.6	55,807	1.6
1910	339,075	18.1	65,064	19.9	58,833	5.4
1920	387,219	14.2	83,252	28.0	67,957	15.5

SOURCE: U.S. Census Reports, 1880–1920.

13. *Atlanta's "new" Kimball House, c. 1895, which was situated almost adjacent to the railroad depot in the heart of the city. When Olmsted first visited Atlanta, he stayed here.*

pavement. Not even one small plot of green space greeted the country's foremost landscape architect upon his arrival. The area adjacent to the depot in front of his hotel, which had served the postwar decade as a city park, was covered by a solid block of recently constructed business buildings. From his hotel window Olmsted could have seen the new State Capital, a Renaissance Revival structure which was the dominant landmark in the smokey atmosphere.[19] His journey from the hotel to the Druid Hills property, which lay beyond the city limits to the northeast, could have been made via Hurt's new electric street railway out to Inman Park on the edge of the city. From this point, the large tract of undeveloped land was accessible only by carriage out Williams Mill (Briarcliff) Road, along its western edge, and thence into the woods by horseback (Map 2). This area must have presented a sharp contrast to the congestion and activity of the central business and hotel district.

Olmsted's visit in 1890 was one of the first steps in the development of this suburban area which later became Druid Hills. Earlier in the year the Kirkwood Land Company, which was to begin the development of the area, was chartered. The group of Atlanta businessmen who signed the petition included a former mayor, James English, a future governor and senator, Hoke Smith, and a prominent banker, Robert J. Lowry, also the owner of a large holding in the area to be developed.[20] Lowry's property, 176¼ acres in Land Lot 242 of the Fifteenth District of DeKalb County, was transferred to the Kirkwood Land Company in July 1890. Two other major parcels of land in the area had already been purchased by the company, and in April 1892 another large tract of 430 acres was added. This addition brought the holdings of the Kirkwood Land Company to more than 1,400 acres.[21] Hurt originally intended to develop only 400 to 600 acres into lots of from 1 to 10 acres for suburban homes. He was gradually persuaded by the Olmsted firm to draw up a general plan for the entire tract before opening any land for development.[22]

Negotiations for this plan were begun not long after the Kirkwood Land Company was chartered, with letters exchanged between Hurt and the senior Olmsted during July 1890 for the purpose of arranging Olmsted's visit to Atlanta.[23] By the end of the year this had been accomplished, and early in 1891 Hurt went to Boston to confer with Olmsted and one of his partners, H. S. Codman.[24] These were the first in a series of visits and letters through which the initial plans for the Druid Hills suburb were developed. During 1891, progress was held up temporarily because of a dispute over a rail line which the Georgia, Carolina and Northern Railroad (Seaboard Airline) ran through the eastern edge of the Kirkwood Company lands. By April 1892, the matter was settled,[25] and during the following month Hurt visited Boston to discuss arrangements for employing Olmsted. Planning details such as land mapping, major thorough-

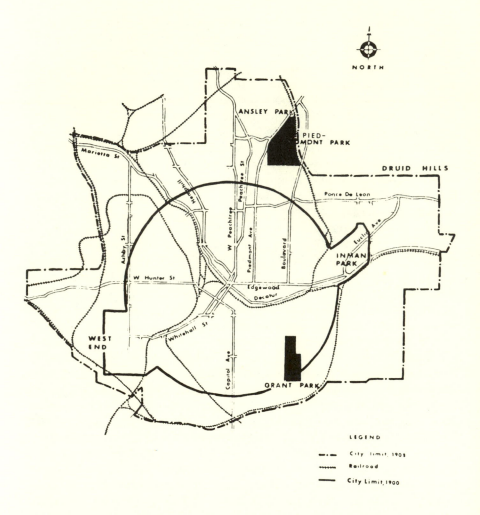

2. *Map of Atlanta, depicting the city limits and main arteries as they existed in 1900 and later in 1908, when a portion of Druid Hills was incorporated into the city.*

fares, and a street railway line were discussed with John C. Olmsted who talked with Hurt in his stepfather's absence. During this meeting, Hurt reported to the younger Olmsted that it was Daniel Burnham who had recommended that the senior Olmsted be employed on a yearly basis to guide the development of his property.[26] By June, Hurt had found a local engineer, Solon Z. Ruff, a graduate of the Engineering School of the University of Georgia, to begin work on the Kirkwood property.[27]

Early in 1893, Olmsted made a second visit to Atlanta. Partly as a result of his observations on this trip—which caused him some uneasines about the project—and also because of the poor health that plagued him while working on the Columbian Exposition grounds in Chicago, he sought to withdraw from the Druid Hills project. He was particularly worried about the possibility of disease in the lakes planned for the project.[28] But Hurt assured him that Atlanta, until it grew into a city of considerable size, had had no cases of malaria, that recent cases were brought in from outside the city, and that only a small minority of citizens were dissuaded from living in the suburbs because of a fear of malaria.[29] Still, Olmsted continued to worry about "fever and ague," and in February 1893, he wrote his stepson that if there should be disease in the area it "would make a great row and we should be held accountable for it."[30]

Persuaded not to drop the project (even though at about the same time he declined personal responsibility for all private work except at Biltmore) the senior Olmsted was once again in Atlanta in March 1893. By this time, a preliminary plan had been prepared and was being discussed.[31] On August 8, 1893, the Kirkwood Land Company was billed $1,358.26 for an unspecified number of trips to the city by Olmsted and for a general plan for subdivision of the company property into roads and building sites, according to agreements worked out in correspondence of June 24 and July 7, 1892.[32]

The exact details of this early plan are not available, but its general outlines are described in correspondence and are suggested by a real estate map published in the *Atlanta Constitution* in 1896.[33] The roadway and open space pattern shown on this map is remarkably similar to that finally carried out several years later from the Olmsted Brothers' plans. The wide and curving avenue mentioned in the correspondence, which later became Ponce de Leon Avenue, was a major feature of the newspaper drawing (Map 3). Hurt wrote Olmsted that he was worried about the expense of the curved driveway but agreed that it would "present a very handsome appearance."[34] Other features which would reappear in the later plan—such as bridges, dams, and lakes—were also discussed in the correspondence.

Letters and reports during 1893 and 1894 indicate that Hurt intended to proceed with the development immediately but was delayed by a series of problems. Olmsted again, and on short notice, appeared in Atlanta on November 20, 1893, to check on the progress of the development. Hurt was in Boston, but Olmsted went to the site with the company secretary and engineer, and asked for a meeting with the company's members. He reports that at this meeting he "made a fairly satisfactory report with a good deal of advice."[35] He found the company divided and financially depressed. "The hard times are on the Atlanta people," he wrote a few days later, "and they are doing nothing, but our visit was timely and

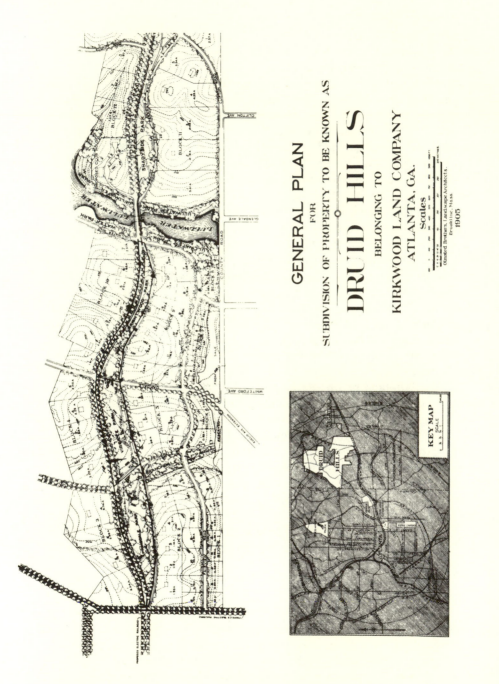

GENERAL PLAN

FOR

SUBDIVISION OF PROPERTY TO BE KNOWN AS

DRUID HILLS

BELONGING TO

KIRKWOOD LAND COMPANY

ATLANTA, GA.

Scales

Olmsted Brothers, Landscape Architects.
Brookline, Mass.

1905

KEY MAP
SCALE

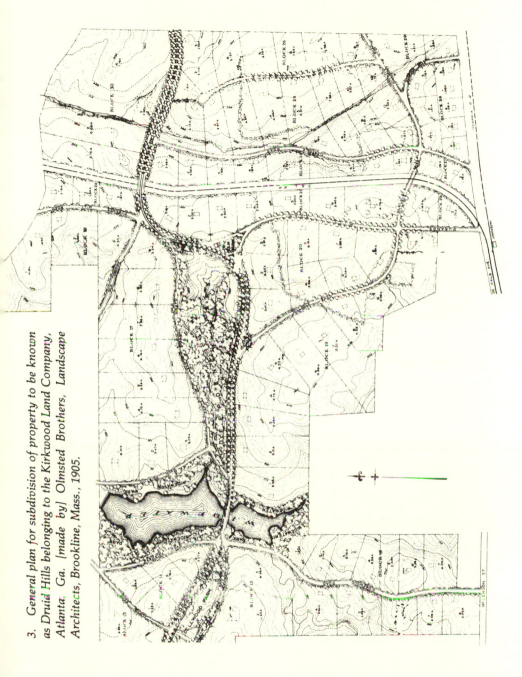

3. *General plan for subdivision of property to be known as Druid Hills belonging to the Kirkwood Land Company, Atlanta, Ga. [made by] Olmsted Brothers, Landscape Architects, Brookline, Mass., 1905.*

made a good impression, and I hope we are yet to make a success of this chance."[36] Thus far, no work had been done on the grounds, but early in 1894, Olmsted sent W. H. Manning of his firm to Atlanta to examine the land and woods, and to make recommendations concerning the choice of plants and their requirements for survival. Plans were made for Kirkwood to hire Henry Miller, a "foreman on the estate" (presumably "estate" meant Biltmore), and for Miller to collect a carload of evergreens in the mountains of North Carolina on his way to Atlanta. In addition, Olmsted was asked on March 17 to write a report on the adaptability of the Kirkwood property for its intended use, for the purpose of helping the company obtain a loan.[37]

Later that spring, however, Hurt was experiencing more trouble with the project. Letters which he wrote to the Olmsted firm reveal his anxiety. Certain stockholders were dissatisfied and suggested changes in the plan. Hurt assured the firm that he was standing behind Olmsted's design concept and that he would resign if it came to a showdown. On May 7, 1894, he reported that "the directors of the Kirkwood Land Company are considering the advisability" of doing the grading necessary to open the drives laid out by Olmsted through the property. Their intention at the time was to complete not only the streets, but the bridges, dams, and aqueduct for the lake as well.[38] Some work was begun, but little was completed.

One major reason for the delay is clear. In the general economic climate of the mid- to late 1890s which followed the paralyzing Panic of 1893, financing was not available. Several loans on the company holdings were made between 1896 and 1898. All of the major tracts of land that had been assembled were used to secure money. Loans were made on the former Kirkpatrick and Lowry lots in March 1896, on one of the Johnson parcels in March 1897, and on the other the following year. One of these loans was repaid in 1899 and another in 1901, but the third tract was still under lien in 1908 when the entire holdings were sold.[39] In August 1899, a Boston lawyer, William H. White, wrote to John C. Olmsted explaining that the Kirkwood Land Company was facing possible receivership because of outstanding claims against it, including one from the Olmsted Brothers. White explained that Hurt wondered whether the Brookline firm could accept half of the bill for services in addition to the money for disbursements, believing that he could, by assessment, get up this amount and save his company from a receiver.[40] In addition to financial problems within the Kirkwood Company, Hurt's other projects had consumed considerable time, energy, and money.[41] It was not until 1902, after funds from the sale of his electric street railway company allowed the repayment of an important loan, that Hurt was able once again to turn his attention to the Druid Hills plans. "He bought at 21 and sold at 75, so he is probably feeling flush," John C. Olmsted reported from Atlanta on this occasion.[42] In addition to repaying the loan, Hurt also bought out some of the stockholders and so tightened his control of the Kirkwood Company.

During the same period when Hurt experienced difficulties with the Kirkwood Land Company, changes were occurring within the Olmsted firm. Frederick Law Olmsted, Sr., who had already given up direct supervision of most of the firm's work, had become increasingly debilitated by illness. By 1895, he had retired, leaving direction of the firm's activities to his stepson, John C., and his son, Frederick Law, Jr. By 1896, he was permanently incapacitated and confined to a sanitorium. He died in 1903.

Thus, when Joel Hurt was again ready to pursue his dream of creating an "ideal residential suburb" in Atlanta, it was to John C. Olmsted that he turned. The younger Olmsted came to Atlanta in March 1902 for several days of consultation with Hurt and his engineer, Solon Z. Ruff. Long discussions in Hurt's Equitable Building office were followed by visits to the property. In the company of Hurt and Ruff, Olmsted toured the lands on foot and on horseback on March 7. The following day, because of rain, he was driven by carriage to Williams Mill (Briarcliff) Road, the western boundary of the property, and from there to the nursery by a small county road. There he found that some of the smaller stock collected several years earlier during the initial phases of planning had succumbed to neglect, but that a remarkable amount of this original material had survived. The reports he sent back to the Brookline firm suggest that the 1893 plan was still being used both as the basis for discussion and as a guide for grading the parkway.[43]

By November 1903, Hurt was making plans to sell lots. He told John Olmsted that otherwise the stockholders would not support any more development. Olmsted urged him not to sell land until utilities had been provided and the landscaping done. Hurt then asked for completion of the general plan, even though, as he explained, he would not have time to devote to Kirkwood because of other business problems. He went on to assure Olmsted, however, that he hoped he could soon get his affairs in order and push the Kirkwood matter.[44] The Olmsted Brothers proceeded to develop a plan which was presented two years later. (Hurt had asked the firm to suggest names for both the suburb and the streets and, after consultation with him, to put them on the plan.) Druid Hills, the name which has since become the common reference for a larger area of northeast Atlanta beyond the limits of the original plan, appears in the records for the first time on this plan[45] (Map 3).

The 1905 plan detailed the development of only the southernmost portion of the Kirkwood Company lands along Ponce de Leon Avenue and includes the parks and parkways which lie to either side of this thoroughfare. Subsequently, the entire Kirkwood Company acreage was developed into a residential neighborhood which in some features resembled the Olmsteds' plans, but in others was considerably changed. Ponce de Leon, which even today gives distinctiveness to the entire area, was structured according to the plans. This avenue, as H. L. Preston describes its development below, was conceived by Frederick Law Olmsted as a double parkway separated by park spaces.[46] The gently curving roads of the subdivision, which work well with the topography of the region, helped to create the natural and informal setting which Olmsted believed should be a feature of suburban living. These roadways also helped to form the chain of parks along the avenue and created, as well, a series of opening and closing vistas. Olmsted's goal, as he had demonstrated in previous park plans for Northern cities, was a hierarchy of park uses: medium-sized parks for rural relaxation and picnicking, smaller landscaped areas with ponds for water recreation, and linear parkland for pleasure drives.

The spirit of his plans still enlivens the area. Springdale Park has slides and swings for recreation; Shady Side Park is an elevated knoll with grassy slopes and clustered trees providing an open scenic vista which contrasts sharply with Deepdene Park a little further along the avenue—a densely forested, seemingly impenetrable depression. Olmsted had written earlier that one should strive to "form passages of scenery contrasting in depth of obscurity and picturesque character of detail with the softness and simplicity of the open landscape."[47] The Druid Hills setting was obviously designed to provide an environment which by its natural and uncluttered space would create a soothing, tranquil scene, one where, as an Atlanta newspaper said, "the repose of nature invites you to leave off toil and enter into rest."[48] The park image appealed to Atlantans. Indeed, numerous newspapers referred to the Druid Hills project as a residential park.

Water recreation for the residents of the park was to have been provided by lakes, one of forty and the other of sixty acres. A casino had been planned for one of these areas, and a golf course and club for the other. Two roads, Lullwater and Lakeshore, were to run along the lakes focusing on water and green space, in much the same way as the driveways and linear park spaces of Olmsted's earlier Riverside, Illinois. Joel Hurt and John C. Olmsted had discussed omitting one of the two planned lakes (the easterly one) because of costs and the number of trees which would have had to be destroyed.[49] As it was, neither lake was ever constructed. The area for East Lake was later subdivided for building sites; and the area planned for Lullwater Lake is today occupied by the Druid Hills golf course and a subdivision called Lullwater Parkway that was created in 1930.[50]

Despite such changes and omissions from the original design concepts, the physical setting of Druid Hills expresses Frederick Law Olmsted's idea of a residential community characterized by a natural appearance and rural attractiveness. It was said of homes in Druid Hills that they would supply "the demand for both a city home and a country residence. With its breezes and ozone laden parks, no one would think of leaving such a home for a trip to a summer retreat."[51] Such an atmosphere was deliberately created by shaping the environment to resemble a pastoral scene. One of Olmsted's outstanding design characteristics was his sensitivity to natural features. No matter how much earth had to be moved or how many new trees and shrubs planted, the intended effect was one of natural or unplanned, if gently tended, nature.[52] So it was with Druid Hills. The early descriptions point up such features as building sites on knolls that nestle into the natural contours of the land, over 250,000 shrubs "bordering the drives and roadways, arising in clumps and clusters on shaded and sodded knolls" a scene in which at first glance it appeared no work had been done because it looked so natural.[53]

In contrast to the picturesque and informal aesthetic of Olmsted's landscaping, the architectural styles of the homes which were built along the curving streets were traditional and formal. The tone was set by the first house built in 1909 at the entrance to the parkway on the northeast corner of Williams Mill Road and Ponce de Leon Avenue. This structure, built for Judge John Candler, was designed by the prominent Atlanta architect, G. L. Norrman, in a French Renaissance mode.[54] The dominant theme of the homes which followed was that of the Georgian Revival. The talented, young, Beaux Arts-trained Neel Reid, who had begun practice with Norrman and who, with his partner, Hal Hentz, would become one of the region's leading designers, established the Georgian mode in several of the early homes which still stand in Druid Hills.[55] There were some exceptions to this classical style—for example, Samuel H. Venable's Stone Mountain granite "Stonehenge" at the corner of Oakdale Road and Ponce de Leon, which has since been transformed into a church. There are also a number of Tudor, half-timbered houses. The earliest of these English houses is one which architect Walter T. Downing designed for himself on Oakdale Road. Another on this same street was designed by Reid.[56] The typical Druid Hills home, however, was a substantial, symetrically composed, block-shaped building with a small entrance portico of classically derived details. These forms were modified by the curving street pattern and landscape features that were carried out in the garden suburb tradition of Olmsted. Thus, the dominant visual impression that was established clearly reflects Frederick Law Olmsted's design concepts.

Between 1905 when the Olmsted Brother's plan was completed and

1907 when the development was announced to the public, the Kirkwood
Land Company graded the main thoroughfare of the subdivision, landscaped the parks along Ponce de Leon Avenue, and laid out the building
lots located in the western section of the area. By this time, nearly
seventeen years had passed since Frederick Law Olmsted's first visit to
the site in 1890; it had been six years since Joel Hurt gave up his interest in
Atlanta's street railway system and turned his attention once again to his
suburban development. Nevertheless, the glowing newspaper account
of 1907 made it clear that Atlantans were still impressed with the results of
the work. Romantically written passages described in detail the skillfully
wrought natural scene and praised Joel Hurt's role in developing this
"sylvan effect."[57] One year after this announcement, however, and in
spite of the long years of distraction and disappointment during which he
fought with stockholders to prevent changes in the plans and struggled to
keep the Kirkwood Land Company financially solvent, Hurt sold the
entire landholdings of the company. The largest real estate sale to that
date of May 1908 recorded in Atlanta—a half-million dollars—transferred
the Druid Hills property from the Kirkwood Land Company to a syndicate composed of Coca-Cola magnate Asa G. Candler, Georgia Railway
and Power Company executive Preston S. Arkwright, and realtors Forrest and George Adair. The new owners pledged themselves to proceed
immediately with "the plans originally suggested by Mr. Olmsted."
"Now that the opportunity is presented to turn the property over to
gentlemen who will carry out my plans and the designs of Mr. Olmsted,"
Hurt told a reporter, "I am willing to part with the property."[58] Privately,
he confided to John C. Olmsted several months later that although an
understanding about the plan had been part of the sale, he feared that
important restrictions would be modified or abandoned , so that "the
property will never be what we had hoped to make it."[59]

It appears that Hurt had sold his property despite his concern that the
plans created and developed over so many years might be altered. The
long delays in the execution of the plans and the press of his other
interests were the reasons he gave John C. Olmsted for his decision. What
role financial gain had played in this decision cannot be determined
because the necessary financial records have not been found. Real estate
values in Atlanta had been climbing rapidly in the early 1900s, but it is
clear from the newspaper reactions to the Druid Hills sale that a half-
million dollars was still considered a very large sum. The Kirkwood Land
Company had paid $209,537 for the land in the early 1890s, but the cost of
several loans had increased this initial outlay. Considerable sums must
have been spent for grading, landscaping, and surface drainage systems,
and a loan of $30,000 was still outstanding at the time of sale. Financial

problems may well have been the precipitating factor which made the sale palatable to Joel Hurt.

The syndicate which purchased the Kirkwood property was incorporated as the Druid Hills Corporation. It held its first stockholders' and directors' meeting on June 30, 1908, on Lot Number One at the northeast corner of Ponce de Leon Avenue and Williams Mill Road.[60] At this meeting, the directors authorized contracts for improvements such as street paving and water and sewer lines along Ponce de Leon Avenue as far east as Lullwater Road. By 1910, these improvements had been extended into the remainder of the western section of the 1905 plan between Williams Mill Road and the eastern limits of the property, and northward along the major roads to Decatur (North Decatur) Road. In 1913, an electric street railway was built along Ponce de Leon Avenue in a strip of land on the northern edge of the parks. In order to get the line into their property, the Druid Hills Corporation had advanced the money to the Georgia Railway and Power Company for an extension of its road from the city limits one-half mile to the west at the Southern Railroad crossing.[61]

Lot sales for the improved areas were also authorized between 1908 and 1910. Forrest and George Adair, the real estate agents who had engineered the Druid Hills sale and who also managed property for Joel Hurt, were named exclusive sales agents.[62] Prices for these first lots were recorded on a list which was apparently passed on to the new company from the Kirkwood Land Company. Lots containing from one and one-third to three acres cost from $4,000 to $12,000; penciled notations in the margins of the company's list of lot prices suggest a similar range for the actual sales.[63] By 1917, real estate sales had almost paid for the cost of improvements and a sizable number of homes had been built.[64] In addition, seventy-five acres of undeveloped land in the northeast corner of the property had been donated to the new Emory University.[65] In 1916, the streetcar line was extended to serve this area, and soon a land boom in the immediate vicinity of this institution stimulated the company to subdivide adjoining lands for development.[66] From the early 1920s, if Oakdale Road is typical, lots north of the Olmsted Brothers' 1905 plan area were plotted into smaller, though still generous-sized, lots and built upon largely by contractors who purchased large blocks of adjoining lots.[67] Following this, in 1924, the area west of Emory University, called Lullwater Subdivision, was subdivided into even smaller lots averaging seventy-five by one hundred feet in area. Many of these were also sold for speculative housing. A few lots adjacent to the university entrances were reserved for business, and soon a service station across from the main gate bore witness to land-use changes.[68] This later development scarcely reflected the original landscape plan of the Olmsteds, except that some of the streets in the new subdivisions were curved.

The original design concepts were thus modified, but some of the ideas about the attributes of a desirable residential community which were present in the Kirkwood Company's plans for the area were continued. Such recreational features as a golf course and country club, planned to attract an upper-middle-class clientele, were retained. The large lots which were laid out in much of the area, as John C. Olmsted had advised Hurt, protected the neighborhood against "the likelihood of poor purchasers."[69] The deed restrictions imposed by the Druid Hills Corporation, as Joel Hurt had feared, were not as extensive or detailed as those which John C. Olmsted had recommended in the early stages of the planning. Single-family occupancy, setbacks, and minimum housing costs were specified; lots were not to be subdivided, and no privies were allowed. But there were no detailed instructions about barnyard animals and servants' houses, such as John C. Olmsted had suggested. Neither was the proposed time span for restrictions followed. Olmsted had advised that at least forty, and preferably sixty, years of restricted use would be necessary in order to protect the exclusive character of the neighborhood.[70] The early deeds from the Druid Hills Corporation specified January 1, 1940, as the limit for restrictions,[71] and in the late 1940s new occupants, such as church congregations and fraternal groups, began to move into the large houses along Ponce de Leon Avenue. Nevertheless, the original section in the southern portion of the old Kirkwood Company tract retained its large lots, parks, and landscaped setting. This section set the tone, if not the details, for the continued development of much of the Druid Hills area, so that the neighborhood today still reflects the Olmsted influence.

A second Atlanta area, Piedmont Park, also bears the imprint of Frederick Law Olmsted's ideas. In this case, the shaping of the grounds for the 1895 fair was given some direction through an early consultation with the senior Olmsted. However, it was not until a plan of improvement for these grounds was submitted by his sons in 1909 that his landscape ideas found expression in the total layout of the park.

The area that is now the park was in use as the driving grounds and race track of the Gentlemen's Driving Club when it was chosen in 1894 as the site for the Cotton States and International Exposition (Map 2). It was not a very inviting place to Frederick Law Olmsted when he visited Atlanta on March 16 of that year and toured the grounds with Joel Hurt and H.E.W. Palmer, the director of the Exposition. Olmsted confided his unfavorable impression to his stepson by letter that very evening.[72] Nevertheless, he went to the site a second time the following day and

spent several hours there. He then made recommendations to a conference of officers and members of the Exposition board. He suggested that
one large exhibition building, placed on the only flat piece of ground (the
race track), would be better than a number of smaller ones, and that such
small buildings as would be built by other states and nations could be
positioned on knolls on either side of the large structure. He advised them
to employ Daniel H. Burnham as adviser on the buildings and urged
further that they make their Exposition a specialized one that would be
distinguished by a clearly defined purpose, for example, a display of the
resources of the South. Having a single focus, he thought, would more
effectively allow them to carry out their purpose than if they sought
simply to compete across the board with the record of the World's Fair at
Chicago. He discussed terms of engagement with them and agreed to
send a more formal draft of terms from his office.[73] For public edification,
Olmsted described the chosen property in glowing terms by claiming that
"it is a beautiful spot and is capable of being converted into splendid
exposition grounds."[74]

Privately, he confided to his stepson, John, that he did not think the site
a good one "from our landscape point of view," but he had been encouraged to keep any unfavorable impressions to himself. His objections were
based on the size (under two hundred acres) and the fact that there were
few trees. He wired John for information on their financial arrangement
for the Chicago fair as a guide for the discussions in Atlanta, assuring him
he was asking for these only as a clue, because the amount of money
available in Atlanta was in no way comparable to that for Chicago.
Nevertheless, he was intensely interested in this job. It would be the best
of the distinctly Southern expositions, he explained, and a more national
advertisement than Chicago. Moreover, it would surely lead to other
things. He further pointed out the advantages of this job which "clusters
in with Biltmore and the Hurt Atlanta affair."[75]

Later in the month, in time for a regular meeting of the Board of
Directors of the Exposition scheduled for March 29, Olmsted sent H. H.
Cabaniss, secretary of the board, a statement of terms under which the
firm would serve the company. The Exposition Company was to furnish a
suitable topographical map, so that the landscape architects could prepare a general plan for laying out the grounds. This plan, when approved, was to be carried out under the immediate direction of a superintendent who was satisfactory to the landscape architects and who would
work under their instruction. For their outlay for draughtsmen, travel,
and other expenses, the firm was to be reimbursed, and for their own
personal services in design and supervision, they would receive a fee of
$3,000 per annum from April 1, 1894, to the close of the Exposition.

Olmsted assured the company that the plan of rights and duties as outlined was similar in its principles to that adopted for the Columbian Exposition.[76]

Subsequently, Olmsted, Olmsted, and Eliot sent Cabaniss a request for a map of Atlanta and for the topographical map mentioned in the proposal of terms. The instructions for this map were explicit and lengthy, and they included requests for all manner of details on the topography and vegetation of the Exposition area. The firm also ordered a year's subscription to the two principal Atlanta newspapers, the *Journal* and the *Constitution*, and asked to be provided with a history of the planning of the Exposition. A separate letter of the same date discussed the position of superintendent. Olmsted had made a conditional arrangement with George A. Parker, who was in charge of the nursery for the Old Colony Railroad in Massachusetts, and suggested the Exposition Company pay him a salary of $2,000 ($200 above his present salary) as well as provide him with a house on the grounds. In a separate memorandum, Olmsted revealed that this same nurseryman was willing to quit his present post with the railroad because his wife had lately been killed by a locomotive at a nearby station; therefore, he was anxious to leave the area. In addition, in expectation that part of the labor force would be black, Olmsted noted that Parker had had experience with Negro labor in Maryland.[77]

Obviously, Olmsted was under the impression that the Exposition Company planned to hire his firm to do the grounds for the fair, and he was making preparations for a general plan of the grounds. Two months later, on May 15, the Olmsted firm wrote to acknowledge a letter of May 12 from the Director-General H.E.W. Palmer requesting a bill for the preliminary visit; the charge was $300.[78] Dated just two days later, a longer letter from the firm explains why Olmsted's name cannot be found in the official report of the Cotton States Exposition. This letter to Palmer began: "Please consider that when, at your suggestion, we offered our professional services for advancing the project of the Exposition, it was with the conviction that we could at once set about the work." Sufficient reason had been given for this understanding, Olmsted continued, and he had therefore begun the preliminary arrangements for carrying out the commission. However, "two full months have passed, . . . A full season in horticultural operations has been lost." The firm had no idea whether Parker was still available. Furthermore, they had not yet been informed whether any action had been taken on their offer or on any of their professional advice. Therefore, while they did not question the necessity of the delay, they could not assume the responsibility for the project, which otherwise they would have gladly accepted. "It is said," the official history of the Exposition reports, "that at the outset the directors sent for the most eminent landscape engineer in America and paid him a large fee

[$300?] to look at the ground and tell them what to do with it. When the report of that eminent gentleman had been received, it was filed but never adopted."[79]

When work on the Cotton States Exposition grounds finally began in July 1894, the plan that was used was drawn up by Grant Wilkins, a local engineer and builder who had been constructing bridges and public buildings in Atlanta since the 1870s.[80] The race track, which Frederick Law Olmsted had envisioned as the site for a large structure, was laid out as a formal space encircling a fountain. The main building was placed on a hill, which, it was said, commanded a view of the grounds, but which had to be cut down twenty-one feet to provide sufficient construction space. One feature of the plan which may reflect Olmsted's advice was the positioning of subsidiary buildings on knolls surrounding the central space. Another may have been the outlines of Lake Clara Meer, the body of water created in the eastern part of the grounds by damming a stream. (Without displaying much understanding of Olmsted's picturesque forms, the grading contractor for the fair declared that the edges of this lake would be "ragged and uneven enough to charm the eye of the spectator."[81]) Still another Olmsted suggestion may have influenced the parkway approaches to the fairgrounds.

The Exposition ran for exactly one hundred days, opening on September 18, 1895, and closing on December 31, 1895. In 1904, the city of Atlanta bought the 189 acres which had housed the Exposition for conversion into what would become Piedmont Park.[82] The following year, when the city's building inspector tendered a report, all the Exposition buildings were deteriorating, some were suitable only for demolition, and others were badly in need of repair. A fire in 1906 destroyed the Fine Arts Building and the New York State Building, which had been in use as a ballroom for the Piedmont Driving Club.[83]

The remainder of the buildings were apparently gone by 1909 when the Olmsted Brothers began preparing their comprehensive landscape plan for the park. Only the general outlines of the Exposition's landscaping and the stone stairways which had led to the buildings and the lake remained. The lake was apparently in danger of filling with mud, and the dam in need of repair. The plan which the Olmsted Brothers submitted early the following year took into account the remnants of the Cotton States plan by utilizing the handsome stone stairways as access and transition paths between different levels. The outlines of the lake were changed and reshaped to make them more graceful. Several features of his sons' plan implemented ideas often expressed by the senior Olmsted, both in his writings and in his park designs.[84] Provisions were made for formal gardens, which would contrast with informal elements arranged along meandering roadways; sections were planned for recreation, baseball, swings and slides, a beach and boathouse; and a five-mile driveway was created to focus on a series of changing views of the lake and landscape.[85] Although Frederick Law Olmsted's proposals for the Exposition grounds had been largely, and apparently deliberately, ignored, it is clear that his principles of park design were later reflected in his sons' plans for Piedmont Park.

While the senior Olmsted's design forms appeared in Atlanta's major park by 1910, his broader ideas about the potential role of parks in the urban environment did not gain wide acceptance. Public officials were reluctant to commit the funds necessary to provide open spaces and recreational areas for the growing city. The central area of the city, whose smoke and congestion had greeted Frederick Law Olmsted on his first arrival there in the early 1890s, was devoid of even one small green space until the 1940s when Plaza Park was built on a one-block square concrete platform over the tracks.[86] Throughout the 1890s and the early twentieth century, numerous grand ideas for parks and parkways that reflected Olmsted's influence were proposed. None was ever carried out.[87] Atlanta's promoters and publicists boasted of the city's many skyscrapers and talked much in the public press about the need for a "City Beautiful,"[88] but the rapidly expanding city was unable to obtain support for comprehensive planning ideas, such as Olmsted's.

On the other hand, elements of Olmsted's residential plans have become a part of Atlanta's garden-suburb image. Picturesque landscapes with irregularly arranged streets, wooded lots, and occasional park spaces are characteristic of many older Atlanta neighborhoods. For example, Hurt used such a scheme in Inman Park as well as Druid Hills[89] (Maps 2 and 4). Ansley Park, begun in 1904, was laid out along curving streets around numerous park spaces by Solon Z. Ruff, the engineer for Druid Hills. During this same period several other subdivisions were plotted around similarly curved street patterns. Many of these separate, individually developed subdivisions became pleasant residential areas. Yet, the privatism[90] which created once fine neighborhoods also contributed to their deterioration and, at the same time, prohibited large-scale, coordinated planning activities which might have prevented decay. Both Inman Park and Druid Hills have experienced periods of change or decline resulting in multifamily conversion of large, single-family residences; subdivision of spacious lots; and invasion by business activities and apartment houses.

The planning and development of Druid Hills demonstrate the strengths and weaknesses of such methods. The success of the subdivision as a living environment depended upon the developer's imagination and sensitivity, financial resources and business ability, as well as will-

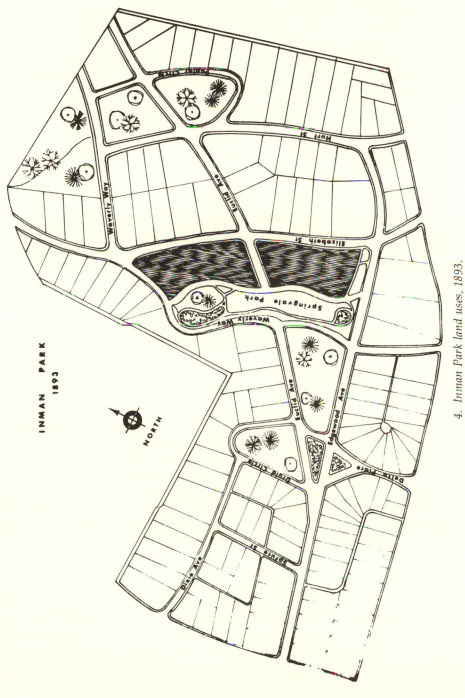

4. *Inman Park land uses, 1893.*

ingness to balance financial gain with the requirements of the planned ideal. Joel Hurt told John C. Olmsted that he had long hoped to build "the ideal residential suburb." To accomplish this goal, he had consulted the foremost landscape designer in the country and had struggled for more than fifteen years to overcome numerous obstacles to its development. That his strong will and self-confidence controlled the work was observed by John C. Olmsted when he wrote, "Although [Hurt] is not president, he is vice-president and chairman of the executive committee and practically runs the whole thing as if it were his own exclusively."[91] Yet, in spite of Hurt's personal goals and abilities, he gave up Druid Hills just as the development was getting under way. Regardless of his reasons for this action, it is evident that, while Hurt was in control of the Kirkwood Land Company, he worked to carry out a consciously designed plan for a particular kind of residential area. After the sale of the property, the new group of developers, without the same commitment to the Olmsteds' several plans, modified the final design and decreased the restrictions designed to preserve it. Later subdivisions of the large tract of land created smaller lots that would produce more income, as well as change the basic plan.

It is clear that the costs of creating a well-landscaped environment in Druid Hills and providing basic services to the residential community were high. Access to such an "ideal" environment was, therefore, limited to an affluent clientele. The early alterations in the original plans of the Olmsted Brothers by the Druid Hills Corporation and the later lapse of restrictions after 1940 both contributed to changes in land use and occupancy in the neighborhood. Some lots have been subdivided recently for new apartment and condominium developments. The privately managed parks were given to the city in 1922 and are now threatened in the 1970s by public officials who propose to destroy them by widening the thoroughfares, so as to provide access to the burgeoning and unplanned suburban areas beyond. This action would substantially alter the environment of the area. To date, Druid Hills has been successful as a pleasant and healthful residential neighborhood; whether it can survive such environmental vandalism is an important question.

The success of Piedmont Park, on the other hand, has continually been limited by the lack of sufficient appropriations for public grounds. The elder Olmsted was well aware of the financial limitations of the Cotton States Exposition, as he indicated to his stepson, John, when he wrote from Atlanta that, because of the scarcity of funds, subscriptions were even being solicited from firemen and Sunday School teachers.[92] Olmsted, Sr., was willing to accept a smaller fee than his usual commission for such a job. However, Exposition officials were either unwilling or unable to commit the funds, and their long hesitation brought an end to

Olmsted's involvement. No detailed financial records for the fair have yet to come to light, but the economic stringency under which the operation functioned is illustrated by its threatened closing several weeks ahead of schedule in late November 1895. With the fair facing bankruptcy and encouraged by the example of Samuel M. Inman, who gave $50,000, the directors raised $100,000 by subscription to keep the Exposition open.[93]

When Olmsted's sons were finally hired to provide a plan of improvement for Piedmont Park, the lake and grounds were deteriorating. Even after work on their plans had been started in 1910, they were concerned about completion. The $10,000 which the city had appropriated for the work was not even a "drop in the bucket," the firm reported to Atlantans.[94] Moreover, recent efforts to rejuvenate the park testify to continued neglect and insufficient support for this public enterprise. In addition, misunderstanding of the park's landscaped features has led to such schemes of "improvement," fortunately defeated, as the recent plan to build four back-to-back grandstands and baseball diamonds, with all the attendant paraphernalia of such an undertaking that would ravage a major open space of the park.

Despite such threats to the physical integrity of both Piedmont Park and Druid Hills, significant and essential components of the Olmsteds' designs remain. These elements continue to enrich these neighborhoods and create visually distinct districts in the changing urban areas of which they are a part. What these landscaped urban spaces provide are those features which, more than one hundred years ago, Frederick Law Olmsted considered necessary ingredients of satisfactory living environments. He felt that the distinctive compositions of gently curving driveways, open, green, meadowlike spaces, bordered by clumps of foliage and contrasted to areas of deep woods, satisfied basic human needs for variety, leisure, and contemplation. Further, the foliage and open space filtered the air and functioned as the lungs of the city. His writings reaffirmed that planned, landscaped areas should respect the ecological balance between human habitation and the natural environment. In residential areas, he suggested, large landscaped suburban lots should be planned to provide for private domesticity, while parks and parkways created spaces for community activities. Olmsted believed that parks, as well as planned residential areas, were important moral as well as physical influences on the lives of urban dwellers, and that, by careful planning and landscaping of the environment, developers could favorably affect the health and welfare of society.

These social and environmental principles are expressed in the physical features of Olmsted designs in Atlanta. These features, if preserved and enhanced, will surely be significant to the increasing population densities now developing in the neighborhoods of both Druid Hills and Piedmont

Park. The physical environment which the Olmsteds, through imaginative and enterprising developers such as Joel Hurt, created in Atlanta thus contains the potential to adapt to and serve changing urban needs. The legacy which Frederick Law Olmsted, through these men, has left to Atlanta is a concern for coordinated planning and a respect for the natural environment.

NOTES

1. Frederick Law Olmsted to John C. Olmsted, March 13, 1894, Olmsted Papers.

2. Sarah Simms Edge, *Joel Hurt and the Development of Atlanta* (Atlanta, 1955), pp. 95–100.

3. See Rick Beard's essay in this book, "Hurt's Deserted Village: Atlanta's Inman Park, 1885–1911." Elizabeth A. Lyon, "Business Buildings in Atlanta, 1865–1930: A Study in Urban Growth and Form," Ph.D. dissertation, Emory University, 1971. The Equitable Building, later the Trust Company of Georgia Building, was demolished in 1971.

4. Edge, *Joel Hurt*, passim.

5. Ibid., p. 129. John C. Olmsted, Report of Visits, May 10, 1892, Olmsted Papers; Frederick Law Olmsted to John C. Olmsted, November 20, 1893, Olmsted Papers; *Atlanta Constitution*, April, 7, 1913 (hereafter cited as *AC*).

6. John C. Olmsted, Report of Visits, May 10, 1892, Olmsted Papers.

7. Edge, *Joel Hurt*, pp. 129–30.

8. Interview with Hurt's granddaughter, Sarah Simms Edge Fletcher, February 1973; list of some of the books in Joel Hurt's library at 85 Elizabeth Street provided by another granddaughter, Bright Bickerstaff West.

9. Edge, *Joel Hurt*, pp. 131–32, 134, 283.

10. Joel Hurt to Frederick Law Olmsted, July 17, 1891, Olmsted Papers.

11. Asa Griggs Candler Papers: Business Records, Druid Hills, copy of land transaction.

12. Edge, *Joel Hurt*, p. 309.

13. *AC*, September 28, 1913.

14. *Atlanta Journal*, July 24, 1895 (hereafter cited as *AJ*).

15. *AC*, March 6, 1896.

16. Edge, *Joel Hurt*, p. 245.

17. *AJ*, August 19, 1897.

18. Lyon, "Business Buildings in Atlanta," pp. 88, 202–203.

19. Ibid., pp. 148–61, 355.

20. Candler Papers: copy of Kirkwood Land Company petition and charter.

21. Candler Papers: deed records; Joel Hurt to Frederick Law Olmsted, June 7, 1892, and July 7, 1892, Olmsted Papers. Lowry received $26,437.50 for his 176¼ acres. On March 28, 1890, 415 acres east of Williams Mill Road were purchased from the heirs of John G. Johnson for $63,000. The 415-acre estate of J. H. Kirkpatrick lying to the east of Lowry's land was purchased from his sons on May 5, 1890, for $45,000. The final purchase of 430 acres was another parcel belonging

to the Johnson family, from which 10 acres around the family homestead had been exempted.

22. Kenneth Ayers, "Olmsted and Druid Hills," unpublished seminar paper, Emory University, May, 1971. Ayers has also contributed additional research from the files of the Library of Congress to this paper.

23. Frederick Law Olmsted to Joel Hurt, July 17, 1890, Olmsted Papers; Hurt, by Litt Bloodworth, Secretary, East Atlanta Land Company to Frederick Law Olmsted, July 29, 1890, Olmsted Papers.

24. Frederick Law Olmsted Reports, December 5, 1890, and January 14, 1891, Olmsted Papers.

25. Franklin Garrett, *Atlanta and Environs* (New York, 1954), 2: 252–54.

26. John C. Olmsted, Report of Visits, May 10, 1892, Olmsted Papers.

27. Joel Hurt to Frederick Law Olmsted and Co., June 7, 1892, Olmsted Papers.

28. Frederick Law Olmsted to John C. Olmsted, February 17, 1893, Olmsted Papers.

29. Joel Hurt to Frederick Law Olmsted, January 30, 1893, Olmsted Papers.

30. Frederick Law Olmsted to John C. Olmsted, February 17, 1893, Olmsted Papers. Olmsted may well have had in mind a similar "row" in Riverside, Illinois, two decades before. See Rick Beard, "Hurt's Deserted Village," below.

31. Julius Gy. Fabos, Gordon T. Milde, and V. Michael Weinmayr, *Frederick Law Olmsted, Sr., Founder of Landscape Architecture in America* (Amherst, Mass., 1968), p. 110. Frederick Law Olmsted to John C. Olmsted, March 14, 1893, March 23, 1893; Joel Hurt to Olmsted, Olmsted, and Eliot, March 4, 1893, Olmsted Papers.

32. Draft copy of bill dated August 8, 1893. Because of $200 paid on account of preliminary visit, the actual balance on that date was $1158.26.

33. *AC*, March 29, 1896.

34. Joel Hurt to Frederick Law Olmsted and Co., March 4, 1893, and July 7, 1892, Olmsted Papers.

35. Ayers, "Olmsted and Druid Hills," p. 8; Frederick Law Olmsted to John C. Olmsted, November 20, 1893, Olmsted Papers.

36. Frederick Law Olmsted to his partners, November 23, 1893, Olmsted Papers.

37. Report of Visits, March 7–11, 1894, Olmsted Papers.

38. Joel Hurt to Olmsted, Olmsted, and Eliot, May 7, 1894, Olmsted Papers.

39. Candler Papers: deed records.

40. William Howard White to John C. Olmsted, August 30, 1899, Olmsted Papers.

41. Most important was the so-called Second Battle of Atlanta, a long, drawn-out power struggle between Hurt and H. M. Atkinson of the Georgia Electric Light Company (now the Georgia Power Company) for control over the city's street railways. For details, see Lyon, "Business Buildings in Atlanta," pp. 216–18.

42. Report of Visits, March 6, 1902, Olmsted Papers.

43. Report of Visits, March 6–9, 1902, Olmsted Papers.

44. Report of Visits, November 24, 1903, Olmsted Papers.

45. Candler Papers: plan for Druid Hills, Olmsted Brothers, 1905.

46. "Parkways, Parks, and 'New South' Progressivism: Planning Practice in Atlanta 1880–1917."

47. Quoted in Fabos et al., *Frederick Law Olmsted, Sr.*, p. 27.

48. Edge, *Joel Hurt*, p. 282.

49. Report of Visits, John C. Olmsted, March 6–9, 1902, Olmsted Papers.

50. Candler Papers: deed records and plat records.

51. *AJ*, May 19, 1908.

52. In the case of Central Park, almost five million cubic yards of earth and rock were moved to create "natural" pastoral vistas. See Fabos et al., *Frederick Law Olmsted, Sr.*, p. 20.

53. Articles in Mrs. Hurt's scrapbook, quoted in Edge, *Joel Hurt*, pp. 279–85; *AJ*, May 19, 1908.

54. Allie G. Funk, "Candler Family Residences in the Atlanta Area," unpublished seminar paper, Emory University, 1970, p. 3.

55. Antoinette Johnson Matthews, *Oakdale Road: Its History and Its People* (Atlanta, 1972), pp. 2, 19, 28.

56. Stephanie Kapetenakos, "The Residential Architecture of Neel Reid" Master's thesis, University of Georgia, 1971.

57. Newspaper clipping from Mrs. Hurt's scrapbook.

58. *AJ*, May 19, 1908.

59. Joel Hurt to Olmsted Brothers, October 8, 1908, Olmsted Papers. The area from Ponce de Leon north to the Byway was built according to plan, but the remainder of the project was carried out according to the designs of local engineer O. F. Kauffmann (Howard L. Preston, "Druid Hills: The 'Ideal Residential Suburb,' " in Rick Beard and Howard L. Preston, "An-Other Atlanta: Turn-of-the-Century Suburbs," manuscript in possession of The History Group, Inc., 1975).

60. Candler Papers: Minute Book, Druid Hills Corporation.

61. Ibid.

62. Ibid.

63. Candler Papers, Kirkwood Land Company, list of lot prices.

64. Charles Howard Candler, *Asa Griggs Candler* (Atlanta, 1950),pp. 270–73.

65. Candler Papers, Minute Book, Druid Hills Corporation. Through the efforts of Asa G. Candler, Emory University, which had been located at Oxford, Georgia, was moved to Atlanta in 1917. According to a report in 1903 by John C. Olmsted, Joel Hurt had also considered locating an educational institution on the Kirkwood Lands. This was to have been a Presbyterian college located in the southernmost portion of the property.

66. Candler Papers, Minute Book, Druid Hills Corporation.

67. Matthews, *Oakdale Road*, passim.

68. Candler Papers: deeds and plat records.

69. Report by John C. Olmsted, c. 1902, Olmsted Papers.

70. Ibid.

71. Candler Papers: deed records.

72. Frederick Law Olmsted to John C. Olmsted, March 16, 1894, Olmsted Papers.

73. W. H. Manning, Report of Visits, March 17, 1894.

74. *AC*, March 18, 1894.

75. Frederick Law Olmsted to John C. Olmsted, March 15, 1894, Olmsted Papers.

76. Frederick Law Olmsted to H. H. Cabaniss, March 23, 1894, Olmsted Papers.

77. Memo attached to letter, Frederick Law Olmsted to H. H. Cabaniss. March 29, 1894, Olmsted Papers.

78. Olmsted, Olmsted, and Eliot to H. E. W. Palmer, Olmsted Papers.

79. Walter G. Cooper, *The Cotton States and International Exposition and South, Illustrated* (Atlanta, 1896), p. 34.

80. Lyon, "Business Buildings in Atlanta," pp. 73, 211–12.

81. *AC*, July 12, 1894.

82. Garrett, *Atlanta and Environs*, 2: 454–55. The property had been offered to the city immediately following the Exposition, but the city had refused the offer because the land seemed too far out from the developed area. By 1904, when the offer was accepted, the city obtained the 189-acre tract for $93,000 and extended the city limits to include it.

83. Report of the Building Inspector, 1905; Garrett, *Atlanta and Environs*, 2: 496–97.

84. Fabos et al., *Frederich Law Olmsted, Sr.*, pp. 18–20.

85. *AC*, March 21, 1910.

86. In 1909, Atlanta architect Haralson Bleckley proposed to cover the entire railroad gulch with a concrete platform several blocks long that would support landscaped areas and walkways. Only the viaducts that were part of his scheme were ever built.

87. Preston, "Parkways, Parks, and 'New South' Progressivism," passim.

88. Lyon, "Business Buildings in Atlanta," pp. 203–11, 362–84.

89. See Beard, "Hurt's Deserted Village," passim.

90. The concept of privatism has been developed most fully by Sam Bass Warner, Jr., in *The Private City: Philadelphia in Three Periods of Its Growth* (Philadelphia, 1968).

91. Report of Visits, March 6–9, 1902, Olmsted Papers.

92. Frederick Law Olmsted to John C. Olmsted, March 16, 1894, Olmsted Papers.

93. Garrett, *Atlanta and Environs*, 2: 329–30.

94. *AC*, March 21, 1910.

Rick Beard

HURT'S DESERTED VILLAGE:
Atlanta's Inman Park, 1885–1911

I need not conceal from you that I am sure that the results of what I have done is to be of much more consequence than any one but myself supposes. As I travel, I see traces of influence spreading from it that no one else would detect. . . .[1]

There was more truth to this observation than even the astute Frederick Law Olmsted imagined when he made it in 1890. His landscape designs for urban parks and residential suburbs set a standard that many of his contemporaries attempted to match, and though these plans usually failed, their influence was often seen. One example illustrative of this influence was Atlanta's first residential suburb, Inman Park. Developed by Joel Hurt in the late 1880s, the suburb ultimately failed to fulfill its design as "the perfect place of residence," despite "all that art and money can do."[2] This study presents the evidence of and reasons for Inman Park's failure and also considers what its failure reveals about turn-of-the-century Atlanta and the nation as a whole.

A number of fundamental issues must be examined here. How many of the ideals supposedly guiding suburban development at this time—in other words, how many of Olmsted's ideas—actually had an impact on the design of Inman Park? Olmsted played no direct role in the design, but Hurt had been corresponding with him as early as 1890. A comparison of Olmsted's plan for Riverside, Illinois, with Hurt's for the Atlanta suburb, however, offers some answers about the Olmstedian ideals of suburban design which appeared in Inman Park. A more fundamental question is whether the landscaped suburb could have worked, and more importantly, should have worked, in Atlanta or elsewhere. Still a third question relating to suburban development is what the effects of American attitudes toward speculation in land and housing were on Inman Park. An in-depth analysis of the development of the Atlanta suburb helps answer these questions as well as another set of questions regarding how the development of this suburb reflects and relates to the re-surgence of Atlanta after the Civil War. The New South of Henry Grady and others was to be both urban and industrial, reconciled nationally and regenerated economically.[3] How much of this creed was at work in the development of Inman Park? And what does the failure of the suburb to accomplish its initial intent reveal about the creed and Atlanta?

Frederick Law Olmsted did not introduce the concept of the exclusive residential suburb to America; rather, he refined it to a level that has not since been equaled. He wrote copiously on the subjects of suburban development and was responsible for the design of Riverside, Illinois, one of the country's most successful residential suburbs. In Olmsted's opinion, "No great town can long exist without great suburbs."[4] This view was frequently echoed in the Atlanta newspaper accounts of Inman Park's development. To Olmsted the suburb was something more than an appendage to a great city: "Probably the advantages of civilization can be found illustrated and demonstrated under no other circumstances so completely as in some suburban neighborhoods where each family abode stands fifty or one hundred feet or more apart from all others, and at some distance from the public road."[5] Such sentiments are much like those revealed by the 1889 advertisement, guaranteeing "first class neighbors of culture, refinement and means" to those who purchased Inman Park lots.

In addition to such general panegyrics to suburban living, Olmsted also wrote numerous concrete proposals for the physical design of the suburban landscape. He identified three essential elements in the suburb: "The construction of good roads and walks, the laying of sewer, water, and gas pipes, and the supplying of sufficiently cheap, rapid, and comfortable conveyances to town centres is all that is necessary. . . ."[6] The roads were to be designed with "gracefully-curved lines, generous spaces, and the absence of sharp corners," and were to have "at intervals pleasant openings and outlooks, with suggestions of refined domestic life, secluded, but not far removed from the life of the community."[7] There were also to be parks, with "the character of informal village-greens, commons, and playgrounds, rather than of enclosed and defended parks or gardens."[8] All of these features were present to some extent in Inman Park: Atlantans were definitely aware of their presence, as numerous laudatory newspaper accounts of the area indicate.

Physical amenities were but one aspect of Olmsted's designs for suburbs. He was quite aware of and concerned about the psychological and sociological implications of his plans. The curvilinear design of the streets, for example, was "to suggest and imply leisure, contemplativeness, and happy tranquility."[9] A writer for the Atlanta *Journal* said much the same thing when he wrote, "The level streets and the quiet freshness of the place will come like a benediction to drivers who have clattered over stones and dodged vehicles in town in a vain effort to get sweetness and light in their daily ride."[10] Olmsted ultimately sought to imbue his plans with elements that would ensure the development of family and community unity:

There are two aspects of suburban habitation that need to be considered to ensure success; first, that of the domiciliation of men by families, each family being well provided for in regard to its domestic indoor and outdoor private life: second, that of the harmonious association and cooperation of men in a community, and the intimate relationship and constant intercourse and interdependence between families. Each has its charm, and the charm of both should be aided and acknowledged by all means in the general plan of every suburb.[11]

Olmsted sought to create this suburban ideal in Riverside, a successful suburban community. Inman Park, although a relative failure, embodied many of the same ideals. The contrasting fates of these two suburbs indicate that factors other than physical design were largely responsible for the failure of the Atlanta development.

Some of these factors can be ascertained through a brief comparison of Riverside's development with that of Inman Park. In 1869, Olmsted was commissioned to design a suburb for the Riverside Improvement Company, a group of eastern businessmen who had purchased a 1,600-acre tract of land west of Chicago. Olmsted envisioned a plan that would "combine the conveniences peculiar to the finest modern towns with the domestic advantages of a most charming country, in a degree never before realized."[12] The physical plan reveals a large subdivision broken into smaller areas by curvilinear streets and open spaces. A large park area stretches along both sides of the Des Plaines River and surrounds the residential areas west of the river. In all, 134 acres were devoted to parks which were protected forever from residential subdivision by deed restrictions dedicating the areas to the public.[13] Riverside, however, was not only a residential community: a $30,000 resort hotel and business block were also constructed there.[14] All of these planning elements —curvilinear streets, park spaces, and a commercial center—were also included in Hurt's design for Inman Park.

A further similarity can be seen in the economic obstacles encountered by both suburbs. Riverside, like Inman Park twenty years later, endured a national financial crisis early in its development. In 1873, the Improvement Company failed after having invested $1.5 million. Causes of the failure were the nationwide panic following the Chicago fire of October 1871, and local rumors that the suburb was plagued by malaria. The company's failure led to a drop in land prices from $300 to $40 per front foot and to the lapsing of all use restrictions. At this juncture, however, the residents of Riverside acted astutely by organizing the Village of Riverside in 1875. This move allowed them to pass ordinances preventing invasion by commercial interests or multiple dwellings and to pass a zoning ordinance in 1921.[15] The village owed its success more to its original physical design, however, than to the political foresight of its residents. An excerpt from an article written in 1932 clearly indicates this debt:

Although Riverside has been without the advantages of stringent private-deed restrictions and architectural control, as we know them today, yet the provisions of adequate open spaces, the setting of houses well back from the streets among trees and shrubs, and the consequent attraction of people with good taste and community pride have accomplished much the same result. . . . How many of our present-day developments . . . are so well planned that they can maintain their original character and identity for sixty years?[16]

In short, Riverside became and remained what Inman Park would not.

Although the physical plans for both suburbs have many similarities, there are some differences in the plans and early development that aid in understanding the failure of Inman Park. Riverside, for example, was more than eight times larger than Inman Park. There was no need to subdivide the individual building lots, a practice which would lead to overcrowding in the Atlanta suburb. The greater size of Riverside, as well as the fact that it was farther from Chicago than Inman Park was from Atlanta, also meant that it would not be so easily lost in the eventual waves of urban expansion. Riverside was nine miles from Chicago and had a distinct design that is still almost immediately visible on a map of the metropolitan area. Its boundaries were quite distinct, and it was protected on two sides by a greenbelt. Inman Park, on the other hand, was only two miles from downtown Atlanta and was small enough that it soon lost much of its identity as the city expanded around and beyond it. The suburb was swallowed up by the surrounding street patterns and is hard to locate on a map unless one knows exactly where to look. The boundaries of Inman Park were not at all distinct, especially after the twenty-foot reserved areas disappeared.

The greater size and distance from the city of Riverside also necessitated some form of self-government. The village government organized in 1875 allowed the suburb greater independence and self-determination than Inman Park ever enjoyed. The residents of the Atlanta suburb had to depend on the city government for services, utilities, and any ordinances designed to protect the area from nonresidential land uses. Such protection was not forthcoming. A final difference between the two suburbs was their attitudes toward open spaces. Riverside devoted more of its land (138 acres, or 11.4 percent of the total) to parks than did Inman Park (5 acres, or 3.8 percent of the total), and it protected its parks better. To some extent, the story of Inman Park is the story of the gradual deterioration of its open spaces. Therefore, while Riverside and Inman Park bear a striking resemblance to one another when viewed two-dimensionally on maps, there were significant differences in size, location, and attitudes toward open space.

These three differences alone by no means account for the failure of Inman Park as an exclusive residential suburb. Another significant factor was the apparent lack of a strong sense of community in the area. Olmsted, as indicated earlier, sought to create such a sense in his projects and was quite successful with Riverside. Evidently, the Chicago suburb quite early developed a sharp awareness of the experimental character and contemporary uniqueness of the development. These created a mystique which combined with the physical design to create a strong sense of community among Riverside residents.[17] The idea of community is an elusive one: Olmsted considered it to be "the intimate relationship and constant intercourse, and interdependence between families." His definition differs from many others and, even if accepted, well nigh defies any definitive sort of measurement. Partial and conflicting views of the sense of community existing in Inman Park may be gained by contrasting an account of life there with the record of residential turnover. Sarah Simms Edge Fletcher, one of Hurt's grandaughters, writes of the lively, cohesive circle of family and friends that centered around Hurt. The Hurt home on Elizabeth Street and the Inman Park Methodist Church served to bring this group into frequent contact with one another.[18] There is some question, however, as to how far camaraderie extended beyond this group. With over two hundred families living in Inman Park by 1911, it would have required more than a few close-knit families to create any real sense of community.

A brief examination of the residential turnover in Inman Park bolsters this last conclusion. With the exception of Joel Hurt himself, no one lived in the suburb throughout the whole period of study. Only seven of the houses built by 1900 were occupied by the same resident over the next eleven years. Although a few of these residents moved from one house to another in Inman Park, most moved out of the area altogether. It would have been very difficult to create a strong community spirit when so many of the residents lived there for only a relatively brief time. It may be assumed that the absence of a strong sense of community led to a lack of identification with the suburb and concern for its development. This factor would surely contribute to the failure of the area.

Whether by design or accident, many of Frederick Law Olmsted's ideas about suburban design were influential in shaping Alanta's first residential suburb. Unfortunately, physical design alone could not guarantee successful suburban development. Other factors such as national economic conditions, social conditions within the suburb, and American attitudes toward speculation in land and housing also played significant roles. Their significance has already been considered in the comparison of Riverside and Inman Park, and must now be considered in light of a detailed analysis of Inman Park's development.

Joel Hurt was one of the prime movers in Atlanta's post-Civil War resurgence. His many business ventures contributed significantly to the city's growth, and no doubt many Atlantans agreed with Georgia Governor W. T. Northen's 1894 statement that "the people of Atlanta have learned that when Joel Hurt touches the button 'we must do the rest.'"[19]

In 1887, the button that Joel Hurt chose to touch was that of suburban development—specifically, Inman Park, which had actually begun as early as 1882, when Hurt began to acquire parcels of land in Lots Fourteen and Nineteen of the Fourteenth Land District of Fulton County (Map 2). He enlisted the aid of Samuel M. Inman, a wealthy cotton merchant and influential citizen who supposedly promised Hurt that "I will do all I can to help you."[20] The help Inman offered was largely financial, for Hurt was apparently unable to acquire all the land necessary for the suburb with his own resources.

Despite this apparent shortcoming, Hurt spent more than $18,000 for property by 1887, when he decided that his project merited a more formal organization. In April, the East Atlanta Land Company was chartered, with twenty-eight shareholders who owned a total of 1,930 shares of stock valued at $100 per share. Control was still very much in Joel Hurt's hands, since he owned 1,035 shares and his wife, another 153. Samuel Inman's brother, Walker P., owned 269 shares, which made him the third controlling stockholder and ensured that the development of Inman Park would remain in the hands of its originators.[21]

By July 14, 1887, the East Atlanta Land Company had acquired 138¼ acres of land at a cost of $74,317. All this land had been sold or traded to the company by Joel Hurt, who paid $68,929 for it.[22] The difference in prices, while it may have represented direct profit to Hurt, was more than likely the cost of initial improvements to the land, such as the laying out of some streets.

Hurt, a trained civil engineer, was able to do much of the surveying himself. To do the landscaping, he retained Joseph Forsyth Johnson in September 1887 and paid him a monthly salary of $400 and expenses. Their accomplishment was glowingly described by the local press: "The two men brought out of the grove the perfect ideal. The curves of the avenues are wonderful in their gracefulness. At various points are grassy plots, reserved to make the place more beautiful and the lots are brought to the grade at which they will remain and the terraces have all been made with artistic effect. The lots are large and are already laid off with a view to a perfect and symmetrical whole." Not mentioned by this enthusiastic writer were the more than seven hundred trees that had been planted to enhance the sylvan quality of the suburb.[23] By May 1889, enough of the work had been completed so that ten lots could be offered at public auction.[24] In the meantime, Hurt had begun two projects designed in large part to enhance the attractiveness of these lots.

As mentioned earlier, Joel Hurt did not conceive of Inman Park as an isolated development. He planned to link the suburb with downtown Atlanta, and as early as 1884 he visualized the extension of Foster Street at both ends to serve such a purpose.[25] Two years later, Hurt reached a tentative agreement with the city. Although the terms are not clearly recorded, Hurt evidently agreed to buy the land needed for widening and extending Foster Street, to pay the city for any amount in excess of $20,000 that it spent in improving the street, and to build a bridge over the Richmond and Danville Railroad. In return, the city was to use its powers of condemnation in clearing the way for extending the street.[26]

By February 1888, Joel Hurt and the East Atlanta Land Company had carried out their part of the agreement, but the city was seemingly reluctant to do its part. An editorial in the *Atlanta Constitution* on February 8 vigorously supported the extension, claiming that it would raise land values, provide a safe railway crossing, and permit quick access to the suburbs. Opposition to the extension, while not clear-cut, centered around fears that tax revenue might be lost and that the East Atlanta Land Company would not be able to pay the costs that might exceed $20,000. To dispel this opposition, Hurt revealed that his land company had capital of $300,000, and he agreed to take over the city's share for improvements, if the city would agree to pay back the $20,000 over the next three years.[27] Even this offer was not enough to gain an immediate agreement. Several editorials critical of the city council and a petition signed by Phil Haralson, Walker P. Inman, Asa G. Candler, Joel Hurt, and several other prominent citizens were needed before Edgewood Avenue (formerly Foster Street) was finally opened.[28]

The ceremonies opening the two-mile, tree-lined avenue brought together many of Atlanta's most influential citizens. Georgia Governor John B. Gordon spoke very briefly, after which Joel Hurt and Henry Grady made somewhat longer speeches. Hurt praised Edgewood Avenue, calling it the equal of such prominent residential avenues as Drexel in Chicago or Euclid in Cleveland. He noted that opening the avenue had required 500 conferences with 132 property owners and 30 condemnations by the city. The expense, he said, came to $125,000, of which the city paid $20,000 and private citizens (meaning the East Atlanta Land Company), $105,000. In clearing the way for Edgewood Avenue, $80,000 worth of buildings had been demolished—ninety-four in all, many of which were small frame dwellings—but at least $250,000 worth of new buildings were anticipated.[29] Grady, who followed Hurt to the speaker's platform, made a speech that reveals the context in which many Atlantans viewed Inman Park and Edgewood Avenue: "I argue from all this that there is no limit to what Atlanta can be, if her citizens will only unite in determined effort. I see around me men of every shade of opinion, and in the face of this auspicious occasion let us bury our differences, heal up these schisms, and determine that Atlanta shall be first in this march of progress."[30] While these comments betray rivalries among Atlanta's prominent citizens, they also evidence the New South idea of growth, of matching Northern achievements. The residential suburb was something that every Northern city of any size could point to: Inman Park was to be Atlanta's first suburb and was to be linked to the downtown by Edgewood Avenue, the equivalent to the finest Northern residential avenues.

The linking of Inman Park to Atlanta was not completed by the avenue, for Hurt had one other part to his scheme—an electric street railway. On August 22, 1889, the yellow car of the Atlanta and Edgewood Street Railroad Company made the first trip from the corner of Pryor Street and Edgewood Avenue to Inman Park.[31] No expense had been spared by the East Atlanta Land Company in building the line. Each car cost $4,000 and had an oak interior and plate glass windows; the steel rails were heavier than those used by the Georgia Railroad and were laid on stone piers; and much of the paving was of Belgian block.[32] In all, $95,000 had been spent on the street railroad, Atlanta's first and one of the first financially successful lines in the country.[33] For a nickel, an Atlantan could now make a quick fifteen minute trip to or from Inman Park any time between 6:00 A.M. and 11:00 P.M.[34]

Judging from newspaper stories and a contemporary map, those who rode the streetcar to Inman Park found neatly arranged, level lots amid trees and gently curving streets (Map 4). According to one writer, "The art of the civil engineer has been made to seem Dame Nature's lackey—perfecting her designs—running her errands in wood and brake. The residence lots are level and grassgrown; the shade trees are trimmed and flourishing, the sidewalks smooth and wide."[35] A plat map dated June 1, 1888, is more revealing about the physical plan for this suburban development. The entire area was bounded by a twenty-foot reserved strip of land to the north, Waddell Street to the west, and Decatur Street to the south. The eastern boundary was irregular, running along the rear lot lines of those lots fronting on Elizabeth Street. The irregularity of this boundary anticipated the eastward expansion of Inman Park three years later when fifty-one acres were added. In 1888, however, the development encompassed only a bit more than 138 acres, with a large amount of this total given over to open spaces and a park. One large open space, located midway between the beginning of the suburb and Springvale Park, was composed of the Triangle, the Delta, and the large area within Druid Circle. The Mesa, initially an open space, linked this area to Springvale Park. The park itself covered five acres and was located in a valley with rather steep walls to the east, west, and south. The main feature of the park was Crystal Lake, which was man-made, fed by water from a mineral spring, and inhabited by numerous goldfish.[36] To the south of Springvale Park was a large open area with the lot number of 139, though it was not sold for several years. To the east of the park between Park Lane and Elizabeth Street, there was another large open area of undivided lots. In short, the residents of Inman Park would not lack open space: 49 of the 130 lots fronted directly on the park or an open space.

With the exception of Waverly Way and Druid Circle, the streets were relatively straight. Their irregular arrangement and the frequent open spaces, however, prevented the monotony thought to be caused by any pattern approaching that of a gridiron. None of the streets traversed the entire suburb, so it was actually faster to bypass Inman Park on trips beyond the development. Trees placed at regular intervals lined all the streets on both sides, and each block had sidewalks. Three alleyways and a cul-de-sac permitted rear access to many of the lots.

The building lots themselves were a half acre or more in size and were generally rectangular with a frontage of seventy feet or more. Trees were plentiful, especially on the lots north of Edgewood and Euclid avenues, and all the lots had been planted with bluegrass. The lots had also all been brought to uniform grade, so that regrading by the purchasers would not be necessary.[37] Indeed, the property did seem to have been brought "to a state of perfection as a residence park," as an advertisement for the first public sale claimed.

The first lots were sold at a public auction on May 9, 1889. Only ten lots were sold, but the excitement surrounding the sale ran high. Excerpts from one of the advertisements announcing the sale indicate this clearly and also reveal that Inman Park was expected to have a regional appeal. It would attract men who were involved in national affairs and would need access to regional and national transportation lines. Exclusiveness, permanence, and refinement were to be its characteristics.[38]

In order to maintain these characteristics, lots were sold with four restrictions: (1) they were to be used only for residential purposes, (2) any residence built was to be worth at least $3,000, (3) all residences were to be set back thirty feet from the front street and twenty feet from any side street, and (4) the violation of any of these restrictions was sufficient cause for voiding the sale. These four restrictions were to remain in effect until January 1, 1910.[39] Occasionally, a lot might be sold to which special restrictions were attached—a different setback, a higher or minimum value, or a specific date by which the house was to be built. These instances, however, were rare, and most of the lots sold had only the original restrictions of 1889.

The first public auction was quite successful: the ten lots offered for sale were all sold for a total of $19,430.[40] In some cases, installment buying apparently led to persons purchasing lots at auction which they later discovered they could not afford or did not want. Then, they would try to find another buyer to assume the payments or would forfeit their initial payment and the lot would revert to the East Atlanta Land Company. As a result, many purchasers listed in the newspaper accounts of the auctions were never recorded as owners in the deeds to the lots. The available records give no hint as to why they did not follow up their auction purchases or how they disposed of the lots. Of the ten lots sold on May 9, only five were deeded over to their initial purchasers. The remaining five went to someone else. This pattern holds true for the entire period under study.

Following the first sale, the company announced that lots would be sold privately at $35 per front foot until the next public sale.[41] This sale was not long in coming, for it was held the next February. In the meantime, work on Inman Park had been continuing. In an interview with a *Journal* reporter on June 17, 1889, Joel Hurt announced plans for building a $50,000 hotel on the Mesa. Hurt planned to raise funds by popular subscription, a method he was sure would be most successful because of the investment possibilities of Inman Park. The hotel was to serve Northern visitors during the winter, Atlantans all year round, and Inman Park residents who did not enjoy cooking or could not find servants. In the same interview, Hurt mentioned plans for extending the street railway to Decatur and expressed hopes that gas and water would soon be available in the suburb.

The immediate lack of such amenities as gas and water (electricity was available) had done nothing to dull enthusiasm for Inman Park. By early 1890, eight houses were already under construction, four by individuals and four by the land company.[42] The second public auction, this time of fifty lots, was held on February 27, 1890. In an interview the day before the sale, Hurt sounded an ominous note for the future development of Inman Park when he discussed the speculative value of investment there: "We do not expect these lots to bring very high prices. It requires a change of deeds for an increase of values. In three years the lots sold Thursday will be worth three times what they bring then."[43] Hurt was not alone in stressing the investment possibilities of lots in Inman Park: of twenty prominent businessmen asked their opinions about the suburb, seventeen spoke of it primarily as a sound investment.[44]

The sale on February 27 revealed that investment was the motivating factor among buyers. Of the twenty-nine lots sold for $68,835, only fourteen were deeded to the purchasers listed in the newspaper, and of these only two established residence. Five of the remaining fifteen lots were eventually used for residences by their initial owners. In short, less than one quarter of the original owners established residence on their lots. This does not mean that the lots were used for purposes other than residence, since the deeds restricted their use. It does indicate that the development of Inman Park became a speculative affair: lots were bought, in many cases left vacant, and then sold when (and if) their value had sufficiently increased. This trend was not immediately clear, for by April, six new houses were under construction and at year's end, fifteen had been built. In September, the city council decided to put in water mains and promised that gas and sewer pipes would soon follow.[45] To all informed observers, the development of Inman Park seemed most encouraging.

The next year, Inman Park continued to grow. Two years earlier, the East Atlanta Land Company had purchased an additional fifty-one acres for $33,333.33.[46] This new acquisition lay in the eastern part of the development, and when it was added to the original land, it completed the irregular eastern boundary and gave Inman Park as a whole the shape of a bent elbow. The new land was ready for sale by April, so Joel Hurt released a new plat map and announced a public auction for April 15.

This sale was advertised as the last that would be held, for the development was now complete and the East Atlanta Land Company wanted to sell all the lots so that houses could be built and the full value of the land realized. Future maintenance of the streets and other utilities was now the job of the city, which had extended the city limits to include Inman Park (Map 2). In Hurt's words: "There is nothing more for us to do, so far as Inman Park is concerned. We shall turn it over to the people by the sale next Wednesday, and give our attention to our other property along the avenue." The company had plans to invest $2 million along Edgewood Avenue, including $750,000 for the Equitable Building, and was anxious to recapture some of the more than $427,000 spent on Inman Park.[47]

The auction on April 15 was not a big success, for only seventeen of the fifty new lots were sold before darkness fell. One week later, however, twenty-one lots were sold at a second auction, and in May a third auction was held at which eleven of the remaining twelve lots were sold. The total income realized from these sales was $137,280.[48] Significantly, only four of the lots were used for residences by their original purchasers: the remaining thirty-four had been purchased as speculative investments.

These three sales in April and May had not disposed of all the Inman Park lots, but the East Atlanta Land Company apparently decided to sell these privately because another public sale was not held for fi⁻e years. During the intervening time, there was a lull in activity in the suburb. By the end of 1891, twenty houses were built or under construction, fourteen by private owners and six by the land company.[49] The hotel planned in 1889 had not materialized, and in April 1892, Joel Hurt announced plans for a conservatory to be built on the same site. The building was to include a three to four thousand seat auditorium, a picture gallery, and a museum. Possible uses included musical festivals, the annual conventions of the education societies, and the numerous Baptist conventions.[50] No mention was made of how the conservatory was to be funded, but whatever means were to be used were inadequate because it was never built.

Two elements combined to inhibit activity in Inman Park between 1891 and 1896. A nationwide business panic struck in 1893 and kept economic activity to a minimum for several years thereafter. A second and more immediate factor was the involvement of the East Atlanta Land Company in other projects, most notably the Equitable Building. The significance of this second undertaking is revealed in Hurt's 1891 comment, quoted earlier, that the company was turning Inman Park over to the people so that it could turn its attention to its other properties. Further proof comes from an 1895 advertisement for a public auction of lots in which it was stated that the expense of the Equitable Building caused a suspension of activity in Inman Park.[51] The fact that only eighteen lots were sold and deeded over in the period is proof of the inhibiting effect of these two elements.

By 1895, the East Atlanta Land Company returned its attention to Inman Park and offered fifty lots and four houses for public auction on May 2.[52] For some reason, this auction was postponed for almost an entire year until April 8, 1896. The most plausible explanation for this postponement was that the company was involved in making some physical alterations in the suburb and that these had not been completed in time for an 1895 sale.

The changes are quite evident on a new plat map dated April 1, 1896. The most noticeable one was the division into lots of much of the open space. Springvale Park remained intact, but thirty-three new building lots now existed where open space had previously been. The Mesa and Druid Circle areas had been sold and divided into eight oversized lots. The area immediately south of Springvale Park was turned into eight building lots, and in the northeast corner of the suburb seventeen new lots were ready for sale. The creation of these new lots left the open space in Inman Park greatly depleted: only the Poplar Circle area and the sections east of Park Lane were of any size, apart from Springvale Park itself. The loss was greatest to the western part of the suburb, where only the Delta and the Triangle remained. Probably the most distinctive quality of the suburb had been the amount and arrangement of open space, which was largely responsible for the area's amenable residential quality. When the open space began to disappear, so did a great deal of the suburb's residential desirability.

Such an alteration took place over time, however, and the sale of April 1896 was still met with great enthusiasm. To conduct the sale, the East Atlanta Land Company had hired William O. Beckenbaugh, a nationally known auctioneer who had conducted the sale of the 1893 World's Fair buildings in Chicago. His verbal advertisement for Inman Park lots was quite a bit different from those heard a few years before and reveals the change in economic conditions: "I tell you that this sale is important to your city. The prices you pay for these lots will settle the price of Atlanta dirt for some time. Upon the success of this sale depends the success of your city as a real estate market for this season."[53] Forty-five of the fifty lots were sold for $65,860. The deeds for the lots sold at this auction contain the usual four restrictions, with the added proviso that the lots might also be used for social, educational, or religious purposes.[54] This is the only time that this addition appears.

This sale was considered only a partial success. In Joel Hurt's words, "In view of the depressed condition of real estate and the financial stringency the company is satisfied with the sale and it realized as much as was anticipated."[55] This auction sale was the last held in Inman Park. From the initial sale in 1889 until the end of 1896, deeds for 153 lots in the suburb had been recorded and a total of $346,807 had been paid, or was being paid, to the East Atlanta Land Company. Only 38 of these 152 lots were used as places of residence by their initial purchasers. The remaining lots were initially purchased as investments. How many of these lots were actually being lived on is impossible to determine with much certainty, but a sensible guess is about 20.[56] In all probability, only 58 of the 152 lots (38 percent of the usable residential space) were actually being lived on by late 1896. This condition would hardly have made Inman Park an exclusive residential suburb of any lasting quality. Indeed, at that point in its development Inman Park might have been more aptly called "Hurt's Deserted Village."

The year 1896 marks a definite turning point in the development of Inman Park. From that point on, the East Atlanta Land Company no longer seems to have considered the suburb an exclusive residential area to which large amounts of money and attention should be devoted. The division of several areas of open space into building lots betrays a desire to realize as much profit as possible rather than preserve the amenities of the suburb. By 1911, only Springvale Park remained undivided. A second indication of neglect is found in a newspaper story which urged the extension of Auburn Avenue to Inman Park because "Edgewood Avenue is so badly paved that life and limb are endangered by driving on it."[57] Although the city was responsible for maintaining the avenue, the land company would surely have pressured the city to repair the avenue or would have done the work itself if Inman Park's development had still been of the first priority. Still another indication of the changed attitude of the company is seen in the 1896 advertisement for the auction, in which Inman Park is described only as a "residence community."[58] In 1889 it had been "the ideal place to build permanent homes," two years later it was "the ideal residence park for Atlanta," and in 1895 it was an "attractive residence community."[59] If advertising is any indication, by 1896 Inman Park was just a nice place to live; it was not Atlanta's ideal suburban community.

There are several reasons why the East Atlanta Land Company no longer considered Inman Park a top priority project after 1896. For one, there were not that many more lots to be sold. Over the next fifteen years, only fifty-nine sales were recorded and sixteen of them were in one year, which means that on the average three lots were sold in each of the other fourteen years. There were no more public auctions. A second, closely related reason is that the sale of lots in Inman Park had become much less profitable, as the figures in Table 2 clearly illustrate.

As lots devalued on the market, more of them had to be sold to realize a profit; as a result, open space began to be divided. It also became necessary to make the terms of the purchase easier. In 1896, a buyer needed only a 20 percent downpayment in cash or stocks, and then only 7 percent interest was charged on the four annual payments. Terms in 1889, 1891, and 1895 had been a 25 percent downpayment with three years to pay the remainder at 8 percent interest annually. In 1890, a downpayment of 33

Table 2
AVERAGE LOT PRICE AT AUCTION

AUCTION YEAR	LOTS SOLD	TOTAL INCOME	AVERAGE LOT PRICE
1889	10	$ 19,430	$1,943
1890	29	$ 68,835	$2,373
1891	49	$138,180	$2,820
1896	45	$ 65,860	$1,463

SOURCE: *AS*, May 10, 1889, p. 3; and *AC*, February 28, 1890, p. 6, April 16, 1891, p. 4, April 23, 1891, p. 5, May 8, 1891, p. 7, and April 9, 1896, p. 5.

percent was required, with two annual payments at 7 percent interest.[60] A third and last possible reason for the loss of interest in Inman Park as an exclusive residential suburb was the incipient development of Druid Hills, which promised to be both more profitable and more exclusive as a residential area. The fact that Hurt commissioned Olmsted to design Druid Hills introduces an ironic twist to the history of Inman Park and Atlanta suburbanization in general.

In the years after 1896, two new tendencies appeared and one old one continued to be evident: lot sales declined and the number of houses built increased, while the old tendency of cutting up open space for residential lots continued. The division, in 1896, of several open areas into building lots has already been discussed. In 1907, this tendency reappeared when the East Atlanta Land Company sold the two large undivided areas immediately east of Springvale Park to Asa G. Candler for $25,000. In October 1909, Candler also purchased the area within Poplar Circle for the sum of $6,000.[61]

Candler's two large purchases left only Springvale Park and the smaller areas of the Delta and the Triangle undivided by 1911. Not even the twenty-foot reserved areas had survived these attacks on open space: several portions of this buffer zone were sold in 1906 and 1908. The Candler purchases, once subdivided, along with numerous minor changes in the lot boundaries, brought the total number of residential lots in Inman Park to 220 (Map 5). Many of the lots added after 1896 were small ones carved out of the original lots or created by dividing the open spaces that had once been one of the most pleasant characteristics of Inman Park. At the same time, a large number of lots were sold by their initial purchasers, who had been interested in a good investment, to people who were interested in a place of residence. This fact accounts for the second new tendency, the increasing number of houses built after 1896. Only about 58 houses had been built by 1896. From then until 1911, building permits for 139 dwellings were recorded. Essentially, this increase in home construction meant that many new families were moving into Inman Park and that "Hurt's Deserted Village" was gradually becoming a misnomer.

The changes in the houses built after 1896 included more than an increase in numbers: the costs of the houses declined and the types of architecture changed. Unfortunately, there is little information available about the costs of the houses built prior to 1896. The Haralson house, a three-storey granite dwelling, reportedly cost at least $8,000.[62] The Gould house was built of marble and also cost in excess of $8,000. These two houses, however, were exceptional. Most of the residences in Inman Park were two-storey frame dwellings that no doubt were less expensive because they were built on a smaller scale with cheaper materials. The

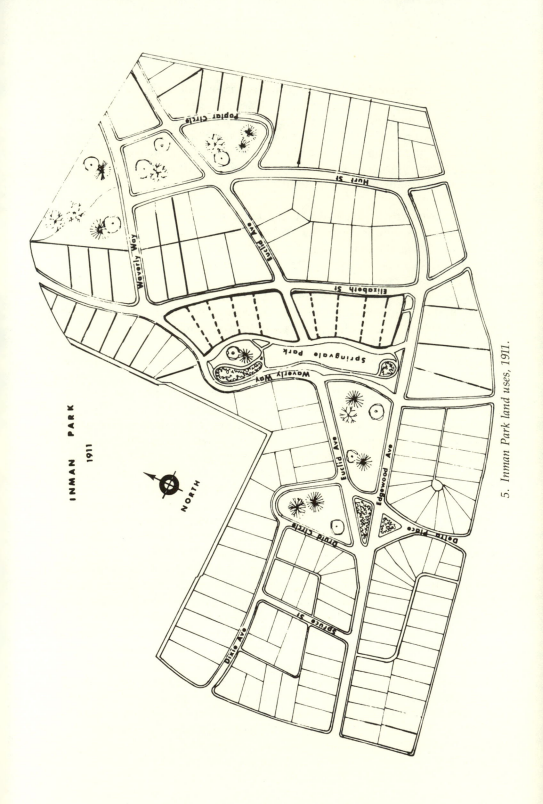

INMAN PARK
1911

NORTH

5. *Inman Park land uses, 1911.*

architectural style of most of these houses is marked by irregular massing, gables, bay windows, and round or polygonal turrets. These features characterize the Queen Anne style, which gained widespread popularity in America following the Philadelphia Centennial Exposition of 1876[63] (Figure 14).

Much more is known about the building that occurred after 1896, for in that year the building department began to keep records. This period was marked by changes in the number of houses built, the costs of the houses, and the style of architecture used. The amount of building in Inman Park fluctuated until 1907, as Tables 3 and 4 illustrate.

This burst of construction activity defies definite explanation, although it might logically be attributed to a large increase in the white population needing housing.[64] These new dwellings were primarily one- or two-storey frame structures; only two brick dwellings were built. Many of these houses still stand and are fair representations of the bungalow style of architecture that had its heyday during the first two decades of the twentieth century.[65] A gabled porch set out from the body of the house, which is usually gable-shaped itself, characterizes this style. However, there are numerous variations on this basic theme, and the main distinction of the bungalow is that it is a one-storey dwelling.

The sixty-four two-storey frame dwellings built after 1906 were largely of the Georgian Revival style. Its dominating characteristic was symmetry achieved through use of a rectangular plan, classical details and facade, and evenly placed chimneys and dormers.[66] The regular, balanced effect of this style contrasted sharply with the irregular massing and ornate decoration of the Queen Anne style. After 1900, however, the two stood side by side in Inman Park.

The suburb also had its churches, for religion was an integral part of the turn-of-the-century society. The Inman Park Methodist Church had been built prior to 1896 on Edgewood Avenue between Elizabeth and Hurt streets. In 1905–1906, the two-storey brick Inman Park Presbyterian Church was constructed for $9,000 at the juncture of Edgewood and Euclid avenues.[67] The Inman Park Baptist Church was located in a car barn on Edgewood Avenue. Originally, the barn was used by the Atlanta and Edgewood Street Railroad Company, but in 1907 it was remodeled for church use at a cost of $1,200.[68] The addition of these two churches provides further evidence of a population influx that led to the 1907 building upsurge. With the exception of a single three-storey brick business building, these churches were the only nonresidential structures in Inman Park until the deed restrictions lapsed. Many of the homes had barns and small servants' houses behind them, but there were no other types of buildings.

14. Residences located in Inman Park on Edgewood Avenue, c. 1895. The open space in the foreground was subsequently subdivided into building lots.

Table 3
TOTAL BUILDING IN INMAN PARK

YEAR	NUMBER	COST
1895	1	$ 3,200
1896	1	4,000
1898	4	15,000
1899	3	19,000
1901	2	9,500
1902	4	38,550
1903	3	12,000
1905	9	37,100
1906	8	26,500
1907	22	83,200
1908	30	142,050
1909	24	81,000
1910	37	123,000
Totals: —	148	$594,100

SOURCE: Atlanta City Building Department Permit Books, 1895-1910.

The pattern of construction during 1910 bespeaks the end of Inman Park as any sort of exclusive residential suburb, an end that had been in sight as early as 1896. In this one year, one frame and three brick stores were constructed. These stores were small and probably catered specifically to Inman Park residents. Unfortunately, they were merely precursors of wider sorts of unplanned-for commercial interests that soon invaded the area and created the mixed residential and commercial character that still marks the area. Along with the stores, a two-storey brick apartment house was built. While apartment buildings are not inherently evil nor destructive to residential areas, neither are they indicative of the type of residential living originally intended for Inman Park. In addition to these particular buildings, the overall decline in the costs of the residences built after January 1, 1910, points to the demise of the suburb.

The sharp decline in the costs of these houses was not the only noticeable difference in 1910. That year also marks the culmination of a trend that had begun in 1906. Until then, most of the houses were built by individuals who were going to occupy the houses themselves. In 1906, however, the speculative builder, usually a real estate or construction firm, first appeared. The houses produced by such a builder were usually crowded close together and were of a similar, if not an identical, style. They were built for whoever could meet the speculator's price rather than for a particular client. In 1906, seven of the nine houses constructed were

Table 4

HOUSING COSTS IN INMAN PARK

1895–1911: Entire period of study

(Type of house)	(No. built)	(Total cost)	(Ave. price per house)
One-storey frame	44	$124,700	$2,834
Two-storey frame	90	$363,250	$4,036
Two-storey brick	7	$ 65,000	$9,286

1895–1910: Until deed restrictions lapse

One-storey frame	26	$ 82,650	$3,179
Two-storey frame	76	$302,950	$3,984
Two-storey brick	7	$ 65,000	$9,286

1907–1911: Period of building upsurge

One-storey frame	41	$114,200	$2,785
Two-storey frame	64	$280,900	$4,389
Two-storey brick	2	$ 13,500	$6,750

1907–1910: Upsurge before deed restrictions lapse

One-storey frame	23	$ 72,150	$3,137
Two-storey frame	50	$220,600	$4,412

1910: After deed restrictions lapse

One-storey frame	18	$ 43,050	$2,336
Two-storey frame	14	$ 60,300	$4,307

SOURCE: Atlanta City Building Department Permit Books.

of this type. Over the next three years, thirty-three of seventy-five houses were speculative ventures, and in 1910, twenty-three of the thirty-two houses were built by real estate or construction firms. Thus, after the restrictions lapsed, 75 percent of the new houses were speculative, as compared to less than 50 percent from 1906 to 1910.

The same basic speculative attitude was revealed by these sixty-three dwellings as had earlier been shown by many of the original lot purchasers. Whereas many of the original purchasers had hindered Inman Park's early development by keeping their lots vacant, the speculative builders helped deliver the *coup de grace* by building nearly identical houses that were crowded together. These characteristics helped destroy the residential amenities and visual identity of Inman Park.

By 1911, it was obvious that Inman Park had not and would not become the "perfect place of residence" in Atlanta. That distinction clearly belonged elsewhere, perhaps to Druid Hills. Now the questions raised at the outset of this investigation must be reiterated and answered. The basic question is why Inman Park failed and what its failure suggests about Atlanta and the rest of the nation at the turn of the century. Could Inman Park have been successful? What insights about nineteenth-century suburban development may be gained from this study? And what effects did speculation in land and housing have on this development?

The logical place to begin is with the first of these questions—why Inman Park failed. Was the original plan at fault, or were other facts responsible? As the discussion at this study's outset indicates, many of Frederick Law Olmsted's ideas about suburban design seem to have been influential in Joel Hurt's plan for Inman Park. The physical design alone, however, was not enough to ensure the success of a suburb; nevertheless, it could hasten the failure of such a development. The physical plan for Inman Park was basically sound: it skillfully used a curvilinear street pattern and initially provided large open spaces. The further consideration of the reasons for the suburb's failure leads to factors present in the city and the nation.

Such a residential area as Inman Park required a stability based on a substantial investment in a lot and house, and with a few exceptions the houses built in Inman Park did not represent such an investment. Only three of the houses built in the suburb cost $10,000 or more, and only sixteen cost more than $5,000. Thus, the vast majority of houses—122 in all—cost $5,000 or less. Overall, the average price of the houses built in Inman Park was $3,992, which did not represent a substantial investment when compared to the average lot price of $2,135. In short, the finest residences were not being built in Inman Park.

This raises the question of whether or not Atlanta had a large enough group of affluent citizens to support both an exclusive residential suburb and the prestigious central city addresses. Although there are presently insufficient data available for the period of this study, in 1880, 20 percent of the city's 37,409 people, or about 7,482, belonged to the upper and upper-middle classes. One year later, only 298 people, or less than 3 percent of the population, reported property appraised at $10,000 or more in the city's tax digests.[69] Assuming that these percentages remained somewhat constant over the following three decades, it would seem logical to conclude that Atlanta did not have a large enough group of affluent citizens to support both Inman Park and the downtown addresses.

Three collections of photographs dating from this era support this conclusion. Among the many pictures of the homes of prominent Atlantans, only four are of Inman Park homes and only two of the homes were occupied.[70] Most of the homes pictured were located in the central city on Peachtree, Washington, and Forsyth streets. These addresses rather than Inman Park were the prestigious ones in turn-of-the-century Atlanta. The New South creed of an industrialized economy had not become a sufficiently real enough force to create an affluent class that was large enough to support both the prestigious downtown addresses and an exclusive residential suburb.

The lack of a large affluent class, a local characteristic, points to several national factors which help account for the failure of Inman Park and lead to some conclusions concerning nineteenth-century suburban development. The importance of such a group to a residential suburb lay with its ability to pay high prices for the land and houses in the suburb. These high prices, in turn, ensured the exclusive nature of the area, for only the wealthier members of society could afford such prices. This circular process points out the speculative nature of suburban development in the nineteenth century. Urban land and housing were considered primarily as investments and as such were immediately responsive to fluctuations in the national economy. When panics occurred, as they did in 1873 and 1893, land prices usually plummeted. The developers of a suburb often failed or sought to sell their property in order to realize some profit during such financial crises. The Riverside Improvement Company failed; the East Atlanta Land Company sought to sell its Inman Park property.

The basic problem underlying this speculative attitude was what Sam Bass Warner, Jr., has called "privatism." The essence of this tradition lay with its emphasis upon the individual and his search for wealth. Out of it sprang the investor who was interested mainly in protecting his equity and making a profit. Any concern for such social amenities as open space disappeared as soon as his interests appeared to be jeopardized. The development of Inman Park exemplifies this tradition at work. After making an investment in excess of $427,000, the East Atlanta Land Company obviously expected to profit. The first five auctions showed much promise, for the lot prices steadily rose (Table 2). The Panic of 1893 put an end to such promise, however, for lot prices had dropped drastically by the time an auction was held in 1896. By that time, the company had apparently adopted an attitude of "take the money and run." Areas that had previously been open space and had been responsible for much of the suburb's attractiveness were subdivided and sold in an effort to reap that much more profit. Although no one took advantage of them, deed restrictions were relaxed to allow for land uses other than residential. Terms of payment were made easier. Hence, the East Atlanta Land Company sought to make as much profit as possible in as short a time as possible. Concern for Inman Park had disappeared amid the exigencies of realizing a return on the original investment. (The East Atlanta Land Company had realized $491,797.45 from the sale of land in Inman Park by 1911.)

The attitude of "take the money and run," a significant cause for the failure of Inman Park and a good example of privatism at work, is at the core of the answer to the question of whether or not suburban development in the nineteenth century could really work. It could work only if the investors were assured a long-term profit or the residents themselves were assured some continuity through self-government. Otherwise, as soon as the investment seemed threatened, such amenities as open space were quickly sacrificed. Neighborhoods like Inman Park all too often suffered from such sacrifices. By 1911, this Atlanta suburb was beginning to assume its present character of mixed residential and commercial land use. Its failure to fulfill its original design resulted from several conditions: the East Atlanta Land Company's speculative attitude, which was shared by many of the original purchasers of lots and several real estate and construction firms; the suburb's size, location, and lack of self-government; the lack of a large affluent class in Atlanta to support such a suburb; and the lack of a strong sense of community among the residents. The original physical design of the suburb was not a contributing factor; rather, to this day it remains the area's strongest point.

This study could quite legitimately end at this point. Were it to do so, however, it would fail to attempt an answer to the most provocative question raised—should suburban developments such as Inman Park have worked? To this writer's mind, there are several valid reasons that justify a negative answer to this question. The first of these concerns the role of such exclusive developments in a democratic society. In most cases when an exclusive residential suburb was spoken of, the emphasis was placed upon "exclusive." Such attempts to single out any particular group for exclusion smacks of an elitism that should have been viewed with the utmost suspicion in a genuinely democratic nation. This most definitely should have been the case in turn-of-the-century Atlanta, where 33 to 44 percent of the population was excluded from Inman Park because it was black.

As is so often the case, however, what should have been contrasted sharply with what was. Undeniably, most nineteenth–century suburban development was highly exclusionary and deliberately so. The realization of this fact calls into question the role of a planner such as Frederick Law Olmsted. Was he an elitist, creating his unequaled landscapes with scant regard for the "huddled masses yearning to breathe free," or was he only a victim of a society that forced him to rely on wealthy clients for patronage and thus to overlook more significant social concerns? He was both, for Olmsted seems to have had both an elitist and social activist side to his nature. No doubt, Olmsted the reformer often felt stymied by Olmsted the achiever, bound to a value system of the age which viewed land and housing as commodities to be bought and sold. Then too, Olmsted was only one man, and whatever his merits as a planner and social critic, he possessed no magical formula for changing the direction of a whole age.

The lack of democratic spirit betrayed by the "exclusive" suburban development stands in clear opposition to the pervasive spirit of democracy that characterizes the typical American view of private property. The tradition of privatism is nowhere better illustrated than in the fee simple system of landownership, which permits and at times encourages gross and even criminal misuse of land. Private land use must be tempered by some sense of social responsibility and accountability. The prevalent attitude towards housing must shift from one of housing as a commodity, which is a product of the spirit of privatism, to one of housing as a human necessity and right.[71]

Essentially, I have concluded that nineteenth–century suburban development should not have worked because it was characterized both by too little and too much democracy. It was far too elitist in its view of who should and could live in the suburbs, and yet it was far too democratic in its view of how land and housing could be used. The irony of the much maligned suburb lies in the fact that such nineteenth–century developments contributed landscapes that are still among the best in the United States today. Although the motives of such men as Frederick Law Olmsted and Joel Hurt might seem questionable when viewed from an egalitarian perspective, their products presented a vision of amenable living that could potentially span all class boundaries and limitations.

NOTES

1. Quoted in S. B. Sutton, ed., *Civilizing American Cities: A Selection of Frederick*

Law Olmsted's Writings on City Landscapes (Cambridge, Mass., 1971), p. 13.

2. *Atlanta Constitution*, February 26, 1890, p. 5 (hereafter cited as *AC*).

3. Paul Gaston, *The New South Creed: A Study in Southern Mythmaking* (New York, 1971), pp. 68–78.

4. "Preliminary Report upon the Proposed Suburban Village at Riverside, near Chicago," in Sutton, ed., *Civilizing American Cities*, p. 295 (hereafter cited as "Preliminary Report").

5. "Public Parks and the Enlargement of Towns," in Sutton, ed., *Civilizing American Cities*, pp. 62–63.

6. Ibid., p. 63.

7. "Preliminary Report," pp. 299, 300.

8. Ibid., p. 300.

9. Ibid.

10. *Atlanta Journal*, June 29, 1889, p. 4 (hereafter cited as *AJ*).

11. "Preliminary Report," p. 303.

12. Herbert U. Bassman, ed., *Riverside Then and Now*, rev. ed. (Chicago, 1958), pp. 72–73. The availability of this book suggested the comparison between the Chicago and Atlanta suburbs. Had there been a similar study of Llewellyn Park, which Inman Park closely resembles in design, such a comparison might have been made.

13. Ibid., pp. 105, 112

14. Ibid., p. 75.

15. Ibid., pp. 104, 116–18.

16. Ibid., p. 106.

17. Harold M. Mayer and Richard C. Wade, *Chicago: Growth of a Metropolis* (Chicago, 1969), pp. 330–32.

18. *Joel Hurt and the Development of Atlanta* (Atlanta, 1955), passim.

19. Ibid., p. 167; see also Elizabeth Lyon's "Frederick Law Olmsted and Joel Hurt: Planning for Atlanta," above.

20. *AJ*, February 22, 1890, p. 2.

21. Fulton County, Deed Book 236, p. 279.

22. Fulton County Deed Books.

23. *AJ*, February 22, 1890, p. 2.

24. *AJ*, May 6, 1889, p. 6.

25. *AJ*, February 22, 1890, p. 2.

26. *AC*, February 18, 1888, p. 7.

27. *AC*, February 18, 1888, p. 7.

28. *AC*, September 5, 1888, p. 5.

29. *AC*, September 27, 1888, p. 4.

30. *AC*, December 15, 1888, p. 22. All the information on the ceremonies surrounding the opening of Edgewood Avenue is taken from this article unless otherwise indicated.

31. *AC*, August 23, 1889, p. 4.

32. *AJ*, February 22, 1890, p. 2.

33. *AC*, February 26, 1890, p. 5.

34. *Atlanta City Directory*, 1891, p. 1215.

35. *AJ*, June 29, 1889, p. 4.

36. *AJ*, April 27, 1889, p. 3.
37. *AC*, February 23, 1890, p. 13.
38. *AJ*, May 6, 1889, p. 6.
39. Fulton County, Deed Book M4, p. 294.
40. *AJ*, May 10, 1889, p. 3.
41. Ibid., and February 23, 1890, p. 13.
42. *AJ*, February 22, 1890, p. 2.
43. *AC*, February 26, 1890, p. 5.
44. *AC*, February 27, 1890, p. 5.
45. *AJ*, April 21, 1890, p. 3; September 5, 1890, p. 5.
46. Fulton County, Deed Book O3, p. 51, and Deed Book S3, p. 680.
47. *AC*, February 26, 1890, p. 5.
48. *AC*, April 16, 1891, p. 4; April 23, 1891, p. 5; and May 8, 1891, p. 7.
49. *AJ*, April 11, 1891, p. 10.
50. *AC*, April 14, 1892, p. 7.
51. *AC*, April 14, 1895, p. 8.
52. Ibid.
53. *AC*, April 9, 1896, p. 5.
54. Fulton County, Deed Book 125, p. 32.
55. *AC*, April 9, 1896, p. 5.
56. This figure was calculated by first subtracting the number of buildings constructed after 1896, as recorded in the permits, from the number of buildings appearing on the Sanborn Fire Insurance map of 1911. The figure arrived at—fifty-eight—is reduced to twenty by subtracting the number of dwellings built by the original purchasers. The possibility that pre-1896 houses may have been demolished and not replaced makes the figure's accuracy open to question, but still probable.
57. *AJ*, January 18, 1897, p. 8.
58. *AC*, April 5, 1896, p. 7.
59. *AJ*, May 6, 1889, p. 6; *AC*, April 14, 1891, p. 9; and April 14, 1895, p. 3.
60. *AC*, April 5, 1896, p. 7.
61. Fulton County, Deed Book 215, p. 403, and Deed Book 268, p. 270.
62. *AC*, February 28, 1890, p. 6.
63. Marcus Whiffen, *American Architecture Since 1780* (Cambridge, Mass., 1969), p. 117.
64. In 1900, 57 percent of Atlanta's 89,800 people were white. Ten years later, 64 percent of 154,800 were white. This means a net increase of 47,786 in Atlanta's white population. While some of this increase can be attributed to the city's annexations, much of it was composed of newcomers to the city. These people needed homes, and no doubt many of them found them in Inman Park.
65. Whiffen, *American Architecture Since 1780*, p. 220.
66. Ibid., p. 159.
67. Atlanta City Building Department, Permit 2947, applied for October 27, 1905.
68. Atlanta City Building Department, Permit 3388, applied for October 9, 1907.

69. Timothy J. Crimmins, "The Crystal Stair: A Study of the Effects of Class, Race, and Ethnicity on Secondary Education in Atlanta, 1872–1925," Ph.D. dissertation, Emory University, 1972.

70. *The Gate City: Atlanta—Historical, Descriptive and Picturesque, 1890*; and *Art Work of Atlanta, Georgia*, 1895 and 1903 editions. Collections, State of Georgia Library, Atlanta.

71. Sam Bass Warner, Jr., *The Urban Wilderness: A History of the American City* (New York, 1972), especially Part One.

Howard L. Preston

PARKWAYS, PARKS, AND "NEW SOUTH" PROGRESSIVISM: Planning Practice in Atlanta, 1880–1917

"The present street arrangement of every large town," wrote Frederick Law Olmsted in 1868, "will at no very distant day require . . . to be supplemented . . . by a series of ways designed with express reference to pleasure." To Olmsted, surface travel over the streets of American cities was simply "far from pleasant" and unless "slowly and carefully done . . . hazardous to life and limb."[1] In nineteenth-century urban America, carefully constructed and well-maintained streets were the exception rather than the rule. Whenever a city did manage to build a public thoroughfare which was deliberately planned and laid out, that route usually stood in bold relief against the rigidity of grid-patterned streets that constituted the overall system of horizontal movement in most cities. In short, the majority of streets and avenues which evolved during this period of rapid urbanization are good examples of the unplanned and uncontrolled growth that was taking place in American cities. Indeed, there was no mistake about Olmsted's conclusion that surface travel was far from pleasant.

Olmsted's answer to the torturous conditions of movement that he saw was to integrate within the general street system of cities a series of broad, smooth, tree-lined thoroughfares that connected with parks. These routes were referred to as parkways. To Olmsted, they not only made surface travel more pleasant, but also provided a means of access to parks for urbanites who lived in other areas of the city and who were otherwise unable to enjoy them. Olmsted incorporated such ideas for parkways into comprehensive plans for street networks in several major American cities. In 1866, he laid out Ocean Parkway and Eastern Parkway as links between the developed portions of Brooklyn and Prospect Park. Five years later, he planned a park and parkway combination for Chicago which included the model suburban community of Riverside, located some nine miles from the center of the city. In 1876, at the Philadelphia

Centennial Exhibition, he unveiled a proposed parkway scheme for Buffalo.[2] And in the 1880s, Olmsted designed a series of parks and parkways
for Boston which encircled the entire city and later received the fitting title
of the "Emerald Necklace."[3]

Some of these proposals and others made by Olmsted and his contemporaries were implemented, but the vast majority never got beyond the
drawing board. Their failure represented the overall failure of American
cities to provide adequate park and parkway facilities for the well-being of
the public. In Atlanta, as elsewhere, the problem that consistently
blocked parkway construction did not stem from any paucity of feasible
schemes, but from the lack of a centralized authority to oversee the
conversion of mere blueprints into realities and to end street-building
practices that worked against efficient movement within the city. Therefore, the underlying question that late nineteenth-century American
planners like Olmsted faced was not whether a genuine need for parkways existed, or whether enough public enthusiasm to support a given
parkway project could be mustered. Rather, it was whether the authority,
and ultimately the power, existed to get the tremendous job of building
parkways in motion.

The best example of the necessary power and forcefulness needed to
accomplish the type of urban street reordering advocated by Olmsted was
evident in the work done in Paris during the mid-nineteenth century by
Baron Georges-Eugène Haussmann. Haussmann designed, and saw
built, a network of boulevards in Paris which constituted north-south and
east-west axial connections, and a double ring of outer encircling
thoroughfares which served as a framework for other minor circulatory
systems in the city.[4] Clearly, the magnitude of Haussmann's work was
never achievable in American cities, which did well to transform plans for
a single parkway into a concrete reality.

Haussmann's success and the consistent failure of American planners
in their endeavors resulted from the existence of two different systems of
authority. A strong dictatorial centralized authority in the form of the
French government and, ultimately, in the person of Emperor Napoleon
III stood behind Haussmann and guaranteed the success of his plans. In
the United States, the decentralization of power did not allow for
achievements on the Haussmann scale. Under the American system, the
support of top-ranking municipal officials, including the mayor and city
council members, meant little. The construction of a parkway through
already built-up areas of the city needed endorsement from a multitude of
individual property owners. Approval would have meant subordinating
private goals to public needs, which would have been directly contrary to
the traditions of city building in America. In the final analysis, the democratic means of change was too slow, too weak, and too inefficient to

ensure that a major overhaul of a city's thoroughfare system could ever be accomplished.

Attempts by urbanites to work within this system and to effect needed changes in their street patterns were met mostly by failure. If the Atlanta experience serves as an example of what took place in most American cities, the failures at providing relief from grossly inadequate street networks far outnumbered the successful building of parkways and boulevards.

After General Sherman burned Atlanta to the ground in 1864, those who rebuilt the city found greater value in concrete and steel than in park space. In 1879, when journalist Ernest Ingersoll came to Atlanta, he reported in *Harper's* that the city had no parks but had an abundance of "substantial business edifices," "new hotels of magnificent proportions," and "churches . . . lofty in gable and spire."[5] In the years immediately following the Civil War, private accomplishments more than public accommodations marked Atlanta's growth, and not until 1882 was the city given the land on which to build its first permanent park, Grant Park. The poor condition of Atlanta's streets further demonstrated the lack of attention paid to public matters. So miserable were they that after a siege of bad weather in 1881, a local newspaperman reported Broad Street, a main thoroughfare in the central business district, to be "half a leg deep in mud" and to resemble a "filthy canal."[6] In 1882, there were only 1.28 miles of improved streets in Atlanta, and when Grant Park opened in 1886, the city had managed to upgrade a mere 12.5 miles of public thoroughfares.[7] Consequently, Atlantans had little reason even to think of parkways until steps were taken to improve the conditions of the city's streets.

During the last fifteen years of the nineteenth century, however, as Atlantans made increasing use of Grant Park, the city did considerable work to improve surface travel (Map 2). The growing popularity of the park increased the demand for access to the city's one "green open space" and resulted in graded streets. More significantly, it produced several plans for a direct route from the central part of town to the park. The first of these plans resulted in the opening of South Boulevard in 1893. The park commissioner believed that the new boulevard, along with the extension of several other streets into Grant Park, would make "access easy from all sections" of Atlanta.[8] But because South Boulevard made no direct connection with the central part of the city, access remained a serious problem. In 1900, Sixth Ward Councilman Henry W. Grady, Jr., son of the famous Prophet of the New South, proposed the construction of a new route that would provide northside Atlantans with a better thoroughfare to the park. Grady claimed that his proposal could be accomplished at minimum cost by renovating existing streets and would simultaneously raise property values along the route.[9] His plan was never implemented, however, and as late as 1904, the need for adequate access to Grant Park still prompted discussion. "Above everything else," pleaded Mayor Evan P. Howell to the City Council, "we need a good road from the city to the park, laid under the direction of our city engineer and built by the city of Atlanta. I have been mortified by strangers who come to the city and want to drive to the park and [I am not] able to tell them a good drive to do it."[10]

A direct route linking the central city with Grant Park never materialized, and by Olmsted's standards the Atlantans' early plans were hopelessly deficient. Nevertheless, the tradition that Olmsted had established elsewhere in his parkway designs was directly felt in Atlanta. In fact, as Elizabeth Lyon has shown, Olmsted himself was quite active in the Gate City. He felt that the future in park design lay in the South, and he was anxious to establish his firm's name there. "Very soon all our northern cities will have been provided with parks," Olmsted wrote. "I am moved by a desire to get a footing at the South, from Southern men, and willing to pay for it."[11] Joel Hurt's planning of Druid Hills, a suburban community located in northeast Atlanta, provided Olmsted with such an opportunity in 1893, when Hurt retained the famous landscape architect as a consultant for the project.

Druid Hills was not a public endeavor, and Olmsted's success in the construction of the main thoroughfare, Ponce de Leon Avenue, around which the entire suburb was built, was entirely attributable to the private nature of Hurt's undertaking. The portion of Ponce de Leon Avenue that Olmsted planned lay within the boundaries of Hurt's property (Map 3). Although Olmsted did not live to see the completion of his scheme, Ponce de Leon Avenue became a reality because it was privately financed and promoted by influential Atlantans who saw to it that Olmsted's plans were followed to the letter. After Hurt sold Druid Hills to real estate magnate Forrest Adair in 1908, Adair remarked: "We are going to work immediately to further carry out the plans originally suggested by Mr. Olmsted."[12] With this kind of backing, Ponce de Leon Avenue was virtually assured of success.

When the boulevard was completed, it revealed Olmsted's skill in combining the practical with the aesthetic. At the outset, Olmsted convinced Hurt that rather than extend Ponce de Leon Avenue on a straight line into Druid Hills, as Hurt had previously done with Edgewood Avenue into Inman Park, a "more natural and economical" plan would provide for varying curves in the route, thus allowing the topography to determine the boulevard's course. Olmsted also addressed the problem of traffic congestion by carefully separating the different modes of transportation on Ponce de Leon Avenue. Arguing that his plan would allow streetcars to travel at greater speeds and with less chance of collision with other traffic, he confined vehicular traffic to the boulevards and located the electric street railway on a strip of land that bordered one of the parkways. The removal of the streetcars from the normal traffic flow, Olmsted believed, would decrease travel time to and from the city and thereby make Druid Hills a more convenient place to live. He argued further that with the streetcar tracks separated from other traffic, their maintenance costs would be reduced and, in addition, that the necessary poles and electrical wires could easily be hidden among the trees, thus making the drive more scenic.[13] Indeed, Ponce de Leon Avenue was a typical Olmstedian creation and demonstrated what careful planning combined with essential power could accomplish.

Olmsted's work in Druid Hills had apparently made a favorable impression on Atlanta's leaders, for in 1894 he was invited back. His return visit was made at the request of William A. Hemphill, the representative of a group of businessmen who were planning a major exposition in the city to promote Atlanta and the South. Olmsted arrived in the city in March 1894 and toured the site of the Cotton States and International Exposition with Hemphill and other officials. Later, in a newspaper interview, he revealed that he found the site to be "a beautiful spot . . . capable of being converted into a splendid exposition grounds."[14] Privately, however, he had doubts. In a letter written to his stepson, John C. Olmsted, he concluded that "the site has been fixed, chiefly by consideration of continuity and means of access. I should not think it a good one from our landscape point of view."[15]

Olmsted left Atlanta with the intention of submitting a report to the Exposition Improvement Committee, but because of a misunderstanding with exposition officials, a finished plan was apparently never submitted. However, at least one aspect of the improvements adopted for the Exposition site reflected the Olmstedian influence. In 1894, street railway tracks covered Piedmont Avenue, the most logical and direct route to the grounds. Rather than radically alter this route, the parallel thoroughfares of Jackson and Fort streets were extended northward to reach Bleckley Avenue, which bordered the Exposition grounds on the south. The extension of these streets linked the central part of Atlanta directly with the Exposition. Also, both streets were built with medians which separated north- and southbound traffic by direction, and no streetcar tracks were laid to obstruct other types of vehicular movement. Jackson and Fort streets, although not specifically designed by Olmsted, certainly reflected the influence of his parkway designs in Atlanta.

In subsequent years, the Olmstedian concept of urban parkways proved to be of continuing importance to Atlanta, for the city patterned its schemes for broad boulevards after those Olmsted had either designed or influenced in other cities. His influence was directly evident in Atlanta's plans for encircling driveways which were copies of parkways that linked parks and open spaces around the perimeter of other American cities. In addition to Boston's "Emerald Necklace," Detroit was the site of a plan in the 1880s for an encircling driveway that was patterned somewhat after Parisian driveways.[16] In 1895–1896, Daniel H. Burnham in cooperation with the city park commission proposed plans for a belt of parkways that would circumscribe the city of Chicago.[17]

News of such impressive achievements apparently sparked envy among Atlantans, who in the last years of the nineteenth century suffered from poor street conditions, a burgeoning population, and an atmosphere polluted by smoke and soot from trains that chugged through the central city. As a result of these deplorable conditions, the Park Commission of Atlanta, in its 1888 annual report, proposed the construction of "a broad driveway—about eight miles long—which will encircle Atlanta somewhat like the fine boulevards of Chicago and St. Louis."[18]

Eight years later, the idea was still alive but somewhat modified. The revised version which appeared in the *Constitution* in early 1896 described, in bucolic terms, an eleven-mile route which connected parks and open spaces on the city's periphery (Map 6). Readers were reminded of the "fresh hills of green, softly carpeted fields and cool, inviting valleys [that] begirt the city." Planned to begin at Piedmont Park and to pass closely by Ponce de Leon Park to the south, the route was designed to continue south to Grant Park and Little Switzerland. Heading west, the route would sweep by Fort McPherson and West End and thus permit easy access to Westview Cemetery, a spot which space-starved Atlantans frequently used for recreational purposes. On its northward course, the route was laid out to connect with Waterworks Park and then swing east, back to Piedmont Park.[19]

The 1896 proposal for the park boulevard was quite popular in Atlanta, at least among city officials. "With the new boulevard built around the city," commented City Engineer R. M. Clayton, "our parks and boulevards would be equal to that [sic] of Chicago."[20] Commissioner Walter R. Brown also compared the scheme to Chicago's:

Now that is just what Chicago is doing, although the city is going to do much more than we propose. Chicago is going to construct a driveway one hundred yards wide and one hundred miles long. This will probably be the best roadway in the world. We only want to build one one-tenth as long as that, and we must do these things in order not to be left behind the other cities.[21]

Another city official, obviously reminded of Haussmann's accomplishments, optimistically envisioned "an opportunity to pleasantly spend

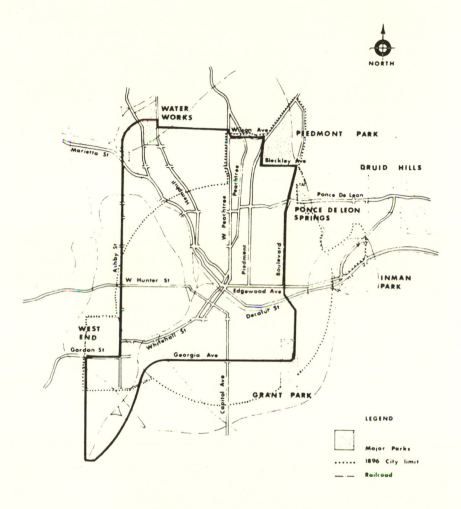

6. Proposed parkway plan for Atlanta, 1896.

summer afternoons in our carriages on the boulevard, as they do in Paris."[22]

The desire for a circumferential driveway did not die with the failure of either the 1888 or the 1896 park boulevard proposals. In late 1899, the federal government, in conjunction with a national park program, became interested in a similar plan. The new idea for an encircling parkway actually included three driveways totaling approximately fifteen miles in length. This undertaking, however, differed from the more conventional application of encircling driveways, as in Chicago and Boston, in that the routes built in Atlanta would link the Civil War battlefields of Ezra Church, Peachtree Creek, and Leggett's Hill (the Battle of Atlanta) rather than parks.[23]

This plan to commemorate Civil War battlefields with the construction of a parkway also got no further than the drawing board, but the idea for a boulevard connecting the historic battlefields located around the city generated enthusiasm among the city's leaders.[24] In 1906, the Atlanta Chamber of Commerce became interested in the idea and attempted to retain the Brookline, Massachusetts, firm of Olmsted Brothers and Associates to devise a suitable scheme. "Our Chamber of Commerce," wrote Walter R. Cooper, secretary of the organization, to Frederick Law Olmsted, Jr., "has under consideration a park system for Atlanta in connection with the proposed National Parks on the battlegrounds around the City, which we wish to connect with a boulevard about 25 miles long, running entirely around the city."[25] Although interested, the younger Olmsted remembered previous experiences in Atlanta and declined the invitation. "If conditions are right for something more than this at present," Olmsted, Jr., wrote back, "my reluctance to take the time for a trip to Atlanta would disappear."[26]

The Olmsted firm's misgivings about working in Atlanta left the proposition of an encircling boulevard open, and real estate developer Edwin P. Ansley jumped at the opportunity. In 1904, Ansley began the construction of his northside suburb, Ansley Park, and four years later he revealed plans for a parkway that would surround the city.[27] Ansley's motivation was the need for adequate sewer facilities for his suburb. In conjunction with the construction of the parkway, he argued that the city could easily install a sewerage system for the northern part of Atlanta and Fulton County. He proposed that the federal government purchase the Civil War battlefields located on the city's periphery, and he indicated that it would be an easy matter to connect battlefields, parks, and points of special interest by extending and improving existing streets. After winning the approval of the Atlanta Chamber of Commerce as well as the Grand Army of the Republic, Ansley employed Solon Z. Ruff, a civil engineer who had worked for Joel Hurt in the early stages of the development of Druid Hills and later designed Ansley Park, to draw up the necessary plans for the new battlefield parkway. However, like previous parkway schemes for Atlanta, the battlefield parkway was never built. Still, in Ansley's mind, such a boulevard would have been nothing short of "the most historic and sacred thoroughfare in all of Dixie."[28]

At the same time that Ansley was developing and promoting Ansley

Park (which he cleverly advertised as "Atlanta Beautiful," thereby seeking to identify the project with the nationally acclaimed "City Beautiful"
movement) Atlantans were made aware that their own parks were markedly inferior to those of other cities. In a series of articles which appeared
in the *Constitution* in 1908, Dan Carey, newly appointed secretary and
general manager of the Atlanta Park Commission, publicized the inadequate state of the parks: "Atlanta is so far behind in the park movement,
so deficient in park development, that it seems almost a shame to write
upon such a matter in the public prints." He went on to point out that "all
writers on the question of the 'City Beautiful' admit that parks are the
basis of everything."[29] In a later article, Carey scorned the city's builders:

We have built as did the builders of the Tower of Babel; we have lifted brick and
mortar and steel and money into the air that all might see the glory of our city; but
what have we done to soften the temper of our people? What have we done
toward giving a chance to the lungs and bodies of the little children of the poor?
. . . We have filled our air with smoke and soot and have provided scantily for the
maintenance of the warehouses of pure air.[30]

Before his appointment to the Atlanta Park Commission, Carey had
worked on separate occasions in the Georgia capital as a reporter for the
Atlanta Constitution and *Journal* and, in 1907, as secretary to Mayor David
Woodward. Carey was well-versed in park and parkway schemes for
other American cities. He pointed specifically to the accomplishments of
Boston's Commons Society, Kansas City's Tree Planters Association,
Buffalo's Forestry Association, and Philadelphia's Fairmont Association
in their respective cities.[31]

During his tenure on the Park Commission (1908–1914), Carey exerted
a positive influence on upgrading the quality of the city's parks. In 1909,
the year after his appointment to the Park Commission, he apparently
helped to secure the services of the Olmsted Brothers firm for the rede-
sign of several of Atlanta's parks. In 1911, one of them, Piedmont
Park—the original grounds for the 1895 Cotton States and International
Exposition—became the city's largest landscaped open space.

Ideologically, Carey combined in uneasy tension the national ideals of
Progressive reform with the regional credo of Southern Bourbonism. On
the one hand, he clearly recognized the social benefits that parks provided for *all* urban dwellers. On the other, he seemed incapable of
carrying that Progressive conviction to its logical conclusion by providing
a place in the city's park system—other than separate, i.e., legally
segregated—for Atlanta's black citizenry. His approach was "New
South."

In 1911, Carey first suggested the construction of a segregated park for

blacks in Atlanta. He based his argument on the premise that "it be-
hooves the white citizens of Atlanta to keep the bodies of the colored
people clean and their minds pure. . . . If the city will open a park for
negroes . . ., the places of vice for negroes will have to close their doors
for·want of patrons."[32] For the next two years, Carey reiterated this
proposal in the annually published Park Commission *Reports*. In 1913, he
made his final and classic plea for a park for blacks in Atlanta:

I again urge you with all the emphasis of which I am capable to use your endeavor
to secure parks and playgrounds for the negroes of the city. Although I would not
be ashamed by any means of urging this for the benefit of the negroes themselves
. . . my main object is for the protection of our own race. Surely it must occur to
you that there is a connection between this fact and the fact that the city is doing
nothing to provide wholesome recreation for the negroes during their leisure
hours. We hear very frequently of the playground and recreation work that is
being done by northern cities. We have heard about the tenement house work.
. . . These works in the north and west have received impetus and are given
attention because they are being done for the class of citizens who correspond in
the north to our negroes in the south. . . . The hospitals are crowded with them,
the insane asylums house a larger percentage of them than of any other race, they
are "our poor." . . . Now I maintain that if it is a function of government to send
these people to jail, to put them on probation for drunkeness [*sic*] and minor
offenses, to treat them after they have contracted tuberculosis, to care for them
after they have become insane . . . then it is obviously a function of government to
adopt such preventive methods as will keep them from becoming our public
charges after it is too late.[33]

Carey's brand of New South Progressivism was apparently too radical
for the conservative Park Commission. Not only did he fail to secure a
park in Atlanta for blacks, but in 1914 he lost the position of secretary and
general manager. While his singular combination of national urban Progressivism and regional "white man's burden" rationale failed to sway
the Park Commission even to consider the construction of a park in the
city for blacks, Carey's earlier denunciation of the miserable state of the
Georgia capital's parks did evoke some response from city officials. In
1903, the city had employed Olmsted Brothers and Associates to plan
improvements for Atlanta's parks. Between 1903 and 1909, however,
Atlanta's leadership refused to appropriate the necessary funds to support improvement projects. Under these circumstances, the Olmsted firm
could do little, and not until 1908, when Carey commenced his searing
newspaper articles, did matters begin to change.
    Indicative of the changed attitude of Atlanta's leadership was the visit
of John C. Olmsted who was invited to the city in the spring of 1909, at
which time he consented to furnish improvement plans for Piedmont

Park, Grant Park, Mims Park, and Springvale Park. The city agreed to pay $1,800 for the Piedmont Park plan and $800 for improvement recommendations for the other parks.[34] Olmsted, remembering how little had been accomplished in earlier attempts to renovate Atlanta's open spaces, quickly pointed out that for the venture to be successful, adequate funds would have to be made available for the improvements. "Atlanta is considerably behind in the matter of parks," he stated frankly. "It will never be able to accomplish anything worthwhile with . . . small yearly appropriations."[35]

Frederick Law Olmsted, Jr., followed his half-brother to Atlanta in the fall of 1909 and spent approximately two weeks with Carey surveying Piedmont Park.[36] Early the following year, Olmsted, Jr., submitted the completed plan to the Park Board. The proposed improvements centered around the idea of a five-mile driveway which would wind through Piedmont Park. The drive was designed to maximize pleasure for the traveler by providing spectacular views of the lake and park landscape at various points along the route.[37] He also intended to use the driveways of Piedmont Park as links to the roadways of adjacent Ansley Park. Indeed, joining the two parks popularized the area, and thereafter it was often referred to as Twin Parks.[38]

With the much publicized beautification of Piedmont Park and Ansley Park in north Atlanta, residents of other sections of the city became interested in improving their areas. In west Atlanta, a group of prominent citizens formed the West Side Improvement Committee for the purpose of calling the city's attention to their "orphaned" section of Atlanta. The campus of Atlanta University dominated this western portion of the city (Figure 12), and at first the West Side Improvement Committee attempted to buy the university property. When university officials rejected this proposition, the committee secured a guarantee from the Atlanta University Board of Trustees that the school would deed a wide strip of property to extend Beckwith Street westward through the campus to Ashby Street.[39] Even though the plan eventually was discarded, the idea won enthusiastic endorsement from many west Atlanta residents and real estate owners who recognized that a new boulevard would raise their property values. "I am deeply interested in this improvement," asserted Samuel M. Inman, a prominent real estate owner and developer in the area. "The First Ward is my old home, and nearly everything I possess is in this section."[40]

Meanwhile, on the city's southside, the Olmsted Brothers' work in Grant Park was drawing the attention of nearby residents. Earlier in the century, the Brookline firm had commended Grant Park's "natural beauty and adaptability for the purpose of a park its size,"[41] but had also expressed concern over the vexing (and long-standing) problem of inadequate access roads to the park proper. In fact, as late as 1903, John C. Olmsted was to describe Augusta Avenue, at the park's entrance, as a "mass of mud."[42] By 1910, however, conditions had improved markedly, as the Olmsteds built new entrances to the park, opened new streets, and widened existing ones. The resulting transformation elicited increasing civic pride from southside Atlantans and prompted the *Constitution* to boast that "the 'City Beautiful' is well shown in some of the fine streets and avenues on the south side."[43]

The newspaper's claim that the southside thoroughfares made Atlanta a "City Beautiful" was, at best, an overstatement. Citywide, between 1888 and 1910, eight parkway proposals had been formulated, but, unfortunately, only one parkway had been built. Seven years later, the city was to receive another chance. On May 21, 1917, a raging fire swept through the Fourth Ward, on the city's east side, devastating approximately three hundred acres of property, destroying 1,938 buildings, causing an estimated $5.5 million in damages, and leaving 10,000 people homeless.[44] Literally all that remained in the burnt district were a few hundred stone chimneys that stood as grim monuments to the disaster.

Recognizing the rare opportunity for significant change now at hand, the Atlanta Chamber of Commerce appointed a special committee to plan new uses for the burnt district.[45] Within nine days of the fire, the first tentative proposal had been mapped out. The plan called for the extensions of Houston Street and Hilliard Street north to Ponce de Leon Avenue, and it then indicated that Houston Street should be widened to one hundred feet and Hilliard Street (to be renamed Grand Boulevard) to one hundred and fifty feet. Finally, the plan accommodated existing racial segregation ordinances by designating the area south of Houston Street and east of Grand Boulevard for blacks, and the area north of Houston Street and east of Grand Boulevard for whites.[46]

In its physical design, Grand Boulevard was very similar to Olmsted's parkways (Figure 15). Trees and hedges were to be planted on a thirty-foot-wide median which separated north- and southbound traffic, and the boulevard was also to be framed by two ten-foot-wide sidewalks. The proposal, however, only covered the area of the city which had been destroyed by the fire, and the Special Committee of the Chamber of Commerce desired to take full advantage of the unique opportunity now open to Atlanta. The Special Committee wanted to use Grand Boulevard as an anchor for a parkway connecting major points of interest on the eastern side of the city. Suggestions to link the city water works in the north with the Federal Prison and Lakewood Park in the south were entertained. Passing through Piedmont Park, Oakland Cemetery, and Grant Park, this route was planned to follow the same course as earlier

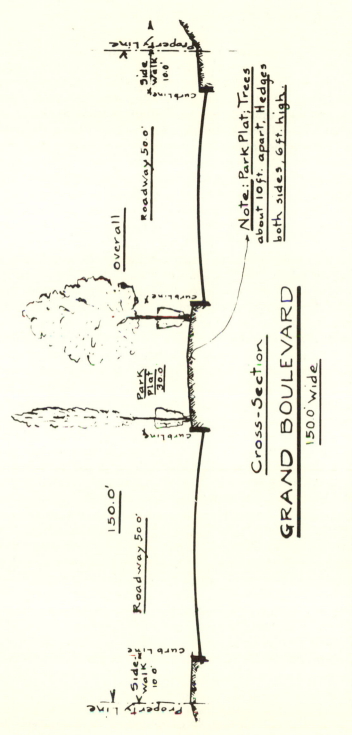

Side walk 10.0'

curb line

Roadway 50.0'

curb line

overall

Park Plat 30.0

Roadway 50.0'

150.0'

curb line

Side walk 10.0'

Property Line

Property Line

→Note: Park Plat; Trees about 10ft. apart, Hedges both sides, 6ft. high.

Cross-Section

GRAND BOULEVARD

150.0' wide

15. Sketch of proposed parkway, May 1917, to be known as Grand Boulevard and to serve as the main artery through the eastern district of Atlanta, which had been destroyed by fire earlier in the year.

proposals.[47] But even though this scheme initially seemed to have a better chance for success than its predecessors, it, too, was discarded.

Thus, between 1880 and 1917, very little changed in Atlanta with regard to park space and parkways. In 1879, Ernest Ingersoll reported that Atlanta had no parks at all, and thirty-eight years later, Warren C. Powell observed that "Atlanta has always been short of parks."[48] During these years, no fewer than nine parkway proposals proved to be of little value to the city of Atlanta. Each plan for better thoroughfares, expressed in Olmstedian parkways, was filed away, one after the other, for possible reference later. The city grew haphazardly, as it always had—by private unrelated interests determining that a street would be built here and an avenue would be laid out there. Private property owners and interest groups continually made the decisions as to which streets would be graded and extended, and their judgments were naturally based on self-benefit rather than any concern for the overall urban environment. No centralized authority existed to stop this unsystematic approach to street building, which in itself had created the need for parkways. Consequently, Atlantans, like most urban Americans, suffered from both a markedly inadequate street network and frustrations caused by a system of government that was unable to respond to this critical urban need.

Under this system of authority, Atlanta's experience was typical. Neither influential groups, like the Chamber of Commerce, nor successive municipal governments had the power necessary to push a park or parkway proposal beyond the mere planning stage or to check the unplanned street construction that was taking place. Unlike other American cities, however, which during the late nineteenth and early twentieth centuries discarded as many, if not more, park and parkway plans than did Atlanta, residents of the Georgia capital were faced with the additional dilemma of being unable to extend nationally accepted Progressive ideals to blacks. The demand for urban open spaces to improve the quality of life for the poor was a useful argument among Progressive groups outside the South. In Atlanta, however, this ideal never gained any degree of acceptability, for in the case of park space, just as with education and politics, the doctrine of "separate but equal"—with emphasis on the separate—always stood as the priority. Therefore, no matter how well-informed, well-meaning, and sympathetic reform-minded Southerners like Dan Carey were to the inequalities visited upon a city's "black side,"[49] their Progressivism still meant dogmatic adherence to racial traditions, which in the final analysis clearly spelled "New South."

NOTES

1. Frederick Law Olmsted and Calvert Vaux, "Observations on the Progress

of Improvements in Street Plans, with Special Reference to the proposed Parkway to be Laid out in Brooklyn" (Brooklyn, 1869), in S. B. Sutton, ed., *Civilizing American Cities: A Selection of Frederick Law Olmsted's Writings on City Landscapes* (Cambridge, Mass., 1971), pp. 40–41.

2. Albert Fein, "The American City: The Ideal and the Real," in Edgar Kaufman, Jr., ed., *The Rise of American Architecture* (New York, 1970), p. 94.

3. Julius Gy. Fabos, Gordon T. Milde, and V. Michael Weinmayr, *Frederick Law Olmsted, Sr., Founder of Landscape Architecture in America* (Amherst, Mass., 1968), p. 71.

4. Georges-Eugène Haussmann, *Memoires* (Paris, 1890–1893), 3: 50. Cited in Francoise Choay, *The Modern City: Planning in the Nineteenth Century* (New York, 1969), p. 18.

5. Ernest Ingersoll, "The City of Atlanta," *Harper's*, 60 (December 1879): 30–43.

6. *Atlanta Constitution*, January 7, 1881, p. 1 (hereafter cited as *AC*).

7. Atlanta Public Works Commission, Report of the Public Works Commissioner, *Annual Reports, City of Atlanta* (1904), p. 288.

8. Atlanta Park Commission, Report of the Parks Commissioner, *Annual Reports, City of Atlanta* (1893), p. 424.

9. *AC*, October 23, 1900, p. 12.

10. *AC*, January 5, 1904, p. 7.

11. Frederick Law Olmsted to John C. Olmsted, March 13, 1894, Olmsted Papers.

12. *Atlanta Journal*, May 19, 1908, p. 4 (hereafter cited as *AJ*).

13. Kenneth Ayers, "Olmsted and Druid Hills," unpublished seminar paper, Emory University, May 1971.

14. *AC*, March 18, 1894, p. 17.

15. Frederick Law Olmsted to John C. Olmsted, March 15, 1894, Olmsted Papers.

16. Blake McKelvey, *The Urbanization of America, 1860–1915* (New Brunswick, N.J., 1963), p. 116.

17. Charles Moore, *Daniel H. Burnham: Architect, Planner of Cities* (New York, 1921), 2: 98–99.

18. *Sixth Annual Report of the Park Commission of Atlanta, to the Mayor and City Council, 1888* (Atlanta, 1889), pp. 1–2. Sidney Root, president of the Park Commission in 1888, was the father of Atlanta-born architect John Wellborn Root.

19. *AC*, February 2, 1896, p. 2.

20. Ibid.

21. *AC*, February 4, 1896, p. 7.

22. Ibid.

23. *AC*, December 5, 1899, p. 9.

24. As late as 1931, plans were submitted for an outer Battlefield Boulevard. While earlier proposals only linked places of military conflict, the 1931 plan took Kennesaw and Stone Mountains into consideration. Robert R. Otis, "Atlanta's Plan, 1909–1932" (Atlanta, 1951).

25. Walter R. Cooper to Frederick Law Olmsted, Jr., September 21, 1906, Olmsted Papers.

26. Frederick Law Olmsted, Jr., to Walter R. Cooper, September 26, 1906, Olmsted Papers. Atlanta owed Olmsted Brothers and Associates $825.14 for services rendered under a 1903 agreement. By 1907, the matter still remained unsettled, and Olmsted Brothers retained an Atlanta attorney to settle the difficulty. The Brookline firm sent a letter to Joel Hurt which read in part: "We very rarely have the occasion to resort to legal measures in the collection of bills due us and it is with great regret that we conclude that it has become necessary in this case. We write, therefore, to ask you if you will be good enough to recommend to us a local lawyer who will be willing and well fitted to represent us in the matter" (March 12, 1907). The problem was settled in 1909 without legal action.

27. AC, May 31, 1908, p. 8D.

28. AC, April 24, 1910, p. 4A.

29. AC, April 5, 1908, p. 6A.

30. AC, April 12, 1908, p. 33.

31. Atlanta City Directories, 1901, 1904, 1907, 1908; AC, April 17, 1908, p. 1, and April 20, 1908, p. 5.

32. Annual Report of the Atlanta Park Commission, 1911 (Atlanta, 1912), pp. 20–21.

33. Annual Report of the Atlanta Park Commission, 1913 (Atlanta, 1914), pp. 32–33.

34. AC, April 21, 1909, p. 9. Mims Park was a small park located in south Atlanta, and Springvale Park was a suburban park situated in Inman Park.

35. AJ, April 22, 1909, p. 10. The city appropriated approximately $50,000 for park improvements and maintenance purposes in 1909.

36. AC, November 3, 1909, p. 11.

37. AC, March 21, 1910, p. 3.

38. AC, April 3, 1910, p. 6.

39. AJ, April 21, 1909, p. 9.

40. Ibid.

41. Olmsted Brothers and Associates to Joel Hurt, March 24, 1903, Olmsted Papers.

42. Report of Visit to Atlanta, John C. Olmsted, March 16, 1903, Olmsted Papers.

43. AC, April 12, 1910, p. 5.

44. Report of the Atlanta Conflagration of May 21, 1917, National Board of Fire Underwriters Committee.

45. Warren C. Powell, "Parks Planned for Burned Area," The City Builder (June 1917): 15.

46. Tentative Sketch #1 submitted to the Special Committee of the Atlanta Chamber of Commerce (in possession of the author). In 1922, the city of Atlanta did "enact segregation along straight social lines by dividing the residential districts into three types: white, colored, undetermined." Seymour I. Toll has examined the legal history of Atlanta's discriminatory zoning in Zoned American (New York, 1969), pp. 262–63.

47. Powell, "Parks Planned," p. 15.

48. Ibid.

49. The division between racial districts in the city was becoming so sharp that the title of the first history of its African-American community was The Black Side of Atlanta (Atlanta, 1894), written by the Reverend Edward R. Carter.

Frederick Gutheim

OLMSTED AT BILTMORE

Olmsted's last great creative effort can be justly regarded as the totality of his Southern projects—the Louisville parks, Atlanta's Druid Hills for the Kirkwood Land Company, the concept of a plan for the Cotton States and International Exposition grounds, and the Hot Springs military reservation—and Biltmore. With the exception of the last, which commenced in 1888, the others all date from about 1893 when Olmsted was chiefly absorbed with the Chicago Exposition and his health was rapidly deteriorating. That he should have risen to the challenge of the New South under these circumstances is a measure of the depth of his conviction that the Southern states were at last demonstrating their potentialities and had become promising territory for the making of urban parks and landscape architecture. But more, and especially of Biltmore, Olmsted saw this as his last great creative effort, and into this work he put his deepest convictions concerning the landscape art and its natural, rural character. At stake was nothing less grand than the American national landscape itself, in all its regional expressions, to be inspired and taught by the Biltmore demonstration, the nursery and arboretum (and be no less significant than Harvard's great Arnold Arboretum), and the school of forestry. Alas, it was a tragic failure.

This is a critical judgment, not one derived wholly from history or biography, although hopefully informed by such studies. It embraces the whole of Olmsted's career, especially those elements of it in which he dealt with the broadest sweep of the national landscape, as in his discovery of western Texas, California, and the Adirondacks. And too, it encompasses the contrast between his comprehensive and constructive proposals for the management of such distinctive regional landscapes and his approach to the landscape of the New South. Much as the environs of Asheville may have been untypical of the South, Olmsted could hardly have been blind to the larger landscape south to Atlanta, or of the coastal plain. Nor could he have ignored the great landscape changes which had marked the passing of the plantation system, the rise of a more diversified postbellum agriculture, and the clear evidence and anticipations of future trends to be seen in the early 1890s.

Preoccupation of earlier writers with the antebellum years of Olmsted's career was dictated partly because it is here that his life was more diversified (and, as Lewis Mumford has argued, more articulated in the writings of those years) and because in landscape architecture his career was more creative and more formative. The tail end of his career shows him struggling against the rising Beaux Arts formalism (in landscape design as well as in architecture), large-scale corporate and government organizations, and the waning of that larger perspective of the national landscape which his work and ideas had exemplified—most strikingly in Yosemite, Niagara Falls, and the Adirondacks, and always through his commitment to the pastoral scenery of his native southern New England. Olmsted's clients, the conditions of work they exacted, even the milieu of his firm—the largest landscape design organization in the world—reflected the new conditions: programs dictated by others, increasingly competitive terms, professional teamwork with architects and engineers, rigid scheduling and tight deadlines, and the inexorable rule of cost accounting and business system. Most of all, as Laura Wood Roper's biography makes abundantly clear, Olmsted was tired and old.[1] Yet, at the age of sixty-six in 1888, his spirits rose as he contemplated the Biltmore project, and they were sustained as its potentialities unfolded during the next five years.

Olmsted at Biltmore also reveals the role and the influence of the professional adviser in the arts of architecture and landscape design. That Olmsted had convictions, that they were indispensable to his advice and necessary to his creativity, and that they attracted clients to him is quite evident. But that his clients could be persuaded to follow his advice seems to have been determined in part by their own desires and the limitations of their own resources, as much as by the intrinsic merits of such beliefs or the force of Olmsted's great persuasiveness. At one extreme, the architect learns to decline commissions from clients whose interests are impossibly incompatible with his own views, and at the other, he can undeniably bring clients to accept advice which unaided they would not have taken. The complex and subtle relationship of architect and client is as inscrutable as in a marriage—and equally to be avoided by those who enter it with the intention to reform the other. And the work of architecture is as strewn with the wrecks of misunderstood commissions and expectations or failed compromises as the world of marriage is marked by separation and divorce.

The relationship between the twenty-six-year-old George Washington Vanderbilt and the sixty-six-year-old Olmsted commenced in 1888 after Vanderbilt had entered upon the acquisition and development of his North Carolina principality. The unfolding of this relationship would be worth reconstructing in detail, but not here.

By the fourth generation, the descendants of the ferryboat, river line, and railroad magnate Cornelius Vanderbilt could attend to interests other than money. True, the sons spread like a dye through the boards of the various national railroad systems, but room was found for some other interests, dictated largely by the style the times prescribed for the monied. In the generation of George Washington Vanderbilt, his brothers were distinguished by an interest in show horses (which extended to giving Rosa Bonheur's *The Horse Fair* to the Metropolitan Museum of Art) and such philanthropies as hospitals, libraries, and the theatre; and they intermarried with the Whitneys and Belmonts.[2]

With his interest in travel, the fine arts, and book collecting and a marked indifference to enterprise, George W. Vanderbilt took an independent line in 1888 when he commenced to assemble the lands in the valley of the French Broad, near Asheville, North Carolina, where he was to create Biltmore. It is not altogether clear what he had in mind at the start, but he was the discoverer of the region, had become attracted to it, and had decided to have a house there in which to spend his leisure and entertain his friends. (He already had houses at Bar Harbor, Maine, and in New York City.)

A modest industrial growth had commenced in Asheville after the railroad reached there in 1880, but the earlier character of the town as a spa and a mountain refuge from the summer heat was maintained. Strengthened by Vanderbilt's conspicuous activities, it expanded into a year-round tourist and resort center which really boomed in the 1920s. The surrounding mountain region was characterized by the poverty and isolation—and the charm—of Appalachia.

The two thousand acres initially acquired by Vanderbilt brought him in 1889 to the simultaneous consideration of appropriate architectural and landscape decisions, and thus to Richard Morris Hunt and Frederick Law Olmsted. The two prominent New York designers had already locked horns over the style of Central Park gateways and the Albany state capital. It would have been hard to imagine any individuals less likely than Vanderbilt and Hunt to have understood the regional situation. What in fact materialized was a New York City Fifth Avenue chateau transplanted to North Carolina. But Olmsted accepted the architectural situation while hoping for more in the landscape.

Indeed, it was hard to know where to draw the line. Vanderbilt had commenced by thinking of a large wood frame house—one recalls the contemporary shingle-style mansions of New England seaside towns or the misnamed Adirondack camps and lodges. But his conception vanished under Hunt's influence as he and Vanderbilt toured the Loire and submitted themselves to the Renaissance splendors of Chambord, Blois, and the garden art of Le Nôtre at Vaux-le-Vicomte. After five years of construction, what emerged was a high steep-roofed *Francois Premier* chateau, with a principal façade 780 feet in length, covering in all four acres. One entered a vast hall 75 feet in height, with a spectacular Guastavino tile ceiling, containing another structural marvel, the self-supporting spiral staircase. Beyond lay endless wonders—banquet halls, dining rooms lined with Spanish leather, fireplaces by Wedgewood, tapestry galleries, special rooms for prints and paintings, libraries—all fitted with great art, decoration, and antiquities of historic association and artistic interest, even down to the red train worn by Cardinal Richelieu. This was not vulgar or ostentatious; everything about it was in good taste—except it. By 1889, Hunt's drawings for this palatial house were shown to Olmsted who raised no objection, intent upon his own part of the project.

It is a reasonable surmise that Vanderbilt approached both Hunt and Olmsted simultaneously and was prepared to play one against the other. The initial question put to Olmsted was what to do with the rather poor mountain land. Olmsted's advice was to limit the garden effort, "to make a small park into which to look from your house; make a small pleasure ground and garden, farm your river bottom chiefly to keep and fatten live stock with a view to manure; and make the rest a forest, improving the existing woods and planting the old fields." A modest program, certainly, but one to prove elusive. Possibly it could already be seen as out of step with Hunt's vast conception. Olmsted soon offered his own general plan for the entire two thousand acres, a plan that followed his initial advice, and within this outline the more detailed features were evolved over time as Olmsted suggested and Vanderbilt accepted them.

New land was constantly being added to the estate. By 1891, the commitment to forestry had been made, and the young Gifford Pinchot, providentially it seems, arrived on the scene and was engaged on Olmsted's advice to direct the forestry work. Vanderbilt became sufficiently enthused to want the forestry program exhibited in the Chicago exposition, on Olmsted's suggestion, and there can be no doubt of its fundamental importance to the origins of American conservation and to the establishment of those national forests Olmsted had urged since his initial efforts to save the California redwood groves. No less than a Secretary of Agriculture expressed his envy that Vanderbilt employed more foresters than the United States government. When he had become head of the United States Forest Service, Pinchot soon changed that balance, but while it lasted forestry was the most successful and significant of Olmsted's contributions to Biltmore.

Olmsted conceived an arboretum as early as 1889, and for years it seemed likely to enlist Vanderbilt's support. But as a scientific arboretum on the model of Arnold or Kew it was ultimately shot down by Charles

Sprague Sargent, the director of Arnold, who judged that such an enterprise should not be left to the uncertain fortune and whim of a single individual. Much as Olmsted hoped for the project, there is no evidence that to Vanderbilt it had ever been more than a whim, or possibly, some murmur of agreement to placate Olmsted while he got on with the principal work. The entire relationship of landscape architect and client, while tranquil, appears lacking in substance, and it seems most likely that Olmsted had misjudged his client's interest. The formal garden itself was compromised when maintenance funds were cut to a quarter of the original budget after 1900; the forestry school was discontinued; and the arboretum passed from Olmsted's control to become something quite different from his original conception.

Before returning to the larger issues of Biltmore for the South, a summary of what it did actually accomplish is in order. This was by no means inconsiderable. The initial two thousand acres grew to one hundred thousand forested acres, ultimately embracing entire mountains, fifteen large farms operated by tenants, a commercial dairy, and the immediate two hundred and fifty acres surrounding the house. Over the years, most of this acreage has been dispersed to form the eighty thousand acre nucleus of the Pisgah National Forest, Biltmore Village, the later residential subdivision, Biltmore Forest, and the house and gardens that are maintained relatively intact as an historic property open to the public. At a later stage, in another generation of Vanderbilts, firmer connections with the realities of the South were established. The Biltmore Dairies demonstrated a new kind of agriculture that could be supported on the local soils and in the upland climate, meeting local market demands. Mrs. Vanderbilt's Biltmore Industries offered training in crafts and industrial skills, and explored new forms of enterprise. Biltmore itself assumed its place in the tourist itinerary of the South. Tourists, summer and winter, came in increasing numbers. And with the maturing of the forests came both forest industries and the creation of the national forest.

What emerged at Biltmore was a manmade landscape, as Central Park, Prospect Park, Belle Isle, or the riverfront parks of Niagara had been carved from rocky ridges and marshlands or reclaimed from human misuse. In the immediate vicinity of the mansion, Olmsted craftily led visitors through a carefully contrived landscape experience. He relocated the approach drive to run along the winding stream with its rich and varied suggestions of the natural forest that would soon surround the estate, clothing the valley slopes with a new growth of trees and making the most of the play of running water, empoundments, and cascades. Emerging from the naturalistic woods, visitors were presented a dramatic change: the great formal gardens surrounding the chateau, and the impressive façade and entrance into the great hall. From the sheltered terraces and balconies and windows of the principal rooms there was the constant reminder of the uninterrupted surrounding mountain grandeur.

While satisfying Vanderbilt and Hunt with these uncharacteristic landscape theatricals, Olmsted searched for more satisfying opportunities. These he found in the larger landscape, in the forestry operations, and in the projected arboretum. Of these, the arboretum most attested to Olmsted's new interest in the South. As an educational institution, it could decisively enlarge the South's understanding of its landscape resources and its potential for a great and distinctive regional style. It could show how the natural resources of forestry, horticulture, and botany in the largest dimensions could contribute to Southern development. Neither did anything of this sort appear in the mind of that cultural carpetbagger, George Vanderbilt; nor was it expressed by Olmsted, intent upon replicating at Asheville his earlier success, the Arnold Arboretum, as a world-renowned scientific institution.

Regionalism was the great and challenging theme at Biltmore, and the failure to realize new regional potentialities was the great tragedy at Biltmore. The instructive contrast is between Olmsted's approach to the new conditions of the West Coast in 1863 and his view of the new conditions of the South after 1888. California had been a *tabula rasa*, virgin territory in which the arid climate, varied conditions of fog, winds, desert, even the hard winters of Yosemite, and the rigors of frontier life were all as stimulating as the new catalog of forest trees and plant materials. Olmsted responded with the enthusiasm of the born traveler for the new, and his reports for the Yosemite Commission and the city of San Francisco, while as barren of immediate accomplishment as Biltmore, showed imaginative brilliance. No similar document illustrates Olmsted's response to the South, but his letters to his son and to his firm provide an adequate tracing of the more pragmatic orientation of his later years. Despite the vast scale of the project and the resources of his client, there are no stirringly vast plans. Instead, there is a greater concern for realizable proposals, the accommodation of the client's view and the terms laid down by his architect, and as the project matured, a more defensive attitude toward the criticisms expressed by the foresters and resident landscape engineers who were carrying out plans they were not in full agreement with and the designer had increasingly diminished control over. Under these conditions, the potential faded for the New South to realize a bold new landscape for city and countryside, born of the South's own needs and reflecting its particular resources—if, indeed, Olmsted had actually formulated the landscape potential. Measured by the articulation of the New England pastoral landscape—that original and durable Olmsted theme and style: the ideas of the Yosemite report, the plan for Niagara Falls, and the Adirondack Park concept (all great national landscapes, reflected at smaller scale in the design of urban parks)—nothing of comparable regional value appeared from the Southern effort. Yet, the regional potential was and is there, and it is probably the most significant aspect of Olmsted in the New South.

But beyond the urban themes as Olmsted enunciated them in Atlanta, the explorer of the Southern landscape needs to contemplate the significance of those carefully designed textile mill towns of the 1920s along the Piedmont crescent; the landscape and urban consequences of the Tennessee Valley Authority; and the design of institutions, state parks, and early city plans. In all of these constituent elements of the Southern landscape can be found today a certain fulfillment of Olmsted's expectations, if not by the hand of the master, then by that of his followers such as Earle S. Draper.[3] The manmade landscape of Florida—past, present, and future—calls for precisely such an historical analysis. The reconstruction and preservation of all of Olmsted's great naturalistic urban parks is a further task of our time that will be enlightened by such research.

In explaining the failure at Biltmore to realize any of his larger hopes and expectations for the New South, three possibilities seem worth further examination. The first is biographical. Olmsted's waning powers simply would not support the great creative effort necessary to make of what he termed "industrial forestry," as interpreted by Pinchot and Schenck, a social rather than the commercial undertaking it rather witlessly became—something comparable to what Benton MacKaye later proposed in the Snoqualamie as an answer to forest plundering and the social unrest that had incited the Wobblies of World War I.[4] (Olmsted's declining powers also explain why he left the arboretum project to the disposition of a cynical Harvard professor instead of transforming it into terms original and relevant to the South.) The second possibility considers the professional evolution of landscape architecture, the professional firm (the largest in the nation), the complicated relations of the aging Olmsted and his partners, and the conflicting demands of the firm's other work—making it impossible for them to reinforce his efforts at Biltmore or even to sympathize with his larger objectives. The third possibility considers the inherent limitations of the professional adviser, both in his relations to other advisers (in this case Hunt, Beadle, and Pinchot) and to a client who willed otherwise. These are all durable and important questions worth further research; here it is sufficient to raise them rather than attempt conclusive answers. If I did not consider all of them significant, I would not have described them.

NOTES

1. The factual content of this paper is drawn largely from Laura Wood Roper, *FLO: A Biography of Frederick Law Olmsted* (Baltimore, 1973). Mrs. Roper's biography shows that Biltmore was Olmsted's last great creative effort and his outstanding professional commitment of the time. His demands for reports and photographs of its progress continued as he entered the long physical and psychological decline which concluded his life.

2. On the whole, to this point, their social career seems to have been correctly summarized by the medieval historian, H. O. Taylor, who once observed to me, "The Vanderbilts jimmied their way into New York society."

3. The outlines of Earle Sumner Draper's activities in the South are sketched out in Norman T. Newton, *Design on the Land: The Development of Landscape Architecture* (Cambridge, Mass., 1971), especially pp. 487–89, 500–502. Draper, "the first professionally trained city planner to locate in the Southeast" and "a pioneer of profession in the South," first set up practice in Charlotte, North Carolina, in 1917, after having served his apprenticeship with the firm of John Nolen in Kingsport, Tennessee. His most notable work during his early years in the South was his design of the planned community of Chicopee, Georgia. Later, he was to direct all regional planning studies for the Tennessee Valley Authority.

4. The best introduction to the thinking of Benton MacKaye is his *The New Exploration: A Philosophy of Regional Planning* (New York, 1928). In his Introduction to the 1962 reprinting (University of Illinois Press), Lewis Mumford has asserted that it "deserves a place on the same shelf that holds Henry Thoreau's *Walden* and George Perkins Marsh's *Man and Nature*" (p. vii).

Dana F. White

ABOUT OLMSTED:
A Bibliographical Essay

The multiplicity of scholarly disciplines and the variety of approaches and emphases represented in this volume made any attempt at a cumulative bibliography for *Olmsted South* impracticable. For references of a specialized nature, both disciplinary and topical, the reader is advised to consult the notes to the appropriate chapter or chapters. The focus here is a more comprehensive one. It begins with an introduction to FLO's works on the South, published and unpublished, and concludes with an examination of major works about the man and the region, Old South and New South.

The two major Olmsted depositories constitute the essential starting points for studies of FLO's ventures south. The Frederick Law Olmsted Papers in the Library of Congress contain some sixty thousand personal and professional items for the years 1838 to 1903. FLO's old studio office in Brookline, Massachusetts (presently occupied by the landscape firm of Olmsted Associates but, at this writing, under review for designation as a national historic site that would be known as the Frederick Law Olmsted Home and Office) contains one hundred and fifty thousand designs and documents. (A preliminary report on holdings, completed in 1977 for the National Park Service by William Alex, is presently the only working guide to this major, endangered collection.) The first of the seven volumes of *The Papers of Frederick Law Olmsted*, under the general editorship of Charles Capen McLaughlin, was published by the Johns Hopkins University Press in 1977. That initial volume, *The Formative Years 1822–1852*, edited by McLaughlin and Charles E. Beveridge, is especially valuable for background information on Olmsted's later writings about his journeys through the American South, for it includes the accounts of his earlier and formative trips to China and England. A volume now in preparation, again with McLaughlin and Beveridge as co-editors, will cover the period 1852 to 1861.

Until the completion of the *Papers* project, the best source for FLO's unpublished writings remains McLaughlin's "Selected Letters of Frederick Law Olmsted" (Ph.D. dissertation, Harvard University, 1960), which contains thirty-five annotated letters from all periods of Olmsted's life. However, a scattering of documents and letters is found in the first volume of *Forty Years of Landscape Architecture: Being the Professional Papers of Frederick Law Olmsted, Senior,* edited by Frederick Law Olmsted, Jr., and Theodora Kimball in 1922 and reissued in 1970 as *Frederick Law Olmsted, Landscape Architect, 1822–1903,* 2 vols. in 1 (New York: Benjamin Blom, Inc.).

Olmsted's initial accounts of his Southern travels were published in three series: the first two, under the pen-name "Yeoman," in the *New-York Daily Times* from February 16, 1853, to February 13, 1854, and, again, from March 6 to June 7, 1854; and the third, under the heading "The Southerner at Home," in the *New-York Daily Tribune* from June 3 to September 25, 1857. Three subsequent volumes drew upon the newspaper series: *A Journey in the Seaboard Slave States, with Remarks on Their Economy,* which was published by the New York firm of Dix and Edwards in 1856 and reprinted in 1968 by the Negro Universities Press (Westport, Conn.); *A Journey Through Texas; or A Saddle-Trip on the Southwestern Frontier; with a Statistical Appendix,* again printed by Dix and Edwards in 1857 and reissued in 1969 as part of the "American Classics in History and Social Science" series (New York: Burt Franklin) and reprinted again in 1978 with a Foreword by novelist Larry McMurtry (Austin: University of Texas Press); and *A Journey in the Back Country in the Winter of 1853–54* which appeared under the imprint of the Mason Brothers (the successor firm to Dix and Edwards) in 1860 and was reprinted in 1970 in "Sourcebooks in Negro History," with a new Introduction by Clement Eaton (New York: Schocken Books). A summary work, compiled by Daniel R. Goodloe under Olmsted's direction, was published in 1861 as *The Cotton Kingdom: A Traveller's Observations on Cotton and Slavery in the American Slave States,* in the American edition, and as *Journeys and Explorations in the Cotton Kingdom,* in the English edition (two volumes each), and reissued in 1953, with Arthur M. Schlesinger's now classic Introduction (New York: Alfred A. Knopf). (The publishing history of both the newspaper series and the books is covered fully in "A Connecticut Yankee in Cotton's Kingdom," above.)

Two other antebellum works by Olmsted that touch upon the "Southern problem" merit attention. The passages on slavery in the two editions of FLO's first book, *Walks and Talks of an American Farmer in England*—the first published in 1852 by G. P. Putnam, New York, and the second, revised and enlarged, issued in 1859 by J. H. Riley and Company, Columbus, Ohio—invite comparison. A modern edition, based on the 1859 imprint, with an Introduction by Alex L. Murray, was released in 1967 (Ann Arbor: University of Michigan Press). Also worth noting is

Olmsted's Introduction to T. H. Gladstone's *The Englishman in Kansas, or Squatter Life and Border Warfare,* printed in 1857 by Miller and Company of New York and republished in 1971 by Bison Books, with a Foreword by James A. Rawley (Lincoln: University of Nebraska Press).

Olmsted's postwar writings on the South have, to date, received little attention from publishers. As concerns his social commentary, this is to be expected. Indeed, we are fortunate to have Thomas H. Clark, "Frederick Law Olmsted on the South, 1889," *South Atlantic Quarterly* 3 (January 1904): 11–15, but FLO's ideas about the Southern landscape should be attended to more seriously. While Olmsted's landscape works in the Northeast (especially New York and Boston), the Midwest (particularly Chicago), and the Far West (California) have been, to varying degrees, documented, only two books in the spate of visual documentaries published in the last decade have given any space to the South: Julius Gy. Fabos, Gordon T. Milde, and V. Michael Weinmayr, *Frederick Law Olmsted, Sr., Founder of Landscape Architecture in America* (Amherst: University of Massachusetts Press, 1968); and Albert Fein, *Frederick Law Olmsted and the American Environmental Tradition* (New York: George Braziller, 1972.

Laura Wood Roper, *FLO: A Biography of Frederick Law Olmsted* (Baltimore: Johns Hopkins University Press, 1973) is the indispensable reference source for all phases of Olmsted's life and work. For his antebellum writings, Charles E. Beveridge, "Frederick Law Olmsted, The Formative Years 1822–1865" (Ph.D. dissertation, University of Wisconsin, 1966) provides a thoughtful analysis of Olmsted's values and ideals of civilization that explain much about his pattern of response to and evaluation of Southern civilization. Broadus Mitchell, *Frederick Law Olmsted: A Critic of the Old South* (Baltimore: Johns Hopkins University Press, 1924; New York: Russell and Russell, 1968) constitutes a dated but still lively "literary biography," with a distinctive Southern bias. Roper's "Frederick Law Olmsted in the 'Literary Republic,' " *Mississippi Valley Historical Review* 39 (December 1952): 459–82, and Schlesinger's Introduction to the 1953 edition of FLO's *Cotton Kingdom* document his travels, the writing of the newspaper series, and the development of the "Cotton Kingdom" books. For the postwar era, only Fein's *Frederick Law Olmsted and the American Environmental Tradition* confronts head on the seeming disparity between the design ideals embodied in Olmsted's early and late work—between, for example, the "democratic" Central Park and the "baronial" Biltmore. Design analyses of the Vanderbilt estate at Asheville are also furnished in Norman T. Newton, *Design on the Land: The Development of Landscape Architecture* (Cambridge, Mass.: Harvard University Press, 1971), pp. 346–52, and in Fabos, Milde, and Weinmayr, *Frederick Law Olmsted, Sr., Founder of Landscape Architecture in America,* pp. 86–89. A most unusual (and rewarding) perspective on FLO's life, which she approaches as "a fable for our times," is found in Helen Yglesias's superb novel, *Family Feeling* (New York: Dial Press, 1976).

In recent years, a more critical perspective on Olmsted has begun to emerge. Robert W. Fogel and Stanley L. Engerman's indictment, "Frederick Law Olmsted: The Micro Evidence," in *Time on the Cross: The Economics of American Negro Slavery* (Boston: Little, Brown and Company, 1974), 1: 170–81, calls into question Olmsted's reliability as an observer; Eric Foner's *Free Soil, Free Labor, Free Men: The Ideology of the Republican Party Before the Civil War* (New York: Oxford University Press, 1970), especially pp. 42–47, places FLO's antislavery views in a new and revisionist historical framework; and George M. Fredrickson's critique of "The Sanitary Elite: The Organized Response to Suffering," in *The Inner Civil War: Northern Intellectuals and the Crisis of the Union* (New York: Harper and Row, 1965), pp. 98–112, raises serious questions about the reform ideals of Olmsted and his contemporaries. Elbert Peets attempted to initiate a reassessment of the philosophy behind the Olmstedian tradition of landscape architecture over fifty years ago, especially in "The Landscape Priesthood," *American Mercury* (January 1927): 94–100, reprinted in Paul D. Spreiregen, ed., *On the Art of Designing Cities: Selected Essays of Elbert Peets* (Cambridge, Mass.: MIT Press, 1968), pp. 186–93. Nearly half a century was to pass before Peets' challenge was renewed. Geoffrey Blodgett, "Frederick Law Olmsted: Landscape Architecture as Conservative Reform," *Journal of American History* 62 (March 1976): 869–89, is the most thorough scholarly critique of the movement to date. Also worth noting are: John Brinckerhoff Jackson, *American Space: The Centennial Years: 1865–1876* (New York: W. W. Norton, 1972), especially Chap. 8; Stanley K. Schultz, "Pioneers of the Crabgrass Frontier," *Reviews in American History* 2 (September 1974): 337–43; Jane Holtz Kay, "Our First Hero of the Landscape," *Saturday Review* (May 14, 1977): 26–27, 31; and Robert Lewis, "Frontier and Civilization in the Thought of Frederick Law Olmsted," *American Quarterly* 29 (Fall 1977): 385–403.

Any effort to separate out from the gargantuan corpus of Southern scholarship a modicum of sources to serve as general background for the study of Olmsted's South is likely to strike some as impossible, others as foolhardy, and many as simply idiosyncratic. Therefore, it must be confessed at the outset that personal preference had a good deal to do in the selection of the works to follow. For a general introduction to Southern studies, Carl N. Degler, *Place Over Time: The Continuity of Southern Distinctiveness* (Baton Rouge: Louisiana State University Press, 1977) is recommended, as are the first two parts of David M. Potter, *The South and the Sectional Conflict* (Baton Rouge: Louisiana State University Press, 1968), pp. 1–198. Potter's posthumously published *The Impending Crisis,*

1848–1861 (New York: Harper and Row, 1976), completed and edited by
Don E. Fehrenbacher, is the most recent attempt at a comprehensive
survey of that critical period when Olmsted first turned south. It should
be supplemented with Clement Eaton's two studies on *The Growth of
Southern Civilization, 1790–1860* (New York: Harper and Brothers, 1961)
and *The Mind of the Old South,* revised edition (Baton Rouge: Louisiana
State University Press, 1967), as well as with Arthur S. Link and Rembert
W. Patrick, eds., *Writing Southern History: Essays in Historiography in Honor
of Fletcher M. Green* (Baton Rouge: Louisiana State University Press, 1965).
For an introduction to the most recent debate over slavery, see David
Brion Davis, "Slavery and the Post-World War II Historians," *Daedalus*
103, No. 2 (Spring 1974): 1–16; Charles Crowe, "Historians and 'Benign
Neglect': Conservative Trends in Southern History and Black Studies,"
Reviews in American History 2 (June 1974): 163–73; Bennett H. Wall, "An
Epitaph for Slavery," *Louisiana History* 16 (Summer 1975): 229–56; and
Thomas Holt, "On the Cross: The Role of Quantitative Methods in the
Reconstruction of the Afro-American Experience," *Journal of Negro His-
tory* 61 (April 1976): 158–72. Kenneth M. Stampp, *The Peculiar Institution:
Slavery in the Ante-Bellum South* (New York: Alfred A. Knopf, 1956) re-
mains probably the best introduction to the system of human bondage as
it operated in Olmsted's day, and Herbert G. Gutman, *The Black Family in
Slavery and Freedom, 1750–1925* (New York: Pantheon, 1976) is the best
beginning point for an understanding of the internal dynamics of that
system.

Travel literature on the American South is rich in variety and sheer
quantity. The most convenient introduction to books in this genre is
found in the "American Exploration and Travel" series of the University
of Oklahoma Press, especially: Thomas D. Clark's three-volume *Travels in
the Old South: A Bibliography* (1956–1959), which covers the period 1527 to
1860; his two-volume *Travels in the New South: A Bibliography* (1962), for
1865 to 1955; and E. Merton Coulter, *Travels in the Confederate States: A
Bibliography* (1948), for the Civil War years. *Travels in the Old South: Selected
from Periodicals of the Times,* a two-volume anthology edited by Eugene L.
Schwaab in collaboration with Jacqueline Bull (Lexington: University of
Kentucky Press, 1973), is intended to supplement the Oklahoma bibliog-
raphies. However, since the editorial procedures established for selection
are vague and since no record of the journals searched is supplied, the
scholarly value of this collection is limited. Still, the section on "The
South in Sectional Crisis, 1852–1860" (2: 477–573) makes for ready comparison with Olmsted's accounts, as does, literally from the "other side,"
the record presented in John Hope Franklin's survey of *A Southern Odyssey: Travelers the Antebellum North* (Baton Rouge: Louisiana State University Press, 1975). For the most part, travel literature on the American

South has been utilized more than analyzed, but an agenda for scholarly investigation of the genre (and its peculiarly Southern expressions) has been provided by Daniel J. Boorstin in "From Traveler to Tourist: The Lost Art of Travel" and "Suggestions for Further Reading (and Writing)," in *The Image, or What Happened to the American Dream* (New York: Atheneum, 1962), especially pp. 78–83 and 275–81.

The final two volumes (9 and 10) of "A History of the American South," under the editorship of Wendell Holmes Stephenson and E. Merton Coulter, provide a comprehensive and authoritative survey of the era during which Olmsted, and later his sons, were at work in the region. These are: C. Vann Woodward, *Origins of the New South, 1877–1913*, and George B. Tindall, *The Emergence of the New South, 1913–1945* (Baton Rouge: Louisiana State University Press, 1951 and 1967). For more specialized approaches to some of the major intellectual and social problems of the period, see Paul H. Buck, *The Road to Reunion, 1865–1900* (Boston: Little, Brown and Company, 1937); Rayford W. Logan; *The Betrayal of the Negro: From Rutherford B. Hayes to Woodrow Wilson*, new and enlarged edition (New York: Collier Books, 1965); and Paul M. Gaston, *The New South Creed: A Study in Southern Mythmaking* (New York: Alfred A. Knopf, 1970).

That elements of Olmsted's South have survived into the present is demonstrated by John Shelton Reed in *The Enduring South: Subcultural Persistence in Mass Society* (Chapel Hill: University of North Carolina Press, 1972 and 1974). That there seems to be a national psychological need for these elements at least to appear to persist is suggested by Patrick Gerster and Nicholas Cords in "The Northern Origins of Southern Mythology," *Journal of Southern History* 43 (November 1977): 567–82. That Olmsted shaped parts of the South's living landscape is manifest on the land itself but, unfortunately, in a discouragingly decreasing portion thereon.

INDEX

ABOUT THE CONTRIBUTORS

RICK BEARD is presently Coordinator of the Center for American Art and Material Culture at Yale University. Previously he was a research historian at the National Portrait Gallery, Smithsonian Institution, in Washington, D.C. Beard, who has published articles on urban topics as well as a number of exhibition reviews, is completing a doctorate in American Studies at Emory University.

KAY L. COTHRAN, who lives in Devon, Pennsylvania, received the Ph.D. in Folklore and Folklife from the University of Pennsylvania in 1972. She has had several articles on folklife in the Southern pineywoods published, including one on the usefulness of travel accounts as ethnographic data. Formerly an Assistant Professor at the University of Maryland, she now collaborates with her husband, Carter W. Craigie, on studies in folklife and related social science fields for Cabrini College, Radnor, Pennsylvania.

TIMOTHY J. CRIMMINS is Associate Professor of History and Urban Life at Georgia State University, where he teaches American urban history and urban studies. A native of Pittsburgh, Crimmins first journeyed south in 1970 to complete a doctoral program in American Studies at Emory University. His articles on southern urbanization have appeared in the *Journal of Urban History*, *Urban Education*, the *American Archivist*, and other scholarly journals. With Dana F. White, he is currently completing a work on the history of Atlanta, funded by a National Endowment for the Humanities grant.

ROBERT DETWEILER studied at the University of Hamburg, Goshen College, and the University of Florida and holds the M.A. and the Ph.D. degrees from the University of Florida. He has taught at various schools, including Hunter College, the University of Salzburg, and the University of Hamburg, and is presently director of the Graduate Institute of the Liberal Arts at Emory University. He is the author of *John Updike* and *Story, Sign and Self* as well as numerous monographs and literary critical essays.

WILLIAM LAKE DOUGLAS holds degrees in Landscape Architecture from Louisiana State University and the Graduate School of Design, Harvard University. He is currently transcribing a mid-nineteenth-century French text on horticultural practices and techniques of that period which was published in New Orleans.

ALBERT FEIN is Professor of History and Urban Studies at the Brooklyn Center of Long Island University, where he serves as Chairperson of the Graduate Department of Urban Studies. Fein is also Visiting Professor of Landscape Architecture at the Graduate School of Design, Harvard University, where he teaches the course "Environmental History of the United States of America and Great Britain since the Eighteenth Century." He is the author of several works, including *Frederick Law Olmsted and the American Environmental Tradition* (New York, 1972), and coauthor of *New York: The Centennial Years, 1676–1976* (New York, 1976).

FREDERICK GUTHEIM is Adjunct Professor of American Civilization at The George Washington University. He was chairman of the 1972 Olmsted sesquicentennial. His interest in Olmsted has been directed toward Olmsted's contributions to conservation, parks, landscape design, and urban environmental quality.

VICTOR A. KRAMER is a member of the English Department of Georgia State University in Atlanta. He has also taught at Marquette University in Milwaukee and was Senior Fulbright Lecturer at the University of Regensburg in Bavaria. He is the author of *James Agee* and the forthcoming book *Thomas Merton,* and is also editor of issues of *Studies in the Literary Imagination.* His articles and reviews have appeared in numerous scholarly journals. Currently he is collaborating on a Reference Guide about Andrew Lytle, Walker Percy, and Peter Taylor.

ELIZABETH A. LYON received the Ph.D. from Emory University, where she was a Lecturer in architectural and urban design history from 1965 to 1975. Dr. Lyon's research has focused on the Atlanta area, and her most recent publication is *Atlanta Architecture: The Victorian Heritage* (1976). In 1976, she became a staff member of the Historic Preservation Section of the Georgia Department of Natural Resources, serving first as Manager of the Survey and Planning Unit and then as Chief of the Historic Preservation Section. Presently she is State Historic Preservation Officer.

HOWARD L. PRESTON has taught in the History departments of Morehouse College and Atlanta University and in the Transportation Program of the Southern Center for Studies in Public Policy at Clark College. He holds the M.A. in History from Atlanta University and the Ph.D. in American Studies from Emory University. His book about the development of Atlanta between 1900 and 1935 will be published by the University of Georgia Press in 1979.

KARLA SPURLOCK-EVANS, a native of Willimantic, Connecticut, was graduated from Barnard College magna cum laude with honors in political science. The recipient of a John Hay Whitney fellowship and a Danforth graduate fellowship, Spurlock-Evans is a doctoral candidate in American Studies at the Graduate Institute of the Liberal Arts, Emory University. She is currently employed as Director of Minority Affairs at Haverford College in Pennsylvania.

PHILLIP ROLAND RUTHERFORD received the B.A., M.A., and Ph.D. degrees in English from East Texas State University. At the present time he is Professor of English at the University of Southern Maine. In addition to being the author of *Dissertations in Linguistics, 1900–1964,* and *The Dictionary of Maine Place Names,* he also serves as the Maine State Chairman of the National Place Name survey.

DANA F. WHITE is Associate Professor of Urban Studies at Atlanta and Emory universities in Atlanta. He has also taught at George Washington University and the State University of New York at Buffalo and was a postdoctoral Research Associate at the Smithsonian Institution. His articles have appeared in *American Studies, Museum News, South Atlantic Quarterly, Technology and Culture, Urban Education, Journal of Urban History,* and other scholarly journals. With Timothy J. Crimmins, he is currently completing a history of Atlanta's development.